The InstitutionS of Education

To Olechka

The InstitutionS of Education
a comparative study of educational development in the six core nations

William K. Cummings

SYMPOSIUM
BOOKS

Symposium Books
PO Box 204 Didcot Oxford OX11 9ZQ United Kingdom
www.symposium-books.co.uk

Published in the United Kingdom, 2003

ISBN 1 873927 69 X

This publication is also available on a subscription basis
as Volume 12 Number 2 of *Oxford Studies in Comparative Education*
(ISSN 0961-2149)

Typeset in Melior by Symposium Books
Printed and bound in the United Kingdom by Cambridge University Press

Contents

Preface

Our history books focus on great wars, technological change, political upheavals, but not on education. At least until recently, we assumed that education was out there doing its job, just like the postal service, or the family doctor. But the steady stream of bad news about education over the past decade – declining test scores, increasing costs, violence in the schools, the high incidence of drop-outs – has surely destroyed our innocence.

At many times in educational history, including the past decade, there are reports of crisis and cries for reform. The successes of foreign competitors are pointed to, new monies are sought and laws passed. Occasionally these reform efforts make a difference. Just as often, they end up as mere rhetoric and the educational indicators continue to slide. Education is a dynamic sector with its ups and downs. To understand these ups and downs and to gain a clearer grasp of the essentials of reform, we need to look deeply into the origins and development of successful and failed reforms. This book seeks to answer that need.

To do so, it stresses two important themes: (a) the essence of educational practice lies in the institutionalized ideals and norms of an educational system, not in how much is spent on education or how many people are involved in education; and (b) while most contemporary (especially American) observers of education tend to think that sound educational practice is pretty much the same around the world, there are at least six distinctive educational InstitutionS currently in place in the modern world, each with its unique strengths and weaknesses. Each also has its own cycle of reform and renewal. And so the landscape of educational reform is much broader than most observers acknowledge.

Most who comment on and work in education have a surprisingly limited perspective, either because they have not been exposed to educational practice in other settings or because they filter their exposure through the lenses of a particular discipline or national experience. The account that follows seeks to broaden perspectives. While most of the study focuses on 'national' differences, the analysis actually begins from the ground, looking at particular schools that emerged early in several modernizing experiences. These early schools are described here as representative schools, for the practices they initiated have had a profound influence on the direction of subsequent reforms in their respective national settings.

Many of the arguments in this book have evolved from personal encounters with schools on four continents, and my reflections derived from these encounters. I began school in North Carolina, but later my father took me to South America and India. And my subsequent work and travels took me to yet other settings.

India initiated my interest in education and development, and my studies at both the bachelor's and doctoral level followed that path. The Indian school I attended during my high school days had once been called the (East India) Company School, and it retained an English orientation, offering a Cambridge Examination Preparatory Stream. All of the students lived in dormitories and followed a strict daily schedule with lots of rules. School took place during the day, sports in the late afternoon, followed by a common meal, study hall, and lights out. The rhythm of this school was very different from my earlier educational experiences in North Carolina and Peru.

Because Japan was described as the only Asian country that had escaped the imprint of colonialism and achieved substantial development, I oriented my early academic studies towards understanding the Japanese approach, and along with teaching in a Japanese university and spending countless hours in Japanese schools I wrote several books on Japanese education.

My Japanese encounter was followed by long sojourns in Indonesia, Singapore and Ethiopia, and shorter visits to many other settings. My stay in Indonesia introduced me to a system that bore the imprint of the continental model introduced through Dutch colonialism, with a tough subject-based primary curriculum that led to high repetition and drop-out rates; much the same can be said for Ethiopia, except that that nation also experimented for two decades with the socialist model. Many of the practices in Singapore, a nation that was and is constantly rethinking its educational approach, had obvious links with the English past. In recent years, more of these visits have been to Western Europe and Russia in an effort to gain a better understanding of the educational approaches of these core societies.

In several of my early comparative studies of educational systems, I tried various ways of classifying educational systems. International agencies like to classify educational systems by regions. But this does not make sense: Singapore is next door to Indonesia, Thailand and the Philippines, yet there are sharp contrasts between these three systems. Similarly, Ethiopia is close to Kenya, Uganda and Mali, but again the contrasts are enormous. Influenced by my personal experiences, I kept coming back to the insight that the key to classifying systems lies in the cultural models they had developed and/or borrowed rather than their physical location.

So these are the experiences that have led to this book. I have tried to keep my eyes open and not be trapped in a particular discipline or theory. Rather, I have concluded that it is necessary to propose a 'new' direction, which I call InstitutionS Theory. Institution was once a prominent concept in sociology and anthropology, but for some time was largely forgotten. Lately, it has experienced a rebirth both in sociology and economics. InstitutionS

Theory is close to this recent institutional theorizing, except that it seeks to be more specific in its propositions, more 'middle range', to use a phrase of Robert Merton's. Also, it seeks to avoid the ethnocentrism that characterizes much of the recent work on institutions.

While the recent approaches treat institution as a macro-concept, the InstitutionS I discuss here begin with the emergence of particular representative schools. These first schools embody values and norms that are later imitated and replicated in successor schools as a particular institution of education is systematized and expanded. The school-based character of this study provides the background for a consideration, in the final chapters of this book, of some thoughts on the shape of future schools.

I have enjoyed the opportunity to think about modern schools. While my thinking is still under way, I feel it now is the time to present my perspective. I hope it will incite reactions, and through future dialogues there will be opportunities to improve on this exposition.

My sincere thanks to David Phillips for his thoughtful review of the manuscript, to Jason Hill for his assistance in finalizing the manuscript, to Olga Bain for her support and encouragement, and to my many friends who have helped to nurture the ideas presented in this study.

PART ONE

Introduction

CHAPTER 1

Thinking about Educational Revolutions and Reform[1]

Social structures, types and attitudes are coins that do not readily melt.
Once they are formed they persist, possibly for centuries, and since
different structures and types display different degrees of ability to
survive, we almost always find that actual groups and national
behavior more or less departs from what we should expect it to be if we
tried to infer it from the dominant forms of the productive process.
(Joseph Schumpeter [2])

Educational Revolutions

Anthropologists report that one of the fundamental needs of human communities is the transmission of culture from generation to generation. In the earliest human communities the family was the primary unit for this purpose; within the family some educational tasks were gender specific while others were shared.[3]

With the advent of writing and the keeping of records, small schools emerged to train a select group from each community to acquire the skills necessary for keeping and developing these records. These differentiated schools constituted the beginnings of the first educational revolution. During this revolution, which dates to the second millennium BC, the primary content of education was the inherited tradition, including the religious and philosophical dogma. This revolution peaked in different parts of the world at different times: in Mesopotamia and Egypt in the first century BC, in China and India soon thereafter, in ancient Greece and Rome in the several centuries before and after Christ, in the Islamic World spreading from Spain to India in the years following the death of the Prophet Mohammed until *circa* AD 1500, and then in Western Europe. In medieval Europe, schooling was limited both in its availability to the citizenry and in its scope. Most schools were run by the churches and placed their primary emphasis on training students for the clerical professions that included, along with the clergy, preparation for positions in public administration and law. If we take AD 1650 as a rough dividing point between the first and second, or modern

13

revolution, it is likely that schooling was most prevalent in the Islamic and Confucian worlds and least prevalent in the Christian world.

Just as the invention of writing facilitated the first educational revolution, the invention of the printing press set the stage for the second, or modern, educational revolution. Until that time, in the West the Church was the principal possessor of the Bible and most other important books. Monks laboriously copied these books in the monasteries and distributed them sparingly to various religious institutions, including the religious schools and parishes. Only a small number of the general public, those with wealth, faith, and an interest in learning, were able to have private libraries. But from the late fifteenth century, important advances were made in the mechanical printing of books (Braudel, 1985, pp. 397ff.) Perhaps the best-known case was the Gutenberg Bible (1455). From that date forth, the Church lost its monopoly on the Holy Book. New religious movements emerged championing the right of individual believers to have direct access to the divine word. A demand was created for the Bible and for the essential skill of literacy so as to read this great book. The Reformation swept across Europe, sowing the seeds of the modern educational revolution. While the major impetus for change was the demand for mass literacy, the revolution had other correlates, including a broadening of the values education curriculum to place at least as much emphasis on love of nation as reverence for God and an increase in the emphasis on such secular subjects as mathematics and science.

The Birth of Modern Education

While the Reformation sowed the seeds of the modern educational revolution, various other changes had to take place before these seeds could germinate. Charles Tilly (1993) observes that there were as many as 500 independent political entities in Western Europe at the beginning of the seventeenth century; many were quite small and lacking in sufficient resources to support an adequate army, not to speak of a popular educational system. Only through the consolidation over the next two centuries of these numerous political entities into twenty or so nation states was there a sufficient concentration of resources to consider such public projects as a mass educational system. Contributing to the consolidation of nation states were new technical developments that altered the nature of military conflict as well as increased the productivity of national economies. The unfolding of these ideological, political, military, and economic changes differed from place to place, resulting in distinctive settings for the birth of modern education. In some settings such as England, the changes unfolded gradually. In contrast was the shock of the French Revolution, which led to the overnight toppling of the French monarchy and the birth of the new republic governed by citizens.

14

Usually it required the emergence of a new polity before bold steps were taken to establish modern education. In France, the toppling of the monarchy was followed within a year by a determination to throw out the traditional Catholic schools of France. Elsewhere in Europe, and later in other parts of the world, there were similar convulsions. In Japan the charter oath proclaiming a modern educational system was announced only four years after the Meiji Revolution. In each instance, a unique confluence of administrative precedent, tradition, utopian ideology, and revolutionary energy created a new ideal for education and a related set of structures and procedures that are considered 'modern' (Archer, 1977; Ringer, 1979; Ramirez & Boli, 1987).

From these ideological and political changes of the long modern century extending into the early 1900s, new 'modern' school systems were established that tended to receive some support from the modern state and strove to provide basic education to a substantial proportion of the populations. Common to these modern educational departures was a concern to rely on a *system* of schools to educate relatively large numbers of the body public in appropriate moral precepts and several cognitively complex subjects, including mathematics, science, and history/geography, and to arrange this education in a series of levels from the lowest elementary grade through intermediate grades to an advanced grade; corresponding to each grade was a class of students who were periodically tested to determine their readiness for advancement. Other commonalities included a bureaucratization of the educational personnel in charge of schools and a standardization of educational materials. While many scholars have emphasized these and other commonalities of the modern educational experience (Meyer & Hannah, 1979; Meyer et al, 1992), our goal here is to highlight some important variations.

The Beginnings of Modern Education

The first steps towards the development of mass systems of basic education are generally believed to have occurred in the Nordic countries. For example, in Sweden, the national church, with the urging of the King, exhorted parents and communities to foster popular literacy, and the literacy rate is believed to have increased from 20 per cent in the seventeenth century to 80 per cent by the early nineteenth century (Johansson, 1981). But this was largely accomplished through home education stimulated by church examinations of each family's progress; in other words, the literacy improvement was not accompanied by the development of an elaborated educational system, and partly for that reason did not gain as much international recognition as subsequent reforms in Germany and France. Table 1.1 indicates the years when basic education was made compulsory in selected states.

State	Year compulsory schooling established
German states	1724-1806
Massachusetts (USA)	1852
Japan	1872
France	1882
England	1900
Russia	1919

Table 1.1. Dates of the establishment of compulsory education in selected states.

Prussia

As in the Nordic countries, the Reformation initiated profound changes in the various German states. Melton (1988) traces the Pietist movement in Germany, and attributes to it the advancement of concern for popular education among clergy and political leaders. The essence of the Pietist argument was that outward piety was insufficient to realize grace; the outward manifestations had to be accompanied by inner understanding, and basic literacy and self-study of the scriptures was essential for this inner understanding. Under King Frederick II of Prussia (who reigned from 1740 to 1786), these concerns were gradually translated into government regulations that had a direct impact on Prussia and were imitated by other German states.

In the eighteenth century the territory now known as Germany was a loose federation of such states under a king and a council of noblemen. Early educational change was largely promoted by religious leaders in local communities, but from the mid-eighteenth century several of the state governments, with Prussia taking the lead, came to propose state-wide strategies. Prussia's General County School Regulation of 1763 was one of the first instances of state interest. By the end of the century Prussian laws declared that the state was the guardian of the child's rights vis-à-vis the parents, while parents had the responsibility to see that their children were educated. The Prussian state in its 1794 General Code set the standards for local school finance and proposed to supply much of the funding for the operation of local schools; the state specified the requirements for the establishment of local schools; and it assumed the authority for appointing teachers (Maynes, 1985, p. 49). These firm steps by the Prussian state to provide a systematic curriculum for public education, to assume a central role in the recruitment and training of teachers, and to specify the details of school buildings and finance were the first instances of the modern system of education.

Behind these changes was the concern of Prussia and other German states to develop a more literate workforce for the rapidly developing industries as well as to ensure a literate cohort of young men for the growing armies they required for their expansionist ambitions. Parallel to these changes in school education, Prussia was also fostering significant changes in the civil service so that the king, rather than local Junkers, enjoyed the final say in appointments.

While several different types of secondary schools prevailed, in the early nineteenth century the *Gymnasium*, with its stress on Latin and a broad humanistic education, was singled out to be the academic bridge between the various local schools and state-controlled advanced education. With the advancement of the *Gymnasium*, other institutions such as the Latin secondary schools came to specialize in more 'realistic' curricula to train young people for clerical and technical positions in commerce and industry. Some of the institutions of this second track eventually evolved into the vocational preparation schools that are currently widely admired in other industrial nations.

The establishment of Berlin University in 1810 by Wilhelm von Humboldt, Prussia's Director of Culture and Education, was an important component of these changes. The new university gradually assumed the role of selecting and educating those individuals who could take up positions in the Prussian civil service as well as in many of the professions (Ringer, 1974). The reliance on examinations to select university students and in turn to certify those eligible for the civil service and other professions has led some observers to speak of the nineteenth century as the 'Age of Examinations' (Amano, 1990). With the rise of modern education through the university level, the state sought to strengthen its control at the expense of the landed classes; those members of the middle class who excelled in education were the major beneficiaries of these reforms.

Over much of the nineteenth century the various states of Germany came to replicate the innovations pioneered in Prussia, so that each state had a comprehensive local educational system crowned by the local university. The result was considerable equality between the states in both the extent and the quality of educational provision. The German approach attracted much interest from educational reformers in all of the other core societies, except the United Kingdom. On the other hand, Germany began late in the European game of building empires, and so it was not in a position to use colonialism as a vehicle for exporting its system. It was only following the Franco-Prussian War of 1870 that Germany became unified in one empire under the Prussian king who was made emperor of Germany.

France

France under the ancien régime was far more unified than Germany in the seventeenth century, and in certain respects France's educational system was more advanced. Certainly, France had more universities and the intellectual life at the French court and elsewhere was more highly regarded. Yet, popular education in France was limited and largely under the auspices of the Catholic Church, which favoured education for the upper and middle classes but had little disposition to educate the working and peasant classes.

Through the latter half of the eighteenth century, various Enlightenment intellectuals, including La Chalotais, Turgot and Rousseau, spoke of the virtues of popular education both for individual growth and national benefit. These ideas were debated in the royal chambers but, as with many other progressive thoughts, were finally left for another day (Chisick, 1981).

The dramatic revolution beginning with the storming of the Bastille in 1789 led to a review of the progressive agenda. Education was not a major concern in the early days, but the stranglehold of the Catholic Church on so many aspects of French life came under immediate attack (Glenn, 1988). Because of the Church's role in it, education thus became one of the foci of reform. Robespierre in 1793 told the National Convention, 'I am convinced of the necessity of operating a total regeneration, and, if I may express myself in this way, of creating a new people' (cited in Glenn 1988, p. 20). A year later, Danton expressed a similar sentiment to the same group:

> It is time to reestablish the grand principle, which seems too much misunderstood, that children belong to the Republic, more than they do to their parents ... We must say to parents: We are not snatching them away from you, your children, but you may not withhold them from the influence of the nation. And what can the interests of an individual matter to us besides national interests? ... It is in national schools that children must suck republican milk. The Republic is one and indivisible; public instruction must also be related to this centre of unity. (Cited in Glenn, 1988, p. 22)

Clearly, the Republicans were determined to build a new society through shaping the minds of children. The Republic proscribed religious teaching in schools and later even forbade priests to serve as teachers, but it achieved little enduring success in promoting school reform. Others who took over abandoned many of the ideas of the revolutionaries. For example, Napoleon soon replaced 'Liberty, Equality, Fraternity' with the dream of a great empire and the need to educate engineers to lead the army and build the empire. To these ends, Napoleon placed his major educational energies on secondary schools (the *lycée*) to prepare young people for training in engineering and the military sciences (Gildea, 1983). Napoleon thus neglected educational equality, and by default the Church resumed its role in basic education.

It is generally accepted that François Guizot in the 1830s was the major architect in France of a national system of basic education. Guizot used the Napoleonic outline of a national school system organized under a central university, regional academies, departments, and local communes. Each level was assigned specific responsibilities with regard to curriculum, personnel, physical plant and finance, with control emanating from the centre. In terms of many of the specifics of administrative and personnel organization, Guizot borrowed heavily from the Prussian experience, which he and several of his staff had carefully reviewed. Thus, as in Prussia, schooling was divided into hierarchical grades with examinations providing the indication that pupils were ready to move to a higher level. Also as in Prussia, a sharp line was drawn between primary education, which was for all young people, and secondary education, which was for the select few. But in terms of curriculum, French education reflected the long-standing French conviction that citizens should have a broad (encyclopaedic) knowledge of all things, and that their thinking should not be limited by the doctrines of a particular religion. Thus, religious education was not allowed and the French curriculum covered more subjects than could be found in the other modern systems.

The main outlines of the French educational system were firmly in place by the 1870s and did not experience significant changes until long after the Second World War.

England

The English story provides an interesting contrast.[4] While England also was an aristocratic society, it was more flexible than France. As early as Runnymede, the aristocrats forced a compromise on the monarch so that power was shared. A civil society was recognized for those who counted, and this allowed for greater adaptivity in the political sphere, including greater autonomy of local areas. A 'national system locally run' is a phrase used to describe English governance in many areas, including eventually education.

The English polity encountered many ups and downs, including the dramatic reign of Henry VIII when England separated from the Catholic Church. The state took over church property and rewrote the privileges of the clergy, including the status of the various church-influenced educational institutions such as the universities of Oxford and Cambridge and the public schools of Eton and Harrow.

At first, the new Anglican Church enforced a new orthodoxy that tolerated no dissent, but later this position was relaxed and various Protestant sects were allowed their freedom, and so in several areas England was able to accommodate pressures that France ignored. But perhaps the greatest weakness in the English solution was the denial of any rights to the rapidly expanding working class except the economic right to seek a job. As Charles Dickens tells us, they endured 'hard times'. Their efforts to organize were fiercely resisted. But various reformers took up their cause, and some gained a hearing in Parliament. At the time these issues were first being articulated, the French Revolution took place. The English were fearful that England might repeat the mistakes of the French. As English society was facing popular discontent easily equal to that of France, those in powerful places decided to respond with charity and minor concessions. Education was low on their reform agenda. Rather, they established poor houses and other like institutions.

Meanwhile, England was facing new challenges – of gains in trade, empire, and smarter factories than elsewhere in the world. England's leaders came to recognize the need for identifying talent if they were to respond effectively. A celebrated reform of 1854 was the introduction of examinations to select employees for the East India Company. Later, the same principle was introduced for the national civil service. At the same time reforms to increase rigour in the public schools and the universities were introduced, as these institutions were the primary recruiting grounds for these posts.

But these reforms did not address the persisting distress of the working class. And so in mid-century a series of popular reforms was launched. Eventually, Parliament turned its attention to popular education with the Education Act of 1870. Forster, in introducing the bill, said:

> *We must not delay. Upon the speedy provision of elementary education depends our industrial prosperity. It is of no use trying to give technical teaching to our artisans without elementary education; uneducated labourers – and many of our labourers are utterly uneducated – are for the most part, unskilled labourers, and if we leave our workfolk any longer unskilled, notwithstanding their strong sinews and determined energy, they will become over-matched in the competition of the world. If we are to hold our position among men of our own race or among the nations of the world we must make up the smallness of our numbers by increasing the intellectual force of the individual. (Cited in Young, 1958, p. 34)*

This was actually a very limited act, as it allowed but did not require local communities to set up elementary schools. Similarly, it did not require local communities to create subsidized grammar schools that might enable working-class graduates who possessed merit to qualify for further education. Thus, it set the pattern for a two-tier educational system, one for the elite and a second for the masses (Johnson, 1987).

The more prestigious English system is the system of public schools, but of course these are public only in name, being funded and governed by private sponsors (Walford, 1986). Many of these schools trace their history back several hundred years. The goal of the public schools is to nurture the polished individual who knows the great books, fine arts, style, and is a sportsman. Through the mid-nineteenth century the curriculum concentrated on the classics and only gradually has broadened to include modern science and mathematics. The graduates of the public schools were once expected to assume positions of leadership both at home and abroad, across the vast expanses of the British Empire. Today they move into the top universities and comfortable corporate and professional positions.

The public school system is highly labour-intensive, with residential schools in beautiful grounds. Reinforcing the curriculum is a co-curriculum of supervised athletics, club activities, common dining, and other events. The programme is expensive and largely self-supporting; the high fees charged are beyond the means of the common man. This system, nevertheless, is the inspiration for many schools throughout the developing world.

The 'modern' English revolution has largely involved the development of a second tier of institutions for the more common English citizen. Many of the English elite were quite disturbed by the revolutionary developments in France and elsewhere and thus reluctant to encourage the enlightenment of the commoner. But others struggled to broaden the English notion of citizenship, stressing the right of all to civil, social and political rights (Marshall, 1964; Bendix, 1969). Education was one focal point for the reformers, leading to a series of education acts that increased the educational responsibilities both of the central state and of local governments.

By the turn of the twentieth century, a new administrative entity known as the local education authority (LEA) had been created for the second tier of 'public' schools that the LEA managed and funded. There are approximately 120 LEAs, each with its own administrative system to manage the schools and teachers in its area. Until recently, the national government has extended considerable autonomy to each LEA. Many of the schools in this second tier are excellent, reflecting the wealth and distinction of the communities where they are located, but others are quite drab and full of problems. Across LEAs there is considerable variation in the particular school forms used for upper secondary work, with most favouring a comprehensive school and a few others still favouring grammar and secondary modern school alternatives.

The curricular emphasis of each LEA has, until recently, been allowed to vary according to local preference. However, the academic track of all LEAs has the responsibility for preparing students for the nationwide General Certificate of Secondary Education (GCSE) and Advanced level examinations prepared by recognized examining boards. The emphasis in these examinations is considerably influenced by the curricular goals common to the elite university and the public school sector. Thus, despite the diversity of the English decentralized and multi-tier system, there is an important strain for consistency in those schools preparing pupils for the academic track.

The national Ministry of Education provides funds to foster some degree of equality in the financial resources available to local school systems, but until recently has been reluctant to intervene in any more substantial way. Partly because of the hands-off attitude of the national authority, it has a comparatively small office and adds little cost to the overall system.

However, over the past several years a number of reports have pointed to the low academic quality of English public education. In response, a number of radical steps have been proposed to elevate and unify national standards (Education Reform Act, 1988). The new interventionist orientation of the national authority will certainly lead to some expansion in the scale of its administrative apparatus.

The USA

The first European settlers came to America to establish God's kingdom on earth. Their concern was to create a setting where individuals could communicate directly with God, rather than through the intervention of church bureaucracies. The ability to read the Bible was an essential element in personal communion, and thus the early settlements placed a strong emphasis on education. Basic skills were taught in the home, but for more advanced ability, including the interpretation of religious and other works, it was recognized that special places of study should be founded. Thus, only sixteen years after the first settlers arrived in New England, Harvard College was founded. By the end of the eighteenth century over 200 small colleges had been founded in the New World (Boorstin, 1958, pp. 177ff.) These colleges were the foundation of American education, to be followed by other institutions at both lower and higher levels.

While religious freedom was the inspiration for many of America's settlers, they had diverse doctrinal perspectives, resulting in the establishment of numerous communities. Other settlers had little interest in religion. The various groups who came to found colonies in the New World had their respective purposes; when, following the revolution, they sat down to devise a new form of government, they agreed that the federal government should have a limited role in most local affairs, including education.

Thus, a decentralized system of control and finance was established for American education. This was intended to make schools responsive to local needs. In the first colonies individual communities were given the responsibility for the provision of education. Over time, the responsibility has tended to shift towards state governments; this pattern is most evident in the western parts of the USA. The decentralized American pattern has fostered much creativity in the conceptualization of new approaches to education. However, the burden of realizing these approaches has rested on the leadership of the respective communities. In prosperous communities that were willing to allocate funds for education, innovation flourished. Elsewhere, education followed a more traditional path.

One of the most distinctive themes in the American dream is the belief that education should respond to individual needs. The Pilgrims and other religious groups that settled in New England stressed basic education so that the individual could directly interpret God's will. In Virginia Thomas Jefferson urged popular education so that citizens could choose leaders wisely. And so from an early stage there developed a notion of learning to enhance the efficacy and enjoyment of the individual. Building on this tradition, other American pedagogues have stressed life adjustment, learning at one's own pace, and learning what is personally relevant.

As with many other core American educational ideas, the curricular implications of the principle of individual development were first explored at the collegiate level. From early in the eighteenth century, college leaders questioned the relevance of teaching the classics and requiring students to achieve mastery of Greek and Latin. As enrolment increased at the more popular colleges, their leaders questioned why all students should be required to take the same courses. Gradually, the collegiate curriculum was reformed to allow more relevance and personal choice. The 'elective principle' was the eventual outcome wherein students were given extensive choice from a wide range of courses (Veysey, 1965, pp. 51ff.) This principle of extensive choice in accordance with personal needs and development has gradually pervaded the lower levels of American education. For example, in contemporary America, at the secondary level, individualized programmes of instruction are made possible by the comprehensive high school and its generous offering of electives. A typical high school will accommodate students interested in both academic and vocational studies, and within each of these tracks there are numerous combinations of subjects and subject quality levels. In the academic track, juniors and seniors can elect advanced placement, honours, ordinary, and remedial level variations of the same subject. Well over half the courses required for graduation are electives, enabling students to follow their idiosyncratic interests. In many high schools, it is possible for every graduate to have followed a unique programme of study.

Boyer (1983) and Goodlad (1984), in their recent critiques of American high schools, speak disparagingly of this freedom, warning of the risks associated with the concept of 'We Want it All'. Many students elect frivolous combinations that do not add up to an education, while the economic burden of providing such a diverse programme is often staggering. While these critics urge a more uniform high school curriculum, the defenders assert that the electives option enables young people to explore their own needs. The prevailing view is that high school is a place for personal exploration and social maturation; rigorous academic work can be postponed to the collegiate or graduate level stage when the young person has found himself.

At the primary level, the concept of individualized instruction has received expression in such experiments as open classrooms and programmes for the gifted and talented as well as for those with learning disabilities or cultural disadvantages. Each student may receive unique treatment. The concern with responding to individual needs through providing many curricular options has led to a preference in the USA for small classes where teachers and students can experience intensive interaction. Reform efforts have consistently promoted this concern, with the result that student–teacher ratios in American education are among the lowest in the world.

The provision of an educational technology responsive to diverse needs requires an extensive support system outside the classroom. At the school level, local districts employ subject specialists to review textbooks, schools employ guidance counsellors and remedial and enrichment instructors, librarians and teacher aids. Administrators are employed to supervise the work of the various specialists.

One of the intentions of the founding fathers was to ensure the right of individual communities to advance their distinctive values through the institutions of family, church and school. Thus, in the US Constitution, they asserted that education was to be the responsibility of local bodies, and not the federal government. But in another part of the US Constitution, the founding fathers asserted the principle of separation of Church and State. When schools were supported by individual donations there were no conflicts. But as American schools came to be funded from public sources, the principle of separation of church and state led to a second distinctive feature, the elimination of religious and moral objectives from the formal school curriculum. Over time, values education in the public school curriculum became narrowed to the conveyance of civic values. Few public school systems are so limited in this regard as the American.

While there were wide differences in the religious and social values of the early American communities, most believed that their young people should learn to read and write, and out of this faith emerged the movement to found common schools. By the middle of the nineteenth century, such schools were widely established. By the turn of the twentieth century, sufficient schools had been established to offer virtually every young person an opportunity for education. In the provision of educational opportunity, the USA moved ahead of all other countries, except possibly Germany and Japan – and the USA has continued to pride itself in this regard.

Over the twentieth century the doctrine of equal opportunity was progressively articulated, gaining especially forceful presentation during the Depression. Minorities were afforded 'separate but equal' opportunity until 1954, when the Supreme Court ruled that separate could not be equal.

While all should be offered the opportunity to pursue education, for much of American history it was up to the individual to take advantage of that opportunity. But in the years since the Supreme Court ruling, American educators have even questioned whether equal opportunity is sufficient, proposing that education should assume responsibility for motivating those who enter schools to achieve equal results. This idea has proved most difficult, given the strict limitations on the curricular goals of schools.

Japan

Japan was far from Europe and essentially oblivious to developments there. Living in virtual isolation, the Tokugawa house coordinated a centralized feudal regime that fostered a reasonable level of economic development and that by the early nineteenth century had enabled approximately one-quarter of the population to achieve literacy (possibly 40 per cent of the males and 10 per cent of the females). In the early 1850s, this peaceful world was shocked by the arrival of Commodore Perry in his 'black ship' with his demand that Japan open up her doors for trade with the USA. Several of the leaders of more peripheral fiefs, fearful of imminent colonization by the ambitious West, decided to join together and create a new centralized political arrangement in order to build national strength and avert foreign domination. What ensued was the extraordinary Meiji Revolution of 1868.

Following their military triumph, the Meiji leaders quickly turned to reorganize national institutions. The vigour of their initiatives was astounding – the abolition of feudalism, the establishment of new factories, and the creation of a central bureaucracy. Educational reform was also key. The new leadership proclaimed the need for Japan to seek knowledge from throughout the world. The Meiji leaders were determined to use education as a means of building national solidarity, developing a technically competent labour force, and identifying and educating the future elite (Cummings, 1980). Every family, whether samurai or commoner, was instructed to send their children to school. Within fifteen years, enrolment ratios at the primary level surpassed those in England and possibly even the USA. The system has steadily expanded and developed since then. These goals have been pursued with surprising consistency down to the present. The only major shift was following the Second World War when the US Occupation insisted on a broadening of the already substantial level of opportunity at the upper secondary and tertiary levels.

While the goals of the new government were ambitious, resources were limited, and so from the very beginning, the government established what might be called a mass-production education drawing heavily on Western European precedent. The following are some of the characteristics of that system that are still in evidence today.

A uniform curriculum with virtually no electives until secondary level tracking. Thus, all students gain a solid grounding in mathematics and science, and all receive a common exposure to moral education. At the secondary level all take foreign languages. In addition, the curriculum stresses moral education, including the important learning principle that spirit overcomes matter, that effort is more fundamental than ability in determining progress in learning.

A national system for the production of textbooks which relies on professional educators and writers to develop the drafts, but relies on bureaucratic committees for a final judgement on content. In earlier times there was one text per subject, while since the Second World War local school boards have been encouraged to choose from several centrally approved texts.

A uniform finance and personnel policy, in keeping with national resources. Due to equalizing regulations, per-student expenditure in public schools is remarkably similar between and within major regions. In the Meiji period, student–teacher ratios were in excess of fifty. Today the ratios are down to thirty, but in a particular class the ratio may be over forty to one as teachers share a class so that they can have more time for lesson preparation.

Concerning the critical area of classroom management, observational studies suggest relatively uniform pedagogy and pace across classrooms of the same grade level in different schools (Stevenson et al, 1986). Underlying this uniformity in classroom management is a widely shared belief in the importance of harmonious and supportive human relations for fostering learning. This leads to a preference for small groups and small schools, and careful selection of the members of these groups (White, 1987). Once the groups are established, close relations are stressed – e.g. the home room principle throughout; automatic promotion, often keeping the same class intact. The stress on holistic education with effort, a resource all can muster, is the key to learning. The group is viewed as the focus of learning rather than the individual.

There have been changes over time. The curriculum was relatively simple in the Meiji period, but gradually has become fuller. Today it is surprisingly rich. At the primary level, along with the standard three Rs, the curriculum includes systematic instruction in music, art, physical education, and both domestic and industrial arts. At the secondary level, a full programme of mathematics and science courses for all students, as well as mandatory study of six years of English and at least three years of a second foreign language, is required.

In the early Meiji period, compulsory education lasted four years. It has gradually been lengthened and in the early 1940s was extended through to the ninth grade. On the completion of compulsory schooling, young people take examinations that determine their place in local high school systems where the constituent institutions are usually stratified by student achievement level; from heterogeneous grouping at the compulsory level, the system shifts to ability-differentiated homogeneous groups. Young people and their parents believe that the particular high school they enter will influence their college choice and their career. Thus, educational achievement becomes a serious endeavour rather early in the educational cycle, typically from the second half of primary school education.

The modern Japanese educational system was established to help Japan catch up with the West. Over time, the national leaders decided they would not only have to catch up with but also compete with the West in the international arena of imperialism. Thus, the values education theme of the schools came to emphasize nationalistic and imperialistic themes. Japan achieved its initial successes in the defeat of China and Russia at the turn of the century, gaining the colonies of Taiwan and Korea. In the 1930s, Japan decided to focus on South-east Asia and entered into the Second World War as an ally of Germany. Ultimately, Japan was defeated and occupied by the Allied powers, who set about introducing many fundamental reforms, including a major reform of education so that the system was demilitarized and more democratic.

Summing up, the Japanese approach is characterized by centralized organization of education which brings about uniformity in major resources and procedures.

The Soviet Union

The last modern pattern emerged out of the Bolshevik Revolution (1917). This system developed very rapidly despite the considerable challenges of widespread illiteracy and the vast size of Russia.

In the territory which eventually was consolidated in the Soviet Union there were many national groups with their distinctive languages and customs. The tsarist government had little to no control over many of these groups. The major influence of the Tsars was in European Russia where the economy was beginning to industrialize. From the time of Peter the Great some important steps were taken to promote technical and higher education, especially in Moscow and in Peter's new capital of St Petersburg.

The tsars obtained their principal support from the rural landowning class, who were afraid of the peasants and reluctant to encourage their literacy (Alston, 1969). Thus, at the turn of the twentieth century no more than one-third of the Russian people west of the Ur7als were literate, and to the east there was nearly total illiteracy (Grant, 1982).

The interaction of Russian elites with their European kindred led to proposals for various political and social reforms, and some argue that Russia in the early twentieth century was on its way towards the same pattern of progressive reform that had occurred in England. But the tsar's decision to involve Russia in the First World War led to great hardships and popular discontent. Various revolutionary groups appealed to this discontent, and eventually proved so successful that the Russian Revolution unfolded. Ultimately, the Bolsheviks triumphed, and one of their top goals was the promotion of mass literacy and a modern meritocratic educational system.

The People's Commissariat of Education was formed in 1918 with Anatoly V. Lunacharsky as the first commissioner. In his first annual report, Lunacharsky set out the principles of Soviet education which continue down to the present day:

> *In place of schools of all varieties and kinds – which formerly were sharply divided into a lower school for the plain people, and the middle school for the privileged classes and the well-to-do people, and divided further into schools for boys and those for girls, into technical and classical secondary schools, general and special school institutions – the*

Commissariat has introduced the Unified Workers' School, covering the entire length of the course of instruction.

The unity of this school should be understood in two ways: first, that the class divisions are abolished and the school adopts a continuous grade system. In principle, every child of the Russian Republic enters a school of an identical type and has the same chances as every other to complete the higher education. Second, that up to the age of 16, all specialization is omitted. It is self-understood that this does not hinder the adoption of the principle of individual attention and of the greatest possible variety of forms inside each school. But specialization in the full meaning of the word is permitted only after the attaining of the age of 16, and upon the foundation of a general and polytechnical education acquired already. The school is declared an absolutely lay institution; diplomas in their character of certificates granting special rights are abolished. The classical languages are declared nonobligatory. (Quoted in Bereday et al, 1960, pp. 51-52)

The proposed system was to have two levels – a primary school of five grades starting at age eight followed by a four-year secondary programme (for those advancing to higher education two additional years of secondary education and for those entering technical areas a specialized programme of the same length). The schools were to be neighbourhood schools with no streaming until the upper secondary level. This basic design has continued to the present with occasional modifications. For example, in 1942 the entry age was lowered to seven, and after the Second World War night schools were established to enable working youth who had to interrupt their study due to war to continue.[5]

The Second Party Programme on Education (1919) emphasized the foundation of schooling in Marxist–Leninist doctrine. Education was to be 'closely connected with useful labour and prepare members for a communist society'. Thus, education was to be free of religious influence, and all schools supported by the Church were abolished.

In 1919, Lenin signed a decree making it compulsory for everyone between the ages of eight and fifty to learn to read and write in Russian or their native language. There was much turmoil during this period as the new government struggled to overcome the threat from the White Russians and other dissident groups in the civil war. But in 1923 a national policy for compulsory primary education was introduced. A key feature of this policy was the elimination of discrimination based on race or gender. Primary schools were made co-educational and allowed to carry out their instruction in local languages while at the same time introducing Russian to those who had a different mother tongue (hence the stress on the bilingual learning theory in Table 1.2).

The Russian state considered education an investment for national development, and it viewed each student to be critical for the state mission.

Thus, the state fully subsidized education and prepared detailed plans both for human resource development and manpower utilization. The technical bias in manpower plans led to an exceptionally strong mathematics and science emphasis in the schools; science fairs and prizes were used to stimulate the enthusiasm of young people. At the same time, Soviet education stressed whole person education, with a strong emphasis on the collective spirit and physical fitness.

The state's commitment to rapid industrial development became particularly evident with the rise of Stalin. Especially from the Third Five Year Plan, many resources were allocated for the rapid expansion of the educational system, and by 1939, 95 per cent of all adult men and 83 per cent of all adult women were literate. The main features of socialist education were in place by the late 1930s, and while there have been various reforms since, only those emerging since glasnost represent major departures (Bain, 2003).

Thinking about Educational Change

We see in these accounts six distinctive trajectories of change. The starting contexts involve unique cultural and political developments, the first steps involve different groups of actors, the announced priorities differ, the rates of change differ, and so do the outcomes. How can these distinctive trajectories of change be explained?

Arguably, the dominant paradigm for thinking about change, at least in the USA, is to assume that societies constantly improve through a graduated series of thoughtful reforms. An additional twist on this paradigm is to assume that these changes are occurring around the world and converging in a common direction, and that that direction has a striking resemblance to the American system. An early expression of this paradigm is what has come to be called modernization theory. Robert Nisbet (1969), in his review of Western theories of social change from St Augustine to the present, argues that certain features of Western, and especially American, character may compel us to see similarities where differences exist. These include the American belief in inexorable progress or the possibility of improving the human condition combined with the missionary zeal that only the Americans hold the key to perfection, so that all are or should become like the Americans.

Concerning education, Philip Coombs (1968), in his initial account of the World Educational Revolution, described the dramatic expansion of schooling following the Second World War. Coombs attributed this expansion to the formation of many more independent states and to the steady economic growth in these new states. He observed that there were certain problems of deteriorating quality associated with this expansion, but overall he projected a promising future so long as the new states could introduce certain reforms, notably the adoption of active learning principles for formal basic education that had a close resemblance to US practice, and the expansion of non-formal education to promote adult literacy. It is somewhat ironic that Coombs (1985) titled the sequel to the above account *The World Crisis in Education*, and focused primarily on an analysis of the World Education Revolution's tailspin. Indeed, in most developing countries educational quality had deteriorated, and in several settings a process of de-scholarization was under way.

In North America, following Coombs, there have been a number of ostensibly comparative studies, but there is a tendency in virtually all of these to minimize the differences between societies, and to repeat the comforting thesis of 1950s US social science that all roads lead to Washington. Alex Inkeles's (1974) *Becoming Modern* is an early example of this tendency. John Meyer and his Stanford group, while initially prepared to reject the US-centric convergence thesis, after extensive research surprisingly conclude that all modern education is essentially the same; for example, in the conclusion to their volume on primary curricula, Meyer et al (1992) assert:

> *The most important finding in our research is the relative homogeneity of the world's primary curriculum outlines in the twentieth century. This is true descriptively – in the sense that there is considerably less variation among curricular outlines than reasonable arguments would have predicted. And it is true in an explanatory sense – factors that vary among countries play a smaller role than most theories would have proposed, in affecting variations among curricula. Further, we notice a pronounced tendency for curricular changes in particular countries to parallel each other and to take the form of conformity to world curricular patterns. (p. 30)*

Meyer (1977), in an important conceptual article titled 'The Effects of Education as an Institution', provides a summary of these arguments, and proposes that the world system is somehow leading all educational systems to converge on a common institutional pattern. Others of Meyer's associates working with parallel data sets and using similar methodologies reach similar conclusions. The main thrust of my argument below is to contest this view, to insist that there is not a single institution of education, but, rather, several that are developing along parallel paths. In other words, the impact of the world system has been vastly exaggerated.

Another interesting recent stream of US theorizing that is as popular in academia as it is on television networks such as CNN is what might be called global theory. Former Secretary of Labour Robert Reich's (1991) *The Work of Nations* is perhaps the most influential development of this thesis. This primarily economic theory asserts that the institutions of modern trade, industry and finance are becoming ever more interconnected and homogeneous and that other institutions, including education, will follow suit. While not explicitly pointing to the USA as the leader, this theory's stress on the information and communication industries, which are most highly developed in the USA, leads it to the all too familiar US-centric predictions for future development.

Among the ambitious US-based comparative studies of education, an important exception to the unilinear theorists is the recent look at socialist education coordinated by Martin Carnoy & Joel Samhoff (1990). This study discovers important differences in the practice of education around the world, highlighting four distinctive socialist models. Prominent in the detailed studies of educational change presented by the authors is the prevalence of major political struggles to bring about changes, changes that are not always positive. For example, educational budgets are shown to decline in some countries before increasing. Enrolment rates go down, as do the ratios of students to resources. In other words, education does not experience continuing progress to some utopian pinnacle, but, rather, experiences and indeed depends on conflict to bring about improvement. Burton Clark's (1983) and Daniel Levy's (1986) interesting comparisons of university systems also dwell on major differences and on cycles of change.

An aid to summarizing these different views of educational change is Ingemar Fägerlind & Lawrence Saha's (1989) suggestive diagrammatic comparison of theories of social change. As illustrated in Figure 1.1, they posited four broad groupings. The first two groupings (classic cyclical and Augustinian Christian) are rarely featured in contemporary comparative work. The two mainstreams of comparative work, at least in North America, tend to reflect either the linear model or the cyclical linear model. I refer here to modernization studies on the one hand and those that draw from the conflict tradition on the other.

The particular approach I am advocating belongs to a fifth grouping, which might be called the parallel cyclical linear model, as depicted in Figure 1.1. It builds on many of the premises of conflict theory, but predicts that the multiple conflicts that occur at particular historical junctures lead societies and educational systems on distinctively separate or parallel paths rather than a common path.

The foundation work for this fifth grouping has occurred largely outside of North America. I think of Margaret Archer's (1977) massive study of educational governance, Fritz Ringer's (1979) and Detlef Müller's (Müller et al, 1987) study and other careful analyses of educational expansion and systematization, Brian Holmes's (Holmes & McLean, 1989) useful comparison of curricula, and Patricia Broadfoot et al's (Broadfoot & Osborn, 1988; Broadfoot et al, 1993) interesting work on teachers. There is also interesting comparative work in Asia by Ikuo Amano (1990) and in Russia by Leo Gumilev (1997) that reflects this fifth grouping.

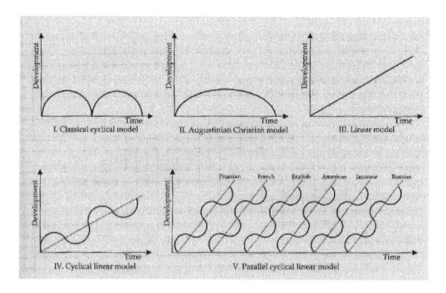

Figure 1.1. Idealizations of five theories of change and development.
Source: Reproduced from Cummings (1999).

InstitutionS as the Key

The concept of Institutions was prominent in early social theorizing. Herbert Spencer (1891) proposed that certain institutions were critical for the survival of societies. Max Weber (1949), in comparing different economic and political institutions, developed the methodology of ideal types to describe the distinctive features of such institutions as patriarchy, patrimonialism and bureaucracy. Talcott Parsons, Alfred Kroeber & Edward Shils (1951), building on Weber, proposed that institutions were formed to realize particular societal values and that the constituent norms, beliefs and regulations of particular institutions tended to derive from these core values; behaviour or social action was seen as following from these normative commitments. Thus, institutional theorists propose that institutions, and more specifically their core values, tend to determine social behaviour. Parsons was particularly insightful in developing this approach in his *The Social System* (1951) and his *Structure and Process in Modern Societies* (1960).

This framework was influential in much of the early post-war thinking about social change and development in the Western democracies. Gabriel Almond & Sidney Verba's (1963) influential work on civic culture assumed that the institutionalization of this culture was critical to the effective working of democracies. Similarly, David McClelland (1976) argued that the achievement motive was critical for the success of capitalism, and Alex

Inkeles (1974) argued that modern values were essential for the functioning of modern factories.

However, from the early 1960s conflict theorists began to suggest that other factors such as class interests or technology played a more critical role in shaping behaviour. They also objected to the characteristic arguments of American institutionalists, such as Talcott Parsons, that social change was following a unilinear evolutionary direction with the USA as the leading prototype. In the process of developing counter-arguments, the conflict theorists and many subsequent theoretical schools tended to engage in a wholesale rejection of institutionalism.

While institutionalism was rejected, those engaged in both the study and practice of social change continually confronted the stubborn reality of institutional factors: one thinks of Clifford Geertz's (1963) exploration of agricultural involution in Java and of Edward Banfield's (1958) description of 'the moral basis of a backward society' in southern Italy which held it back from the economic take-off of northern Italy. And after a decade or more of tiptoeing around these realities, in recent years a new generation of institutionalists has emerged in a variety of disciplines ranging from anthropology to sociology, political science and economics. An interesting illustration of this shift is a recent World Bank study (1993a) of economic growth in East Asia through the early 1990s, which places considerable stress on institutional as contrasted with market factors. And the subsequent publications about the Asian economic flu also stress institutional factors.

Douglas North (1990), in his theoretical argument for the role of institutions in economic change, notes that neoclassical economic theory predicts that all societies will converge around a common economic system. But that has not transpired. North suggests that there must be flaws in the theory, particularly concerning the accessibility of economic actors to accurate information. Given imperfect accessibility and the threat which that implies, actors agree on various informal and formal constraints, in other words, on institutions such as polities that intervene in economic transactions, property rights and contracts. North notes that the specifics of these institutions differ widely from one locale to another. They set up different incentive structures, some that are favourable and some that are antithetical to development. The challenge for the researcher is to clarify these differences and their consequences.

The work of North and others has spawned a major industry of interdisciplinary theorizing which frequently evokes the code word of social capital. Such phenomena as the differential developmental success of small villages in the Andes and the relative prevalence of the Mafia have been considered by these theorizers. The central concern of this new theoretical school is to understand why some societies achieve better outcomes than others. That, I believe, is also our central concern, the only difference being that we focus on educational outcomes. The following are some of the main tenets of institutional theory.

- Institutional theory's focus is on the patterns, or constellations, of ideals and norms, that govern day-to-day transactions.
- Patterns change rarely, and usually concurrently with radical shifts in other institutional patterns, in periods of major upheaval.
- These patterns have a certain hierarchical order to them, beginning with core ideals or commitments and working down in layers of specificity to rules about process, technique, and resources.
- Patterns are articulated through specific organizations – in the case of education, through representative schools.
- Patterns, while difficult to change in their fundamentals, are easily imitated and replicated.
- While patterns are powerful shapers of change, they are typically the focus of criticism which may or may not be articulated in counter-institutions.
- When patterns change, the magnitude of the change will be related to the magnitude of the upheaval and its abruptness.
- When patterns change, the new patterns are likely to inherit many of the features of their predecessors.

The Six Core Educational Patterns

Drawing on the insight of institutional theory, we will propose here that six core 'modern' educational patterns or InstitutionS emerged. In order of their appearance, they are the continental pattern (which is best broken into the Prussian and French variants, with the Lowlands as a third possibility), the English, the American, the Japanese, and the Russian socialist patterns. Some commentators on the modern educational revolution tend to minimize the differences between these patterns, but it will be argued here that the differences are considerable and enduring. Moreover, these differences have been diffused widely throughout the modern world. A seventh 'pre-modern' pattern, Islamic education, survived despite the aggressive advance (through colonial governments) of the core modern patterns, and in recent years has achieved a new vitality.

Each modern pattern is unified by a core set of ideals (much like the genotype of biology) that can be at least partially captured in a slogan such as nineteenth-century aristocratic England's ideal of the educated gentleman or, in the American case, the continuous development of the individual. Over subsequent decades these national ideals were continually refined, but in the six cases under consideration they were never fundamentally altered. These ideals thus had an enduring influence on various structural features of the respective systems, including the type of school that is most esteemed, the range of subjects covered, the prevailing theory of learning, and preferred teaching methods. In other words, there is a *gentle degree of determinism* implied (Müller et al, 1987), with the ideal placing some constraints on curriculum, learning theory and so on. For example, to realize the comprehensive educational goals implied in the English concept of the educated gentleman, a boarding school is essential along with close monitoring by tutors; and as a gentleman is expected to dabble in everything, the co-curriculum is highly valued. A contrast might be made with France where formal education was intended to train experts, outstanding in a particular intellectual area but with no expectation that they play cricket or polo. The distinctive characteristics of each of these patterns can be summarized with an ideal-typical schema (Table 1.2).

	Prussia	France	England	USA	Japan	Russia
Period of genesis	1742-1820	1791-1870	1820-1904	1840-1910	1868-1890	1917-1935
Ideal	Loyal mandarin	Technical elite	Educated gentleman	Continuous development of the individual	Competent contribution to the group	Socialist achievement
Representative school	Primary schools	*Lycée/grande école*	Public school	Comprehensive high, liberal arts college	Primary school	General schools
Scope	Whole person, many subjects, humanistic bias	Cognitive growth in academic subjects arts/science	Academic subjects, civic & religious values, culture & curriculum	Cognitive development, civic values, social skills	Whole person, wide range of subjects, moral values, physical & aesthetic skills	Whole person, broad curriculum, technical bias
School & classroom technology	Lectures & self-study	Lectures & exams	Tutors, co-curriculum boarding school	Individualized courses & instruction	Teacher-centred, groups, school as units	Collective learning
Learning theory	Natural unfolding	Mental discipline	Hereditary brilliance	Aptitude & growth	Effort	Interactive
Administration	Quasi-decentralized	Centralized	Private	Decentralized	Quasi-decentralized	Centralized
Administration style	Autocratic	Authoritarian	Leadership	Management	Cooperation	Collective control
Unit costs	Moderate	Moderate	High	Variable	Moderate	Moderate to high
Source of finance	Local state	State (church)	Fees	Local taxes	State	State

Table 1.2. The core educational patterns.

These patterns were developed in the core nations of the world system and later diffused by their respective colonial and/or ideological systems. Thus, the French variant became influential in Africa, Indochina and Latin

America; the English pattern was widely diffused through Asia and Africa; the American pattern had some early influence in Asia and since the Second World War has had global influence; the Japanese pattern had a profound impact on Korea and Taiwan and more limited influence elsewhere; and the Russian socialist pattern influenced China, Eastern Europe, Cuba and many other developing societies.

Core Propositions of the InstitutionS of Education

The following are ten core principles of institutional theory as applied to education.

1. The concept of the ideal person is the core of an educational system. All of the great educational proposals begin with a vision of the type of person that society prefers. Confucianism stressed the virtuous official. Medieval classical education favoured the devout servant of God. The French Enlightenment favoured the savant with encyclopaedic knowledge and quick wit. American educators came to believe in the individual with his or her possibilities for continuing development throughout the life cycle.

2. In times of rapid ideological, political and economic change, new thinking about education may emerge, leading potentially to educational reform. Education, like other institutions, has mechanisms to buffer itself from outside influence. But under the pressure of the triple revolutions that began in the mid-eighteenth century leading to the modern era, traditional institutions, including those providing education, experienced much stress. The temporal peaking of these triple revolutions differed in each of these settings, as noted in Figure 1.1. Modern education was first conceived in Prussia and France, last in Russia; and in the settings of France, Japan and Russia this stress was relatively severe and temporally compact, leading to major change over a relatively brief time span. In contrast, in Prussia, the USA, and especially England, the stress was less severe and thus change was more gradual.

3. The most fundamental educational reform is the creation of a new concept of the ideal person. In the early modern period, doubtless many new concepts emerged. But for various reasons, only six of these survived. Each of these concepts was the invention of prominent leaders who were, at the same time, advocating a socio-political revolution that favoured rising class interests. The leaders often remarked on foreign examples in promoting change. The American proponents of the common school cited Prussian and French precedent. Forster, arguing in 1870 for England's first Education Act, said, 'If we are to hold our position among men of our own race or among the nations of the world we must make up the smallness of our numbers by increasing the intellectual force of the individual'.

The six new concepts and the institutional patterns that evolved from these concepts eventually largely displaced the former educational traditions. Yet each pattern built in some degree on the prior traditions of education, which were resident in the geographical space where they were conceived. Thus, the new French pattern, while rejecting the sacred thrust of earlier education, retained the prior emphasis on encyclopaedic knowledge and other Enlightenment principles such as the stress on oral recitation and examinations. In contrast, the new English and Prussian patterns retained the prior sacred emphasis. In Japan, the traditional emphasis on moral education was retained while all other subjects were replaced by a Westernized curriculum. The new concepts were constructed through combining tradition, foreign ideas and indigenous creativity.

4. Notions of who should be taught, what they should be taught, how people learn, and how education should be organized follow from a society's conception(s) of the ideal person. Institutions are built with a concern for internal consistency, and the foundation of this strain for consistency is the values or goals the institutions seek to realize. In education, these values or goals are embodied in the ideal person. Where the ideal person is an elite (as in the case of England and France), the educational system is likely to be more restrictive. Where the ideal person is expected to have diverse functions, the curriculum is likely to be more holistic. Table 1.2 summarizes my understanding of the key decisions made by the leaders of selected early modern societies as they constructed their new educational systems.

5. The representative school is the principal vehicle for nurturing the ideal person. Among the first acts of educational leaders was the creation of a new 'representative' school to embody their new ideals. In the Japanese case this was the new primary school; within four years of the Charter Oath on education, some 22,000 new primary schools had been established following a common ideal. American educational leaders were fixated on the college. Only sixteen years after the Pilgrims landed at Plymouth Rock, Harvard College was founded; by the time of the American revolution there were eighty-five colleges in the thirteen colonies, compared with only two universities in all of England. Napoleon, concerned to build a new technical elite from the ranks of the French bourgeoisie, placed his greatest stress on the *lycée* and the *école polytechnique*.

6. A society is likely to establish numerous schools, which, while they vary in level, size and location, reflect the institutional pattern of the representative school. The initial thinking about schooling was instituted in these first representative schools. Later thinking about education for other levels tended to derive from this initial thinking. For example, the organization of Japanese middle and high schools tends to follow from the primary school; at all three levels there is a common curriculum with no electives and students stay in the same home room classrooms throughout the day while teachers move from class to class. In contrast, in the USA, high schools and junior highs tend to adopt the institutional pattern of the college, with students enjoying numerous electives which they pursue by moving from one classroom to another throughout the day.

7. Educational change, since the emergence of these six concepts and their representative schools, has largely focused on their refinement, expansion and systematization. As will be noted below, in each of the core societies there are periodic cries of crisis followed by much reform rhetoric. Despite all of that, education today in all of these societies bears a very close institutional resemblance to the education conceived in the early decades of the respective modern revolutions.

8. Educational leaders, in the process of systematizing education, seek to buffer the 'core' educational processes from external influence. Mechanisms such as boards of trustees, school boards and public examinations are instituted for this purpose. In times of economic strain, the buffers established for universities and the vocational/technical sector are most vulnerable. In times of political/ideological strain, the primary levels are most vulnerable.

9. Each institutional pattern provokes counter-patterns that have some impact on educational practice, the magnitude of which depends on the openness of the political system and on the strength of opposition politics. Just as each of these new educational reforms replaced a prior pattern, critics soon emerged to suggest yet other alternatives. Over time, the thinking of these critics became more elaborate and was either promoted by independent educators or opposition political organizations. For example, in Japan, some of the early Meiji leaders withdrew from the ruling oligarchy to found their own private schools (later enlarged as comprehensive school systems). In England, the socialist party was persistently critical of the elitist education favoured by the dominant Conservative Party, and especially after the Second World War, when the socialists enjoyed power over an extended period of time, they translated their critical thinking into new schools such as the comprehensive secondary school and the red brick universities. In the Soviet Union, there was always a strain between the proponents of education to cultivate the Soviet citizen and those stressing the need for a higher level of technical expertise; yet another group stressed the need for a more humanistic education (Bain, 2001). Diane Ravitch (1983) has provided an excellent account of the persisting American dialectic between excellence and equity.

10. The six patterns have had a profound impact on the educational landscape, resulting in the worldwide diffusion of six distinct patterns of education. I feature only six institutional patterns in this schema as, over most of the modern period, these were the only societies that both enjoyed continuing national integrity and were sufficiently powerful to have extensive influence, through empire, trade and other means, over other nations. Education in most other modern settings came to emulate the educational institutions of these six core nations, as I will illustrate below.

So, to reiterate, in this schema there are six InstitutionS of modern education, each developing along a distinctive trajectory. There is at least one pre-modern pattern, the Islamic pattern, that also deserves note as it resisted the onslaught of modernism and has continued to exert a major influence on the practice of education.

Comparing the Major Patterns

The core patterns emerged at different periods in the global process of modernization. In each instance there were unique confluences of internal and external forces, necessarily inviting distinctive responses. Several generalizations about the nature of educational reform can be derived from these accounts.

- Educational reform is closely associated with political shifts; economic forces are an important contextual factor.
- The magnitude and abruptness of the political shift influences the extent of the educational reform.
- Political shifts are closely associated with major class realignments, and these in turn influence the focus of the educational reform.
- Educational reform, while bold on rhetoric, tends to focus on a limited set of changes concerning a particular level of schooling, at least in the short run.
- Educational reform, while often mentioning foreign examples in its rhetoric, tends to draw extensively on indigenous resources, indigenous ideals, and indigenous educational practices (both past and present).
- Thus, even after a seemingly dramatic educational reform, the memory of past ideals and practices will persist to exert influence on the new and even possibly at some later date to replace the new.
- In developing rules and procedures for reformed educational institutions, there is always pressure to harmonize with the rules and procedures of other institutions.
- Thus, educational reform, in its particulars, tends to turn inwards, reproducing and creating indigenous patterns, rather than outwards, converging on internationally approved patterns.

Those patterns that emerged as one outcome of major social revolutions tended to express a greater departure from the past and to move towards systematization and expansion at a more rapid pace. The French, Japanese and Russian systems were most closely associated with revolutions, and in each case the main pieces of the new system were articulated in a decade and largely realized within three decades. In contrast, the English system evolved at perhaps the slowest pace, reflecting the ability of English parliamentary democracy to avert a major revolutionary rupture.

Those patterns created out of peasant and/or worker revolution tended to place a greater stress on equality for all. The American revolution gave birth to the phrase 'all men are created equal' and the French revolution proposed 'liberty, equality, fraternity'. But both of these revolutions were essentially urban middle-class bourgeoisie revolutions and the major educational beneficiaries were these same classes; for example, school funding in the USA became related to the wealth of local communities, thus sharply handicapping most rural areas. In contrast, in Japan, many of the core revolutionaries were lower samurai from rural and comparatively peripheral areas. These samurai insisted on the development of provisions in various social services that ensured equal treatment for rural people; for example, special regulations and allowances were introduced to attract qualified teachers to mountainous areas and offshore islands.

The latecomers, reflecting their genesis in a period of heightened nationalism, tended to place a greater stress on moral education. Most emphatic was the determination of the Russian system to develop a socialist consciousness and of the Japanese to emphasize moral education and imperial statism. In contrast, the French system, formed on the basis of Enlightenment ideas that stressed the separation of Church and State and the supremacy of reason, tended to minimize the school's socializing role. Similarly, in the USA by the late nineteenth century, family and church were looked to for values education rather than the school. Prussia would seem to be an exception to this generalization as piety and loyalty were strong themes in Prussian popular education from the early eighteenth century.

Those patterns that were created later tended to be more centralized, and to receive relatively more state support – and they incidentally also had a leaner administrative system. By the middle of the nineteenth century it was widely accepted that both work and war required literate men; the presumed national benefits of popular education encouraged the newer nations to assume responsibility not only for funding but also for ensuring its effective realization. Japan, on the advice of an American, briefly experimented with local funding of education only to discover that the people would not pay; and so after only a few years of this experiment, the Meiji state took over the full burden of financing the public school system. The new Soviet Russian state from the very beginning determined to use central government funds for the finance of education. The reliance on state support was associated with a uniform curriculum, a central system for examinations and textbook production, and other centralizing tendencies. These apparently led to greater efficiency. For example, in Japan today only one-eighth of all educational personnel are involved in administration whereas in the USA over three-eighths are involved in administration and support.

These later patterns moved faster to universal mass education – and to place more of their funds in basic education. The commitment of the late developers to mass literacy, and to the use of schools for promoting officially approved values, led them to place an especially strong emphasis on the early school years, for it is in these years that it is possible to have the greatest impact. Nations such as Japan and Russia place a considerable stress on basic education. In contrast, France under Napoleon looked to the educational system to train engineers for the army and the empire; thus, the major stress was on the *lycée* and the *grandes écoles* for this advanced technical education of the few. The USA developed a fascination with higher education. Thus, as recent studies show, a greater proportion of US educational expenditure goes to higher education, a greater proportion of Japan's expenditure goes to basic education, while on the European continent, a greater proportion goes to secondary education (Organization for Economic Cooperation and Development, 1995). This difference is illustrated in Figure 1.2.

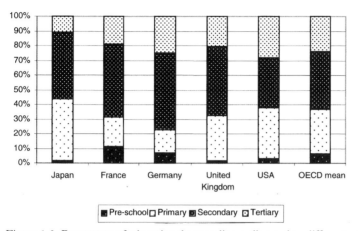

Figure 1.2. Percentage of educational expenditure allocated to different school levels.

Methods to Fit Theories

Linear theories of change such as modernization theory have tended to be accompanied by linear methodologies involving the decomposition of social structure into minute discrete subsystems. These subsystems are depicted as being composed of sets of interrelated concepts. At an early stage, the interrelations were depicted as organic patterns, but with the passage of time the interrelations have come to be viewed as more problematic, dynamic. Thus, each concept has come to be viewed as an independent variable and the assumption of the organic whole has weakened. As far as possible, linear methodologies prefer to develop measurements for these variables that have continuous or interval scale points.

This linear approach encourages a differentiated focus on the respective subsystems. Hence, Western universities divide themselves into departments that focus on the respective subsystems. Because the economic subsystem is most amenable to the preferred methodology, those who focus on this subsystem have tended to gain the ascendancy in Western social science. Increasingly, the economists assume that the other subsystems are irrelevant – thus there is a rational theory for politics, an economics of love, and so on. The penchant for linear models and specialization has its analogy in modern medicine. Western medicine tends to divide the body into various parts and develop specialized studies of these various parts. This can be contrasted to holistic Eastern medicine.

While linear social science has made many advances, the fact is that the explanatory power of these methods is surprisingly weak, especially in the field of education. For example, studies of educational achievement typically only account for 25 per cent of the variance. But if one approaches these same educational phenomena holistically, it is possible to achieve full explanation. For example, if dummy variables are entered in an equation to represent the respective units (each country, or each school, or each student) 100 per cent of the variance can be accounted for. Of course, statisticians may object to this strategy. But the impressive power of the dummy variable approach does provoke a different line of thinking: Might there be more value in looking at patterns than the prevalent methodologies encourage?

Going back to the early days of social science, Max Weber stands out as one of the great intellectual giants. He proposed a methodology of ideal types that has tended to be ignored in recent decades (Weber, 1949). It would be useful to review his proposal. He did not seek a perfect accounting of reality, and in this regard he claimed no more than the linear methodologists. Yet, Weber was able to shed impressive light on some of the most profound changes of our times, from feudalism to capitalism. He had the advantage that assumptions about the interrelations within ideal types were made explicit. The holistic approach involves great intellectual demands and there were great difficulties in carrying out measurement, especially in the early days of social science. And so while the approach had many European adherents, it tended to be neglected in the more pragmatic USA. Fortunately, in recent years there are new adherents who are proposing significant methodological innovations that enable an amalgamation of holistic and linear approaches. Charles Ragin (1987) has been especially prominent in this regard.

What Lies Ahead: early modern, mid-modern, late modern or postmodern

Our methodology stresses ideal types. Many pre-modern institutions were followed by a smaller number of early modern educational systems. In most instances there was significant systematization and expansion over the modern period, and at least in the case of the Japanese pattern there was a second revolution leading to major revisions of the early modern pattern. Today, in the late modern period, education is said to be under stress, and many assert that we are moving into a postmodern era without boundaries or structure. While this claim is appealing, it does not fit the facts. While modern education is yet to be dethroned, there is the prospect that the information revolution may have as profound an impact as did the earlier inventions of the printing press and movable type. That is the topic for the last section of this book. First, we will review in greater detail the causes of the modern revolution and its consequences.

Notes

[1] An earlier version of this chapter appeared as 'The InstitutionS of Education: compare, compare, compare!' *Comparative Education Review*, 43 (November, 1999), pp. 413-437. This article was recognized as 'The Most Outstanding Study of the Year for 2000' by the International SIG of the American Research Association.

[2] From Schumpeter, 1947, pp. 12-13.

[3] The information available in the Human Relations Files indicates that every human community ever studied by anthropologists has recognized the family as their primary social unit (Goode, 1963).

[4] In that the location of the principal 'representative schools' is in the area known as England, I usually refer to this Institution as the English model. Over the course of English history, England was united with Wales in 1284 and England, Wales, and Scotland became Great Britain in 1707. The United Kingdom (UK) came into existence in 1801, inclusive of Great Britain and Ireland. With the independence of Ireland, from 1927 the UK has included England, Wales, Scotland and Northern Ireland. The English model has had the greatest influence on schools in England but it also has had considerable influence throughout the United Kingdom. Thus as the book moves forward and I discuss more contemporary events I use England and the United Kingdom as somewhat equivalent institutional concepts.

[5] In the late 1980s, the Ministry of Education encouraged schools to open classes for six year-olds. Currently, some schools admit six year-olds, others seven year-olds, and yet others admit children of both ages depending on parental preference.

CHAPTER 2

The Great Transformation and the Demands for Modern Education

It no longer suffices to know how to babble a few words in a lamentable tone or to trace a few lines. It is necessary that children who are entering this era of equality, of industry and of emulation be capable of gaining knowledge extensive enough to get out of the rut in which they unavoidably find themselves with the old methods of instruction ... The material improvement which accrues to you as a result of these innovations is equally precious, above all for those who are without fortune. Your children will not have to supply books or papers or pens. We require of them only good conduct and the desire to learn and to become good citizens. (Poster announcing the new Monitorial School in Bollène, France, 1831)

In the early 1400s the predominant mode of production was agriculture, and the most important political units were relatively modest in scale, deriving revenue from taxes on the agrarian economy. Peasants were linked to lords by reciprocal feudal bonds of privilege and loyalty (Moore, 1966). The core feudal units were relatively large in China and Egypt as the land was flat, thus limiting possibilities for local defence, and there was a practical need for careful coordination to harness the potential of the great rivers. Over the relatively large territory of China, there were perhaps fifteen warring lords, and Egypt was essentially unified under Ottoman control (Goodwin, 2000). The feudal units tended to be smaller elsewhere, as the topography was more hostile and the human settlements were more dispersed. Over the much smaller territory of Japan there were at least 250 distinctive units, and similarly, over what is now known as Western Europe, there were at least 500 units (Tilly, 1993). 'Religion' was important in defining the rules of conduct. In Europe, the Holy Roman Empire was the main binding force, whereas in China Confucianism provided the political and social glue. But in Europe, as elsewhere, the integrative ties were weak. The level of inter-unit interaction was modest, deterred by various strictures on trade and migration. Similarly, this period failed to stimulate much of note in the realms of artistic and intellectual creativity.

But towards the end of the fifteenth century, rates of change in belief, technology and social structure sharply accelerated in Western Europe (McNeill, 1963). Popular accounts point to Columbus's brave journey across the Atlantic as a pivotal event. In the ensuing centuries there were new discoveries in religion, in military and industrial technology, in commerce, and in science and medicine. Starting from an economic level on a par with the rest of the world, by the end of the eighteenth century Europe's average per capita standard of living was ten times greater than that of Asia and Africa; by the end of the nineteenth century it was twenty times greater. Among non-European countries, the USA and Japan were the only rivals to European supremacy.

The political outcome of these events was the consolidation of the many small fiefdoms of Western Europe into several nation states with productive economies and powerful armies.[1] By the middle of the nineteenth century, the leading European states were forcing their will on less fortunate areas throughout the world. Outside of Europe, only North America and later Japan were able to remain independent and competitive.[2] The USA claimed independence from Great Britain at the end of the eighteenth century, and, while limiting its imperial ambitions, came to play an increasingly important role in international political and economic affairs. Under pressure from the West, Japan shed itself of the former feudal system with the Meiji Revolution of 1868. By the first decade of the twentieth century, Japan had achieved an impressive degree of industrialization and established a small empire of its own.

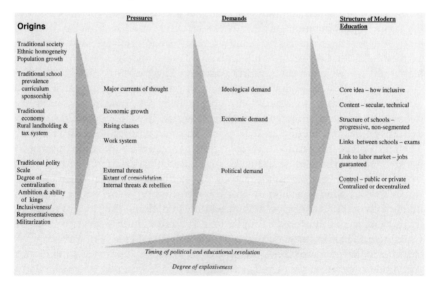

Figure 2.1. Factors influencing the institutions of modern education.

The new political entities of Europe, the USA, and Japan eventually decided to build systems of mass education, the principal concern of this book. This chapter will highlight the distinctive characteristics of the beliefs, economies and polities of the core pioneers of the modern transformation as well as the timing of these changes. It will conclude with a consideration of the implications for education. The principal concepts featured in this and the next chapters are presented in Figure 2.1.

Changes in Belief

The Reformation

Relative to more recent times, during the medieval period in Europe (AD 300 to AD 1500) there was remarkable stability in ideas and in social structure. An aristocratic class had claim to the land and a peasant class worked it. Commerce existed on a limited scale in the cities and castle towns but was restrained by law and by the prevailing means of transportation.[3] The Holy Roman Empire provided the legal framework for daily transactions. While the daily life of most people was full of activity during this period, over time conditions were remarkably stable – except when the status quo was threatened by external invaders or the ravages of disease. At least in Western Europe, neither the size of the population nor the average standard of living shifted very much during the medieval period. Life was according to God's will (Cantor, 1994).

But somehow, out of this stability, towards the end of the sixteenth century, Europe began to seek a new direction, whereas in other parts of the world there was a tendency to stick with tradition. Historians dispute why Europe ultimately rejected the medieval order while China, the Ottomans and other lesser empires persisted in their time-worn ways. It is impossible finally to point to any single factor; rather, it is apparent that the explanation lies in a combination of several interrelated developments. But among these, is it not possible to determine which was most important? The classical debates contrast technology and ideas, ideology and class conflict. But perhaps these opposites go hand in hand. At any rate, it is apparent that there were important breakthroughs in thinking in Western Europe that led to political and technological change while the intellectual accomplishments in other areas were less innovative.

The most fertile minds of the medieval period from Saint Augustine to Thomas Aquinas were involved in understanding God's ways. Over time, the focus of inquiry shifted from a focus on God's word to a focus on God's will as expressed in the laws of nature (Durkheim, 1969, esp. pp. 215 ff.) This shift, often referred to as the Renaissance, began in Italy and is associated with such notable thinkers as Leonardo da Vinci, Pico della Mirandola and Francis Bacon. Of course, during this period there were many innovative thinkers in other areas of civilization, for example, Averroes of Moorish Spain (van Doren, 1991, p. 116) – but the continuity or momentum was most evident in Christian Europe.

Among these innovative thinkers, Martin Luther posed perhaps the most fundamental challenge to the old order. He questioned the practices (and hence the authority) of the Pope, who was the ultimate political as well as religious leader of the Western world. Luther's initial protest was against the sale of indulgences as a way of compensating for past misdeeds and acquiring a ticket to heaven. Prior to the Pope's promotion of this opportunity, the influence of Rome in the area where Luther served as priest had been weak and its impositions modest. But the promotion of indulgences with the suggestion that their purchase was the only means to salvation was perceived by Luther as both an unwelcome imposition and as patently hypocritical. Luther posted his objections on the door of the cathedral at Wittenberg.

At first, Luther attempted to work within the Church and entered into dialogue with his superiors, resulting in a trip to Rome to discuss his thinking with the Pope. But the differences were irreconcilable, and as Luther became more prominent his criticisms raised other questions. In particular, he argued that salvation was achieved through faith and that individuals had the responsibility to build a relationship with God. In order to develop this relationship, individuals needed to read and study God's word. These ideas tended to undermine the status and role of the Catholic Church.

While the Reformation focused almost exclusively on religious liberty, it encouraged the ordinary lay people to think for themselves as well as to critically examine new approaches. Where Protestantism prevailed, popular schools were more likely to be established (Lamberti, 1989). Some have linked the emergence of the Enlightenment to the new atmosphere of inquiry fostered by the Reformation. Max Weber (1930), through a careful study of the rise of capitalism in Western Europe, developed the argument that the Protestant areas were more likely to foster entrepreneurial economic activity. And it can be argued that the new independence of thinking fostered in this period extended to popular questioning of political authority. Indeed, the language of the Enlightenment had a strong egalitarian thrust. On the other hand, Robert Gildea (1983) reminds us that despite its universal rhetoric the Enlightenment was reserved for the elites whereas the ordinary people were considered beyond the pale.

Some seem to suggest that the Reformation had a uniform effect across Western Europe (Ramirez & Boli, 1987). But from a spatial and temporal perspective the impact was chequered. This is no better illustrated than in the decisions on state religions that were formulated in the Peace of Augsburg. The preceding conflicts had sought to establish a common religion across the numerous principalities that later were unified in modern Germany. But the fighting ended in a stalemate, and this peace allowed neighbouring states to practise Catholicism and Protestantism depending on the preference of their princes. These differences persist to the present. In general, those states that adopted Protestantism were more inclined to promote mass popular education at an earlier date.

Concurrent with the Reformation in Europe, Japan also experienced significant religious and economic shocks (Sansom, 1962). New streams of Buddhism had entered from China and were threatening the feudal order. Also, international trade was picking up. But Japan, rather than accept these new developments, made a conscious decision in the early seventeenth century to close its doors to foreign influence and to social and religious reform. It was only following the Meiji Revolution of 1868 that Japan experienced the themes of intellectual ferment that had earlier excited the West.

The 'Myth' of Nationalism

In seventeenth-century Europe there were numerous independent political units, loosely held together by a common legal framework established long before by the Holy Roman Empire. These units were culturally diverse, speaking different dialects and even distinct languages. Especially in the case of the German states, neighbouring states might adhere to different religions.

The modest size of most states naturally was associated with small armies. The inadequacy of these small armies was especially evident in the German case where the various states proved easy prey to Napoleon's advances. The defeat of the German states in the early nineteenth century provoked a new wave of nationalism in Germany that was soon imitated throughout Western Europe. The Prussian philosopher, Johann Gottlieb Fichte, who had been an admirer of Napoleon, was devastated by the military collapse of Germany and the strict conditions of disarmament imposed in the Treaty of Tilset (1807). Fichte began to pronounce a new vision of the genius of the German people. His arguments were picked up by other German thinkers, and soon were evident in the statements of political leaders. Inspired by the new rhetoric, these leaders worked around the constraints imposed by Napoleon and built up a new military presence that involved a new level of cooperation across principalities. The combined German armies played an important role in the eventual collapse of Napoleon and fostered German national pride and ultimately German unification.

The same drive for national unity was evident in other European settings. In France during the revolution the national myth took a more secular direction, with the Church experiencing a purge of many of its privileges. Under Emperor Napoleon II, the French centralists launched a campaign to advance French culture and a single French language which led to pressure to reject the rights and privileges of the various ethnic minorities who resided in France.

The USA was born as an outpost of England. As immigrants came from other parts of Northern Europe there were expressions of discomfort over language, culture and religion. But the common bond of anti-Catholicism was shared. However, from the 1840s, with the Irish potato famine, an increasing number of Catholic Irish arrived, and soon thereafter there were new waves of immigrants from Southern and Eastern Europe. The cultural clashes that ensued provoked the Great Awakening, with its persecution of these new 'un-American' groups. Nationalistic sentiments were stirred that ultimately became expressed in the American drive for empire and grandeur. By the end of the nineteenth century, through the Spanish–American war, the USA acquired its first colonies in the Philippines and Puerto Rico.

Japan, with the Meiji Revolution, also stressed national unity and strength as a counter-measure to the decentralized and culturally diverse Tokugawa feudal arrangement. The Emperor was hailed as the enduring symbol of Japanese nationalism, universal conscription into the Japanese army was introduced as a means of building national strength, and the new mass education system was launched to build a common culture.

As E.J. Hobsbawn (1990) and Benedict Anderson (1983) argue, nationalism is a convenient myth to forge unity among previously diverse and splintered political and cultural units. Nationalism has the powerful implication that all who meet national criteria are entitled to similar privileges. And so it erodes the claim of aristocratic privilege and supports populism and democracy. In general, nationalism involves reaching out to include more people in the nation state and to motivate those included to identify with this entity. Education is looked to as an important vehicle for fostering this common identity, and for promoting patriotism (and in some instances racism).

Socialism

While the rise of nationalism was associated both with the consolidation of states and the ideology that all within a state shared a common national identity, this national equality was not extended to the realm of politics or economic life. Rather, in most of the new nation states, power was concentrated in the hands of a small group and there were great disparities in wealth, property and income.

The Enlightenment language of liberty and equality questioned the appropriateness of these political and social equalities, and the French Revolution provided a concrete expression of that challenge. But the immediate outcome of the revolution was to imply the empowerment of the bourgeoisie while relegating the peasant and working classes to a subordinate position. Yet the numbers of people engaged in these lesser positions were steadily increasing, especially the numbers residing in the expanding towns and cities and involved in industrial production. The close proximity of the urban workers to each other encouraged a common understanding of the difficulties they faced relative to the good life enjoyed by their employers; what Karl Marx described as 'class consciousness'.

50

A variety of intellectuals commented on the disparities between the privileged and the poor, presenting arguments both through their writings and their actions for a reduction of these inequalities. For example, Robert Owen, an English industrialist, took the unusual measure of providing housing for his workers and encouraging their participation in cooperatives for the purchase of their food and other necessities. Owen and others focused on the material and social rights of workers, thus fostering a new movement and ideology known as socialism.

Certainly, the most renowned socialist of the nineteenth century was the German economist-philosopher, Karl Marx, whose writings were so inflammatory that he was forced to leave his own country and eventually took up residence in England. One of Marx's best known compositions was the 'Communist Manifesto', prepared with Friedrich Engels in the wake of the French workers' revolt of 1848. In this essay, Marx and Engels asserted that the spectre of communism was haunting Europe. The Manifesto both outlined the key tenets of this spectre and its inevitability. The Manifesto was followed by many other writings which inspired political activists during the nineteenth century and ultimately provided the theoretical underpinning for the Bolshevik Revolution that led to the formation of Soviet Russia.

Marx argued that the means to the production of economic goods should belong to all the people rather than some small privileged group that acquired this capital through some chance event such as inheritance or speculation. As capital belonged to all the people, they should share it and its fruits equally. On the other hand, the people varied in their skills and ability to make use of the capital; some were too young and others too old, some had disabilities while others were healthy, some were well trained for operating the current means of production, whereas others were not. All that should be expected is for each individual to contribute to the best of their ability: 'To each according to his need, from each according to his ability'.

Marx saw the state, led by a dictatorship of the proletariat, as the coordinating body for managing the process of economic production and distribution during the transition period from capitalism until a smoothly operating communist society could be developed. The state's task was to promote ability so as to maximize the income enjoyed by all. Thus, an important duty of the state was to provide education and training for all and to effectively place the trained workers so that they could make their contribution to the common good.

The articulation of socialist thought became increasingly popular over the modern period and had a profound impact on European politics where nearly every nation witnessed the emergence of an expanding labour movement and a socialist political party. Due in part to the socialist movement, the right to education became an inevitable pledge of the modern state. Thus, it can be said that the ideas of socialism are parallel in importance to the Reformation and the Enlightenment in shaping the modern era.

Economic Change

The European Miracle

Paul Kennedy, in *The Rise and Fall of the Great Powers* (1987), observes that there would have been no obvious reason in the year AD 1500 to expect 'the European miracle'. At that time, economic strength and military might were far more impressive in China and the Ottoman Empire. Yet, over the next three centuries the locus of world leadership shifted to Europe, ultimately leading to the subjugation and colonization of these former great powers.

The European miracle, which only in the twentieth century was surpassed by the American, Japanese and Soviet miracles, became possible due to the concurrence of several developments in the technical, social and cultural realms. In the technical realm, these included the improvement of shipping and the design and mass production of cannon and rifles, thus enabling the mobilization of large armies and armadas for outward conquest. The revenues flowing both from trade with and exploitation of the subjugated areas added to the strength of Europe. But underlying the emergence of the new military superiority was, as Michael Polanyi (1944) has so eloquently described, a critical transformation in the nature of work. Work in the Europe of 1500 was primarily agricultural; by the mid-1800s it had shifted towards the production of manufacturing goods and various services.

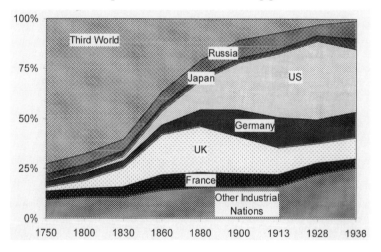

Figure 2.2. Global shares of manufacturing output, 1750-1938.
Source: adapted from Kennedy (1987), pp. 149, 202.

This transformation was not a uniform process. England and France were the setting for the earliest phases, with other areas following their lead. Outside of Europe, America and then Japan were the first and most successful followers. While prominent social theorists (Spencer, 1891; Rostow, 1960;

Kerr et al, 1960) suggested that the latecomers in the process would or should replicate the earlier experiences, this was not to be. Bairoch (cited in Kennedy, 1987) has compiled comparative information on the global shares of manufacturing output of various nations, as summarized in Figure 2.2. This information suggests essential parity across nations, including those in the so-called developing world, in the early 1700s. But from that point on, the modernizing societies begin to separate from the pack. By the 1770s, France is taking the lead, with the United Kingdom a close competitor. Germany's share begins to increase in the early 1800s, peaking in the first decade of the twentieth century. The USA follows on Germany, and is in turn followed by Japan and Russia. As will be stressed elsewhere, the timing of the economic prominence of these societies imperfectly coincides with their political consolidation, leading to distinctively different patterns of political economy.

The Variety of Work Systems

Common to many social theories is the assumption that the world of work provides the key building blocks for the core structures of society. Marx argued that particular modes of production were displaced by more advanced modes, but subsequent experience and research indicates that a wide range of modes of production can coexist. Essentially, five modes of production have been discriminated by industrial sociologists, each of which has implications for the associated relations of production, as detailed in Table 2.1. The totality of these implications, which can be called work systems, will be introduced here, drawing primarily on European experience.

The first of the five work systems is what will be called the feudal system – this type is a reduction of Weber's feudal and patrimonial types that were used to manage large agricultural estates. Workplaces that adopt the feudal system provide each of the members of the labour force with lifetime tenure. The workplaces give low-ranking workers considerable discretion concerning day-to-day operations, but this is within a framework of customs set by those of higher rank. These customs can be adjusted at any time by higher ranking members, and the lower ranking members have no recourse but to comply. The lowest ranking members are not given a fixed income, but the taxes operate in such a manner that they can expect to receive an income within a certain range. Higher ranking officers tend to be given a fixed income, but again there may be some latitude. In general, this system provides little opportunity for vertical mobility for those of the lowest rank, whereas those in the middle ranks who demonstrate exceptional service may achieve some mobility. Election into the feudal system is typically based on the principle of family succession.

Type	Feudal, subsistence agriculture	Self-employed entrepreneur	Market	Organization	Professional
Principles	Authority	Effort, Risk	Skill, Scarcity	Commitment, Seniority	Knowledge, Networks
Investment	Property	Capital	--	Career	Education
Nature of Work	Traditional, labour intensive	Own choice	Usually manual, routine determined by employer	Often complex techniques. Must be mastered, jobs linked to others through a hierarchy	Application of professional knowledge on a case-by-case basis
Degree of Independence	Varies	High	Low, careful supervision	Moderate, but group decisions important	Considerable
Characteristic of workplace	Large overall, some with small subunits. Poor conditions	Variable size and conditions	Varies, but tendency to large scale	Large scale, good conditions	Moderate scale, may have multiple places
Hours	Long	Own choice	Fixed, 40-50 hours a week	Fixed	Long, but flexible
Rewards	Subsistence, in kind	Profits, depending on success, fame	Hourly wage, based in part on productivity	Seniority-based salary, pensions, prestige	Fees and salary according to reputation, prestige
Security	High	Moderate to low	Low	High	Moderate to high
Workplace/ Home link	Same place	Often same, at least in early stages	Separate, home own responsibility	Separate, but organization may provide assistance for home, health	Usually separate
Commitment	Life, or contracted term	--	Short-term	Until retirement	Lifetime
Mobility	None	Expansion of activity	Frequent inter-workplace. Both occupational and industrial	Often occupational. Rotation in early career	Moderate inter-workplace, inter-industry
Typical Industry	Agriculture, mining	Commerce, service, manufacturing	Manufacturing, service	Service, government, education	Education, service, manufacturing
Typical Occupation	Serf, tenant, small farmer	Shop owner, free-lancer	Non-union, blue collar, day labourer	White collar, unionized blue collar	Professor, lawyer, applied chemist
Personality Traits	Hard-working, obedient	Ambitious, active, independent	Self-reliant, short-time perspective	Cautious, other-directed	Cautious, independent
Ideology	Conservative	Nineteenth century liberal	Apolitical	Liberal to progressive	Progressive
Selection Criteria	Hereditary	Individual ambition	Skill, physical strength, availability	Education attainment, personality	Professional education, reputation
Selection Process	--	Trial and error in early ventures	Family connections, employment agencies	Special tests at last year of college	Continual process beginning in final stages of education

Table 2.1. Work systems of pre-modern and modern economies.

As the work at all levels is based on time-worn technology, the system does not lead to major educational demands – primarily, it is the middle ranking people who seek education so as to acquire the skills necessary for processing their records. Nevertheless, education is often promoted by the leaders of this system as a means for legitimating the status quo. Schools emphasizing moral education may be provided for lower ranking members. And as those in the higher-level schools are destined for different status positions in the feudal government, schools tend to emphasize general qualities of virtue (that all can acquire) rather than intellectual skills (where differences in performance might prove embarrassing). The feudal pattern has by and large disappeared from the agricultural sector of most modern societies, but we sometimes find it in the mining industry and low-productivity manufacturing firms.

An offshoot of traditional fiefs was the numerous entrepreneurs who attempted to provide special services or products. Often, these entrepreneurs developed their businesses as a supplementary activity to their agricultural pursuits. The entrepreneurs would typically involve their entire family in the business (creating the now familiar model of the family firm). After achieving some success in the new venture, the entrepreneurs might work full-time at their business venture. As the upper classes of the feudal society came to depend on the entrepreneurs for their special services, the demand for this sector became more predictable; while individual ventures failed, the opportunities for entrepreneurs improved. In order to gauge their performance, entrepreneurs gradually developed the concept of a business profit and procedures for computing the costs of the various inputs into their businesses. While the prime ingredient for success in entrepreneurship continued to be the courage to take risks, it became increasingly advantageous for entrepreneurs to gain command of the basic skills underlying this computation – and thus in this limited sense the entrepreneurial sector came to depend on education (Weber, 1930; McClelland, 1976).

An important elaboration of the entrepreneurial system was the establishment of guilds composed of a number of entrepreneurs specializing in a common craft such as leather making, carpentry, copper work, or printing (Heilbroner, 1962). The craft guilds came to agree on standards of production as well as common pricing so as to prevent destructive competition. The guilds sought the authorization of local governments, for with the weapon of local approval the guilds could control the number of entrepreneurs producing the common product. In order to guarantee standards, the guilds arrived at conventions for the training of new members and established apprenticeship programmes. The guilds, once prevalent in Europe and other pre-industrial cultures, have gradually receded in importance. However, many of the principles of guild organization influenced the character of the professional work system, to be discussed below.

In some of the pre-modern systems, large numbers of free labourers emerged – either because of rapid population growth relative to a fixed land base or because of the enclosure movement, as in England (Thompson, 1963). These free labourers, lacking a secure source of income, sought to sell their labour for periodic compensation. In response to the availability of this labour, various traditional producers – whether in agriculture or the entrepreneurial sector – increased the scale of their routine work so that they could offer short-term employment to the free labourers at modest wages. As long as the employers had business, they might continue to offer employment to the same labourers, but if business slacked off they would release them. On the other hand, the labourers felt free to leave their employers if they could obtain a better wage from a different employer. In the early stages of this market system, most free labourers had little to offer their employers other than their physical strength. However, some developed special skills such as welding (through work experience or attendance at short-cycle vocational skills), and this became an asset for them in their efforts to obtain higher wages from a different employer. On the other hand, employers began to suffer from the costs of rapid labour turnover, and thus sought to develop mechanisms to prevent this situation.

Bureaucracies emphasizing specialized rules, a hierarchical chain of command, formal modes of communication, and record-keeping first developed in ancient military organizations (Bendix, 1956; Wilson, 1989). However, most states have evidenced some degree of bureaucratization in their other government services. The upper ranks of the feudal system were organized along essentially bureaucratic lines, though their work was largely of a peaceful nature. As modern states emerged, they borrowed many of the principles of feudal bureaucracies to organize their systems for public service and tax collections. The core idea in bureaucratic organization is the creation of a condition of tenure for carefully selected public servants, with gradual stages of advancement for those who demonstrate loyal and competent service. As the industrial organizations of the private sector expanded their administrative operations, they came to adopt a similar employment concept, at least for their white-collar employees (Mills, 1951), and in many instances, they even extended the concept of secure lifetime service to their core blue-collar workers so as to discourage these workers from moving to other organizations.

The large organizations stress merit criteria in the selection of their personnel, and they often provide various extra benefits to employees. Workplaces using the organizational system tend to be large, and hence have to recruit large numbers of new personnel each year. Typically, minimum educational requirements are relied on as a screening device in selecting personnel, supplemented by personality tests and other devices (Collins, 1979). The organization attempts to construct normative career lines for recruits that have starting points and maximum levels of promotion geared to qualification at entry. Thus, high school graduates can expect at best to rise to clerical positions, whereas graduates of leading universities can hope to at least rise to the lower managerial ranks.

The final major type of work system is the professional system. Professionals apply the specialized knowledge they have mastered through long years of study to the solution of relatively unique problems; they find they need considerable freedom as well as resources (library, equipment) to solve these problems, and thus while they may work in an organization, they resist the bureaucratic principles characteristic of the organizational work system. In that professionals gain command of a universal body of knowledge that can be applied in many different areas, they may actually be simultaneously involved in several workplaces. They also find it relatively easy to move to new workplaces. The training to become a professional is lengthy, and each aspirant sets their own pace. Professional associations judge whether individuals measure up to professional standards and confer on individuals the right to claim a professional status.

Work systems, once institutionalized, are remarkably resistant to change. Arthur Stinchcombe (1965), in a fascinating analysis of the structure of American workplaces, shows how those workplace groups that first emerged in the pre-industrial era – e.g. hotels, retail shops, farms – still tend to have a familistic employment structure composed largely of owners and unpaid family workers. Those founded in the early industrial era – lumber, clay, glass, textiles – still maintain a familistic managerial structure supplemented by blue-collar wage earners. Those founded in the railroad age – the railroads, the postal services – retain a bureaucratic structure, and so on. These structural tendencies by industry have persisted even a hundred years after the workplaces were initially founded, and despite the fact that there have been innumerable new developments in managerial principles that, if applied, could enhance their productivity. Stinchcombe's breakdown of different phases in the organization of work closely parallels the five work systems described earlier.

Work Systems and Ideology

Each of the systems generates a characteristic ideology to legitimize its activities. The feudal system develops elaborate metaphysical justifications for the right to rule and celebrates the virtues of obedience and hard work expected of the selfless peasant (Bendix, 1956). The entrepreneurial system emphasizes the virtues of calculated risk-taking and the rights to profit of those who are most clever (and lucky) in their endeavours; often, a Darwinian claim of superior qualities is used to legitimize the privileges of the successful. At the same time, through emphasizing boundless opportunities, the entrepreneurial ideology holds out hope to the aspiring entrepreneurs.

The market system portrays society as having various needs that are being differentially served. Those who are able to serve the highest needs deserve, and, according to the market ideology, actually receive, the largest rewards. Those who serve lesser needs receive lesser rewards; however, to mollify the poor, the market ideology celebrates the value of these lesser rewards – the pride the worker can take in his physical strength and in his capacity for drink.

The organizational ideology emphasizes the virtues of loyalty, competence and maturity. It emphasizes the need for and prevalence of objective evaluations and for decency and fairness in human relations (because these are often lacking). Finally, the professional system celebrates knowledge and technique, and suggests that all problems can be solved through their systematic development and application. While major achievements are often the product of individuals, the professional system also praises collegiality and cooperation as important means to the achievement of professional goals. The professional ideology also stresses the need for public support of scientific research and development.

The above ideologies reflect the exigencies of the respective work systems. To the extent that a particular work system prevails in a society, the corresponding ideology will tend to be prominent in the national culture.

Historical Evolution of Work Systems

Work systems are institutionalized in specific workplaces or groups of workplaces such as might compose an industry. However, when the focus is shifted to the societal level, it is found that modern societies at various points in their history have placed special emphasis on one or the other or some combination of these systems. A preliminary proposition about the differential contemporary emphasis of leading societies is presented in Table 2.2.

	Dominant work system	Secondary system
France	Entrepreneurial	Organizational
UK	Entrepreneurial	Market
USA	Entrepreneurial	Professional
Germany	Organizational	Feudal
Japan	Organizational	Entrepreneurial
USSR	Organizational	Feudal

Table 2.2. Works systems emphasized by leading nations.

Tradition and timing are key factors in understanding the observed differences in emphasis. Feudalism was never established in the USA and comparatively weakly established in the United Kingdom and thus could be easily displaced by other systems, whereas feudalism was more firmly established in Russia, Germany, France and Japan. Whereas the entrepreneurial and market systems emerged in the early stages of the great transformation and become relatively firmly institutionalized in the lead societies, these same societies gave birth to other work systems that ultimately proved more appropriate for high energy industrialization and the service industries. Late industrializers such as Japan and the USSR could adopt these later work systems, and even use them for objectives that were not typical of their forerunners: for example, Japan's large industrial firms are more organizational than are those of the United Kingdom (Dore, 1973).

Most societies, prior to their modern stage, organized work primarily along feudal lines, yet they allowed a certain amount of entrepreneurial activity. According to Weber, societies with the patrimonial variety of feudalism, such as China, placed the most severe restraints on entrepreneurship, whereas in many of the European systems entrepreneurs were allowed a relatively free hand.

Gradually, members of the entrepreneurial sector began to create many of the technological innovations that became the basis for industrialization. However, it was in the United Kingdom, where large numbers of people sought new employment as a result of the enclosure movement (and population growth), that the industrial revolution initially took place. This free population was anxious for work, and as entrepreneurs sought to expand their production through hiring day labourers they found that the members of the free population were prepared to work on their terms. In this setting, the United Kingdom gradually developed the market system as a major extension of entrepreneurship, and despite subsequent developments such as the labour union movement and the growing scale of organizations, the principles of the labour market system have remained entrenched. Other European societies have in varying degrees followed the British model. However, none has become as thoroughly committed to the market as Britain.

In France, the entrepreneurial sector has shown exceptional growth, especially in the provinces, whereas in major cities (especially Paris) one finds many workplaces that have adopted the organizational system (Crozier, 1964). However, one special characteristic of European economies often noted is the pattern of dual structures: an upper layer composed of nationals employed in entrepreneurial and organizational work systems, and a lower layer of 'immigrant workers' employed according to the market principle.

Among advanced nations, the USA is the major case without a feudal past. America's early years involved the fostering of a nation of small independent entrepreneurs (both in the city and on the farm), though there was much flux and ambiguity in this pattern. For example, many southern cotton planters depended on slave labour. And gradually in the north industries were established that employed the new immigrants, especially those from southern Europe. This mix of entrepreneurship and the market created a restless condition in America somewhat hostile to the development of the organizational principle. Nevertheless, by the end of the nineteenth century, America had developed many large workplaces in the mining and service industries. As mass production and mass technology became refined, ever larger workplaces emerged in the manufacturing and service sectors, and small entrepreneurs (as distinguished from franchisers) became increasingly uncommon. In the post-war period, mass production extended to agriculture.

In many respects, these large workplaces were organized along organizational principles; however, in contrast to the Japanese example, the American workplaces did not grant security to most blue- and grey-collar workers, nor did they offer these workers a career. Rather, they treated the workers as labourers in a market. Under these conditions, other devices, such as union pension plans and social security, evolved to provide the workers with some security. Also, the American manager was not provided with unequivocal security, but, rather, was judged in terms of his performance and expertise. Some mobility developed in the managerial ranks, and increasingly managers developed a professional self-image. Similarly, American manufacturing organizations began to create research branches staffed by professionals, and more generally, in the broader society, growing numbers of the labour force began to pursue professional careers. By 1970, nearly 20 per cent of the American male labour force reported that it was engaged in professional or technical work compared with no more than 10 per cent in most other advanced societies. Thus, the USA has taken unusual strides towards institutionalizing the professional work system alongside the organizational and entrepreneurial systems (Reich, 1991).

Japan, like Europe, had a feudal background and allowed moderate freedom to the entrepreneurial sector, and in the early stages of Japan's modernization, the entrepreneurs played a major role. But in Japan, unlike Europe, there was insufficient 'surplus labour' to allow the development of a substantial market. In these circumstances and also given Japan's urgent desire to industrialize, it was only large organizations offering security and generous employment conditions that could draw workers from their traditional workplaces. The government took the lead through creating large organizations to produce ships and munitions, and to manage the railways. Significantly, Japan was able to draw on its highly elaborated feudal past in deciding on the principles for structuring these organizations. As the private sector developed, the larger workplaces began to model their structures on the government examples – especially from the early years of the twentieth century. Over time, growing proportions of the labour force have become employed in large-scale workplaces structured according to the organizational principle. At the same time, Japan retains a large subsector of low-productivity, low-wage small businesses and farms organized along the entrepreneurial principle, and thus it is often said that Japan has a dual economy (though structured differently from most European examples) (Cummings & Naoi, 1974).

The Russian experience somewhat resembles that of Japan. During the nineteenth century the tsarist state took the lead in establishing a limited number of state enterprises while also encouraging entrepreneurship in the cities. On the other hand, unlike Japan, the state made no effort to break down the feudal pattern of agricultural production. In 1917, with the Bolshevik Revolution, the pattern of state leadership in industrial production was sharply strengthened, while urban entrepreneurial activities were discouraged. Eventually, the state turned to the establishment of agricultural collectives in place of the old feudal domains. Thus, the state sought to introduce the organizational pattern for all productive endeavour. However, this reform faced difficulties and was only partially implemented.

Implications of Work Systems for Society

Most societies have workplaces which employ all of these work systems, but particular societies place a greater emphasis on some than on others – and the particular work system emphasized has pervasive consequences not only in the sphere of work but in other spheres as well. Among contemporary advanced societies, we have suggested that the United Kingdom places a special emphasis on the market system, Japan on the organizational system, and the USA on the professional system. These emphases mean that workplaces producing essentially the same product may have quite different characteristics in each of these societies. For example, Ronald Dore, in *Japanese Factory, British Factory* (1973), indicates that compared to its English rival the Japanese electrical firm places a much greater emphasis on education in selecting personnel and builds much more obvious rewards for seniority into its wage and salary schedules. Also, the Japanese factory provides many extra benefits to its employees. On the other hand, in the United Kingdom, layoffs are more common and worker mobility is higher. A study of an American electrical firm would result in a picture much closer to the British factory, with the exception that the American firm would have a much more substantial research operation and would hire many professional scientists and managers for this purpose.

Workplaces in the United Kingdom make clear distinctions between management and other blue-collar workers, but do not make so many distinctions within these categories. Japanese organizations make elaborate distinctions within each sector in terms of seniority rank, though not necessarily in terms of functional role. At the same time, the Japanese organization superficially tends to blur the dividing line between white- and blue-collar workers (all may wear uniforms, belong to a common union, and eat in the same dining facilities). American workplaces, affected by the professional ethic, are likely to have an unusually large number of both professional-technical and managerial positions. From a strictly technical point of view, many of these positions may not be necessary. For example, an American firm may create the position of 'sanitation engineer' – that is, a professional position – to clean the workspace. And many of those in the American organization with managerial positions perform work that ordinary white-collar workers might perform in Japan.

The emphasis in a society on one or the other of these work systems has many implications that range far beyond workplaces. In the next section, as we review the patterns of political development in the focal societies, we will note how the different work systems foster different economic classes and class relations, and how these in turn influence the political economy.

Political, Military and Demographic Change

The Religious Wars and the Rise of Nation States

One outcome of the Reformation was to plunge Western Europe into a long period of 'religious' wars between those political entities that accepted the new thinking and those which sought to preserve the old order. The first such war took place in Germany between those princes who approved of the new Protestant thinking and those who accepted the authority of the Pope. These skirmishes continued for nearly three decades until it was agreed in the Peace of Augsburg of 1555 to let the differences prevail. But in the decades to follow, as the Reformation spread to Switzerland, France, England and Scotland, new conflicts ensued. These finally converged in the Thirty Years War (1618-1648), the worst conflict ever experienced in Europe up to that point. Over 2 million were estimated to have died, the largest number of casualties in a conflict until the First World War (Levy [1983] as summarized by Tilly [1989], pp. 165-166.). These extended conflicts often took place on German soil and involved German soldiers, leading to a depletion of the German economy relative to its neighbours, from which recovery was only realized in the late nineteenth century.

England often participated in these conflicts but enjoyed the privilege of physical separation from the Continent. While the English kings continued to support the Catholic Church, the new religious ideas were circulating in England. But when Henry VIII's request to the Pope to annul his first marriage was rejected, he also decided to break with Rome and establish the Anglican Church as the new English orthodoxy. This Church was like the Catholic Church in everything but name, and so it failed to respond to the Reformation impulse. Only after several decades did England come to express some tolerance for the new religious movements.

Behind the religious issues, however, were the political tugs of war, especially those between the French Bourbons and Austrian Habsburgs. These more political issues continued to surface and provoke conflicts for the remainder of the seventeenth and much of the eighteenth century.

During this period, Western Europe did not hold an exclusive monopoly on war. Indeed, in the late sixteenth century the Mughals were conquering India, the Manchurians were beginning their raids on China that ultimately would lead to the formation of the Ching dynasty, and in Japan Hideyoshi had just completed at the Battle of Ashigahara (1602) the struggles that ultimately led to the formation of the Tokugawa shogunate. In most of the non-European cases, over subsequent years there was extensive consolidation in loose networks of quasi-independent units. Japan's numerous fiefs were held together in a centralized feudal arrangement that left considerable autonomy to the respective local lords. The various local units of China and India were joined in a common federation led by an emperor with divine powers. But in Western Europe, the outcome was possibly the most innovative. The number of political units was reduced from approximately 500 'state-like units' to about thirty-five (Tilly, 1993, p. 25) by the early nineteenth century, a number that has remained essentially stable down to the present. The new states, while amalgamations of several smaller entities, defined their mission in terms of advancing the interests of a particular national group. These 'nation states' proved to have a great influence on the course of history over the next two centuries.

Charles Tilly, in collaboration with others, has sought to account for the unique outcome in Western Europe of consolidation and national integration. They note that Europe, despite its considerable diversity, enjoyed a common legal culture, based on the Church. Also, the new religious developments in Europe had disposed politicians to be open to new proposals for political realignment. Finally, they stress the importance of the changes in military technology and strategy. While these general conditions were prevalent, there still remains the issue of explaining why certain of the original political entities were winners – Spain, England, France, later Sweden, Prussia, and many smaller states – while others were absorbed as territories of the new nation states. Such factors as the availability of extractable resources, a strategic location (England being blessed by a peripheral or offshore position which maximized the impact of her navy), a strong coalition of the central power with major segments of the landed elite, and a continuous supply of political entrepreneurs are said to have characterized the winners. But above all, the winners enjoyed military success.

The Military Revolution

The last factor, military success, has received increasing recognition by historians.[4] In the early modern period, most wars were modest affairs conducted by small professional armies that met in open fields and relied primarily on muzzle-loading rifles for firepower; the combat was often over in a few days or weeks. But since those days the scale has grown exponentially. Kennedy indicates that the size of the typical army doubled from the early 1600s to the early 1700s, tripled from that base by the early 1800s, and doubled again by the early 1900s (Kennedy, 1987, pp. 56, 99, 203). The scale further increased through the First World War, after which there were temporary reductions. But growth was again evident from the 1930s. After the Second World War the major powers maintained large standing armies that only began to be downsized in the early 1990s. Associated with the increase in scale has been the rapid evolution of military technology. Transportation has shifted from land and sea to air, firepower has rapidly escalated, and in recent years computer technology has come to be deployed for missile guidance and military surveillance.

One corollary of these technological changes has been the shift in the requirements for the ideal soldier. Eighteenth-century war depended on sheer numbers of soldiers to fill battlefields, with the strategy by generals an important secondary element. But with the increasing role of technology in military affairs, smart generals need to be complemented by smart soldiers. Prussia was the first to recognize this in the mid-eighteenth century. From that point on, mass education was advocated as a component of national defence. The French educational reforms of the 1830s were justified as essential to match the competence of the German soldier. Japan's Meiji government authorized universal basic education in 1872 so that future conscripts to the army would have an adequate educational foundation. The proponents of England's Education Act of 1870 cited the need for the English people to have the same level of education as their European counterparts if England was to compete and be safe. And in the USA, every major national educational initiative since the First World War has been rationalized as contributing to national defence.

Demographic Change

While political leaders during the great transformation were often engaged in external military conflict, they also encountered internal rebellion. This internal protest varied in magnitude from decade to decade, but Jack Goldstone (1991) suggests that it peaked in England in the mid-seventeenth century and in France towards the end of the eighteenth century, leading to the major revolutions experienced in these two settings. In examining the causes of the patterns of rebellion in France and England, Goldstone points out that the price of basic commodities began to accelerate prior to these two critical revolutionary eras, thus creating mounting hardship, especially for the urban population. The root cause of inflation, according to Goldstone, was population growth:

> State institutions are like buildings on a plain, and population pressure
> is like the seismic pressure that shifts the plain on which the buildings
> are constructed. From 1500 to 1660, and from 1730 to 1860,
> population pressure all across Eurasia created 'seismic pressures' that
> undermined the foundations of states. This explains the synchrony of the
> state breakdowns. (1991, p. 175)

Population growth in combination with minimal improvements in agricultural technology led to a shortage of grain and hence to rising prices. Not so coincidentally, the national treasuries of England in the mid-seventeenth century and France in the late eighteenth century were under strain. And popular discontent combined with elite charges of fiscal irresponsibility led respectively to the Cromwellian revolution and the fall of Louis XVI. Goldstone extends his argument to consider the causes of the fall of the Ming dynasty in China in the mid-seventeenth century and a major challenge to the Ottoman Empire at about the same time.

A key strand in Goldstone's argument is the balance between the size of a population and the resources available to the population. The demographic accelerations from the sixteenth century on are generally attributed to a combination of economic growth and improvements in sanitation and health that helped to lower infant mortality. These changes were more evident in some areas of the world than others and were more long term in some areas than others. Figure 2.2 presents the trends in population growth for the six nations this study will focus on from the mid-1700s. France evidences some growth during the 1700s which later slows. German growth is modest from the 1700s down to the twentieth century. England experiences substantial growth over the nineteenth century before levelling off. The three late developers have the most rapid growth thereafter, with the USA experiencing continuous growth, Japanese growth picking up in the mid-nineteenth century at the time of the Meiji Revolution and Russian growth accelerating in the first decade of the twentieth century.

When economic growth slows and population increases, as occurred in Western Europe in the mid-nineteenth century, hardship is felt, leading both to popular unrest and immigration. The USA was the recipient of a continuing stream of immigrants from Europe, and later from Asia and Latin America, thus augmenting its growth.

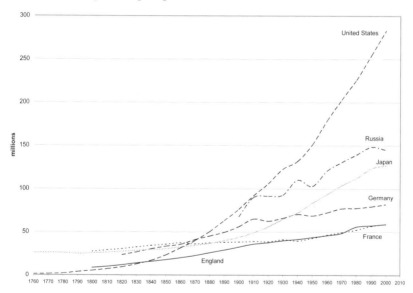

Figure 2.3. Trends in population growth of the core societies, 1740-2000. Sources: Sansom, 1963; Mitchell, 1982; Anderson, 1988; Marshalck, 1987; Gemery, 2000; Population Division of UN Secretariat, 2001.

While population growth puts pressure on governments to expand the provision of social services, effective governments are able to respond. The

65

modern educational revolution is the story of governments responding to the expanding demand for popular education by building more schools and hiring and training more teachers. The European nations with their slower population growth had the easiest task whereas the educational systems in the USA and Soviet Russia continuously faced the challenge of keeping up with an expanding population.

Democracy or Autocracy and Other Variations

The Holy Roman Empire provided the legal framework for most of Western Europe prior to the modern era. Within this legal framework, feudal lords exercised control over territories that varied considerably in terms of size and income. The fiefs in the areas now known as France and Spain tended to be relatively large, while those in the British Isles and Germany tended to be smaller. Partly for this reason, the traditional patterns of governance in the respective areas differed. In the former areas, where there were a small number of lords, patterns of authority tended to be more centralized and hierarchical. In contrast, especially in England, the many lords insisted on the formation of a large assembly to discuss matters of common interest before reaching a decision. This decision at Runnymede (1215) is an example of England's nascent democracy. As the modern era unfolded, the members of the new urban-based classes of merchants, artisans and workers increased in number and importance, and there was increasing pressure to incorporate these new groups into the political process.

One outcome of these pressures was the process of political consolidation into a small number of nation states that was discussed earlier in this chapter. The process of consolidation was largely effected by the ruling classes of the constituent political units, who either used force or diplomacy to do so. The new governments certainly included representatives from the various states that had been consolidated. Less predictable was the extent of inclusion in the political process of representatives from the middle and working classes. The tendency of including ordinary folk was most evident in the more peripheral European states of Scandinavia, which had long experience with local self-government. Political inclusion was firmly resisted in other parts of Europe and the United Kingdom out of a concern to preserve aristocratic and, later, middle-class privilege. The rise of the working class and the steps taken by workers to join in unions led to frequent conflicts over inclusion throughout Europe. In contrast, the USA and later the new republics in Latin America and elsewhere were more receptive to the inclusion of a broad spectrum of popular groups in their democratic processes. Even so, women were not allowed to vote in the USA until well into the twentieth century.

A second outcome was the structure of governance that each new nation state selected. Those states that emerged in the nineteenth century tended to allow individuals and corporations to possess private property (capitalist assumptions) while those that emerged in the twentieth century entrusted all property to the state (communist assumptions). In the former cases, systems of representative government were formed that tended either to be based on individual or corporatist interests. In the communist cases, representation was organized by the unitary state. A final dimension differentiating the governance structures was the extent to which local governments were accorded some independence or subordinated to a unified central government. Table 2.3 portrays the major dimensions of governance.

	Capitalist		Communist
	Representative Democracy	Corporatist Autocracy	People's Democracy
Centralized	France	Japan Germany	Russia
Decentralized	United Kingdom USA		

Table 2.3. Governance structures of the core societies.

While there is widespread agreement that the core states arrived at different governance structures, there is less agreement on the reasons for these differences. Barrington Moore (1966) provides one of the most intriguing explanations. Focusing primarily on the more prominent examples, he observed that those with a more democratic form of government, such as the United Kingdom and the USA, had been characterized by a strong commercial impulse, first expressed through agricultural innovation and later in the more urban activities of industry and finance. The transition from an agrarian to an industrial society caused much hardship but was not accompanied by a significant incidence of peasant revolt. Market forces were championed to facilitate the distribution of resources, including labour, and so displaced rural workers moved to the cities to join the working class. While initially repressed, the workers eventually were allowed the right of organization, and they used this right to mobilize unions and exert pressure through the political system. Democracy was strengthened.

France, while weaker on commercial impulse, nevertheless experienced a significant peasant resistance, perhaps due to the excessive state taxation. The outcome was the creation of a political system to guarantee some protection for various stakeholders. While more centralized than the United Kingdom and US models, it still has a democratic character.

In contrast to the democratizing path were the examples of Germany and Japan where the commercial impulse developed at a slower pace. German commercialism was perhaps restrained by continuous involvement of the various fiefs in military conflict that drained the economy of free resources. In Japan, the Tokugawa regime placed significant restraints on commerce, and, furthermore, curbed political organization, both of rural and later of urban workers. Those with the financial resources to promote economic modernization were able to dominate political life; the economic elites crafted mutually beneficial alliances with the commanders of the forces of order (the police and the military). Together, these fascist elites used their prominence to promote commercial and imperial policies that favoured their interests, with little fear of opposition.

Moore (1966) argues that the main difference between the fascist paths of Germany and Japan on the one hand and the communist paths of Russia and China on the other hand was that, in the latter cases, labour and peasant revolts did finally take place despite the considerable efforts of repression by the state. The conflicts were so severe that they ultimately led to the toppling of the capitalist state and the emergence of communist regimes.

Moore's arguments have had a major influence on the comparative analysis of political development, but some question whether his analysis considers all of the important political components: Above all, what about the military, who in so many settings seem to be the guiding hand? And as Downing (1992) points out, Moore also fails to appreciate the extent to which proto-democratic forms of government were widely prevalent in the early modern era, even in Germany, Italy and Russia. But over the course of industrialization these democratic seeds were encouraged in some settings and repressed in others. So what is missing?

Downing suggests that it is important to consider the nature of the wars each emerging state engaged in. Where the wars were offshore and financed largely by externally derived resources, as in the case of the United Kingdom and the USA, the state could continue to encourage a participatory government. But when the war effort had largely to depend on domestic resources, the state had to assert a stronger hand in order to command resources, and this stronger hand led to curtailing the right to vote in the case of Japan and Germany and even the right to private property in the cases of Russia and China. The French case is especially interesting. The constant threat of war disposed France towards monarchical absolutism, but the abuses of the monarchy ultimately provoked a massive popular revolt. The First Republic sought to replace the monarchy with a representative system, but it ultimately collapsed to be replaced by state absolutism under Napoleon Bonaparte. Over time, France was able to achieve a balance between the pressure for centralism and representation.

Comparing these alternate forms of government, the more democratic governance patterns look to the people for informed participation whereas the more autocratic forms seek to limit popular participation. The extent of dependence of the state on popular participation is yet another factor influencing the disposition of the state to encourage mass education. To the extent that state power is based on the support of a more restricted group, it will be disposed to limit the right of education to that group.[5]

Impact on Education

This chapter has sought to highlight several of the shifts associated with the rise of the new states and their economies (summarized in Table 2.4). Some of these shifts, such as the development of printing, the spread of commerce (including the commercialization of agriculture), new procedures of bookkeeping, and advances in military and industrial technology, 'originated' in Western Europe and were rapidly diffused throughout the western hemisphere and elsewhere and thus became the possession of all modern societies. The principal import of these universal shifts was that they occurred in some areas first, thus giving these areas a head start. The United Kingdom was first in harnessing waterpower and later steam, thus enabling it to pioneer in industrial production. France and Prussia made the earliest advances in modern weaponry, with repeating rifles, long-range cannons, and later with tanks. Thanks to their head starts, these nations were able to assert their military dominance over others, thus becoming the core of the newly emerging world system (Wallerstein, 1976, 1980). But eventually these universal developments diffused to most areas of the advanced world as part of the 'great transformation', and thus did not contribute to distinctive patterns of modernization.

	Prussia	France	UK	USA	Japan	Russia
Changes in Belief	Reform-ation & nationalism	Enlighten-ment	Reformation	Reformation & Enlightenment	Restore Emperor, nationalism, Westernize	Socialism
Period of economic ascendancy	1880s	1770s	1800s	1920s	1960s	1950s
Dominant work system	Organiz-ational	Entrepre-neurial	Entrepre-neurial	Entrepreneurial	Organiz-ational	Organizational
Secondary work system	Feudal	Organiz-ational	Market	Professional	Entrepre-neurial	Feudal
Rising class	Bourgeoisie	Bourgeoisie	Bourgeoisie & working	Stable class relations	Peasants	Working
Political pattern	Centralized corporatist autocracy	Centralized represent-ative democracy	Decentralized represent-ative democracy	Decentralized representative democracy	Centralized corporatist autocracy	People's democracy
Military challenges	Extensive	Extensive	Moderate	Minimal	Minimal	Extensive
Domestic rebellion	Moderate	Considerable	Considerable	Minimal	Moderate	Considerable
Demo-graphic Change	Moderate growth, with some downturns	Peaks in late 1700s	Peaks in mid-1600s	Steady to rapid growth augmented by immigration	Steady growth from mid 1800s	Steady growth from early 1900s

Table 2.4 Contexts affecting the institutional development of the core societies.

Facilitating the dominance of the lead European nations was the trend toward political consolidation and the emergence of new national identities. Austria under the Habsburgs took the lead, followed by France, and later Germany. Similarly, the American colonies concluded that their initial

69

confederation of states was inadequate and committed in 1787 to the formation of a federal republic. And Japan with the Meiji Revolution also began its path towards national consolidation and strength. While each of these political paths had their unique characteristics, they all shared the common dimension of building a strong nation state.

In contrast to these universal developments were the more qualitative changes – changes in belief, in the nature of government and administration, and in the structure of work. These latter changes were more grounded in the experience of particular peoples and proved less imitable, either because the information was not shared or it was not viewed as of great import. This is not to say that there was no sharing of these qualitative changes, for, as we will see in our reviews of institutional development, reformers always pay much lip-service to foreign examples. But often their attention is self-serving and deceptive. The foreign references are as likely to be mythical as factual.

Timing also seems to have played a critical, albeit often under-appreciated, role in encouraging distinctive modern outcomes. For example, the French Revolution's championing of human rights put enormous pressure on later polities to recognize this principle and to foster democracy. Thus, the various Latin American republics that asserted their independence in the first three decades of the nineteenth century borrowed heavily from the French precedent. But because of the 'excesses' of the French experience with radical democracy, the United Kingdom was reluctant to attempt similar reforms (Moore, 1966, p. 442). As the new nation states increased in strength over the nineteenth century, they became more competitive in claiming new colonies and trade routes, and in using nationalistic ideologies to justify their claims. Prussia and Japan were perhaps most notable for their nationalism. And so the dominant ideas of different periods also shaped the tone of new initiatives.

Irrespective of these debates on causal factors, most observers agree that there are important differences across major societies in these three areas of belief, including nationalism, polity and economic structure. In this chapter, we have highlighted the major differences. The distinctive patterns and timing of change in these three areas go a long way towards accounting for the six patterns of modern education we consider in the next chapters.

	1750	1800	1830	1860	1880	1900	1913	1928	1938
France	4	4.2	5.2	7.9	7.8	6.8	6.1	6	4.4
UK	1.9	4.3	9.5	19.9	22.9	18.5	13.6	9.9	10.7
Germany	2.9	3.5	3.5	4.9	8.5	13.2	14.8	11.6	12.7
USA	0.1	0.8	2.4	7.2	14.7	23.6	32	39.3	31.4
Japan	3.8	3.5	2.8	2.6	2.4	2.4	2.4	3	5.3
Russia	5	5.6	5.6	7	7.6	8.8	8.2	5.3	9
Third World	73	67.7	60.5	36.6	20.9	11	7	3	1
Developing World	9.3	10.4	10.5	13.9	15.2	15.7	15.9	21.9	25.5

Table A.2.1. World's share of manufacturing output.
Source: Kennedy, 1987, pp. 149, 202.

Notes

[1] Russia, while it occupied a vast area extending to the Pacific, was essentially a European nation at this time. Politically and economically it was behind the major European powers, but under the leadership of such exceptional tsars as Peter the Great (1672-1725) and Catherine the Great (1762-96), Russia made bold efforts to catch up.

[2] While a number of new nations were formed in South America during the early nineteenth century, none played a significant role in global politics or the world economy until the latter half of the twentieth century.

[3] In both China and Japan, according to Confucian orthodoxy, merchants were regarded as a lower class. Despite that, Sansom (1950) argues that they were becoming more prominent in the sixteenth century only to have their activities once again curtailed in the seventeenth century by the rise of the Manchu dynasty and the Tokugawa shogunate.

[4] Behind the new consciousness of military affairs is the growing recognition, stimulated by the Vietnam War and the global arms race, of the remarkable scale and tenacity of the military–industrial complex and its enduring impact on national and international politics.

[5] Of course, there were important after-shocks in some of these states – France after Napoleon, Japan and Germany after the Second World War, the United Kingdom under socialism, etc.

PART TWO

The Foundations of
Modern Education

CHAPTER 3

The Call for New Schools

There is one experiment which has never yet been tried ... Education has never yet been brought to bear with one hundredth part of its potential force, upon the natures of children, and through them, upon the character of men, and of the race ... Here, then, is a new agency, whose powers are just beginning to be understood, and whose mighty energies, hitherto, have been but feebly invoked ... Reformatory efforts, hitherto made, have been mainly expended upon the oaken-fibred hardihood and incorrigibleness of adult offenders; and not upon the flexibleness and ductility of youthful tendencies. (Horace Mann. 12th Report to the Commonwealth of Massachusetts, 1849)

Each of the lead modern societies faced distinctive challenges that led to unique responses, including a new assessment of the importance of literacy and learning. The process was often chequered, but by a certain point in all of the core societies a new vision of education came to be implanted. And since that time, this initial vision has had a profound influence on all that was to follow. To sharpen understanding of these differences, the following issues will be considered.

- When did the respective modern projects begin?
- What was the priority given to education in the respective modern projects?
- What were to be the main purposes of modern education?
- Was the modern school to be for everyone, or was it to be for a select group?
- What were the outstanding characteristics of the representative modern schools?

The Birth Periods of Modernity

Modernity is an intellectual construct to summarize a constellation of changes rather than a single fact or event that is easily pinpointed. Thus, there are understandable differences concerning the birth period of modernity. The French Revolution is sometimes viewed as the first step, as it was dramatic (Johnson, 1991), providing the bold proposal for 'Liberty, Equality, Fraternity' as the new principles for rebuilding one of Europe's richest and most highly stratified societies. Of course, many have observed that the equality promoted by the Revolution mainly benefited the new commercial class or bourgeoisie and was essentially indifferent to the needs of the peasants. Concerning education, the Constitution of 1791 declared:

> *There shall be created and organized a system of public instruction common to all the citizens and gratuitous in respect to those subjects of instruction that are indispensable to all men. Schools of various grades shall be supplied according to need over the entire kingdom.*
> *Commemorative days shall be designated for the purpose of preserving the memory of the French Revolution, of developing the spirit of fraternity among all citizens and of attaching them to the constitution, the country and its laws. (Reisner, 1923, p. 12)*

Others point to the long-term intellectual shift fostered by the Protestant Reformation as the true harbinger of modernity (McNeil, 1963). The Reformation began in Germany, and had the effect both of empowering the common people with greater control over their religious development and of strengthening the position of local kings and barons vis-à-vis the authority of the Pope and the Holy Roman Empire. To a considerable extent the Reformation leaders and their kings collaborated in mutually reinforcing political and religious revolutions, and thus the language of the new churches was full of expressions of devotion to the local royalty. At any rate, this collaboration hastened the retreat of Rome and led to the creation of new institutions of law and governance to fill the gap. Educational reform was required to provide the personnel for these new institutions as well as to satisfy popular demand.

England in its insular position geographically separated from the continent had always seemed to enjoy greater intellectual and political independence from Rome. Thus, from the thirteenth century the English aristocracy had taken steps to devise new forms of governance that were more democratic than those found on the continent, and that provided a more attenuated role both for the English King and the Roman Pope. Then England took yet another bold step away from the mainstream when Henry VIII decided to reject the authority of the Roman Pope and founded the new Anglican Church. Soon thereafter, England was hosting diverse sects of the new Protestant churches. While England did not pioneer in the Reformation, it did play a lead role in the transformation of economic life through its fascination with technical innovation and its openness to incorporating new innovations into new ways for producing goods and services. The industrialization of England brought more people to the cities and expanded the working class.

The modern shift began later in other parts of the world. The USA, formed by European settlers that felt oppressed by the conservatism there, was born with the spirit of modernity, but it took some time for American institutions to take shape. The revolutionary war, the convening of the

Continental Congress that followed, and eventually the framing of the American Constitution were important early steps in institution building, though it was not until the middle of the nineteenth century that the USA had a fully developed set of institutions and a clear direction.

Russia under the tsars seemed to take two steps forward and one back on its journey to modernity, and so it took the Bolshevik Revolution to truly launch Russia into the modern era. And for Japan, it was the threat of invasion by Commodore Perry and the US Navy that pushed Japan to the Meiji Revolution and a rapid reform of its institutional structure.

And so the timing of the emergence of modern institutions varied among the lead societies. Hence, so did the timing of modern education.

Education as a Priority?

All of these modernizing societies paid much lip-service to education, but they differed widely in their actions. Traditionally, education had been a private affair provided by family tutors or by the Church. With the rise of the modern state, arguments were advanced for governments to assume greater responsibility in the field of education.

These arguments highlighted such diverse benefits as a more devout commoner, a more productive worker, a smarter soldier, and a more thoughtful mother. But there were also counter-arguments that popular education might foster a disloyal and rebellious public. Thus, some nations were more influenced by the positive arguments, others by the negative. To the extent that the positive arguments prevailed, education was elevated in the ranking of the various new projects that the modernizing nations chose to undertake.

While France and Germany were neighbours, several of the German princes proved more open to the new arguments for popular education. As early as 1716 Frederick William I of Prussia published a rescript making attendance at village schools compulsory unless children were not otherwise provided with instruction. Similarly, in Weimar, village folk schools were widely available by the middle of the eighteenth century.

Whereas Germany demonstrated much receptiveness, France during the reign of the Bourbon kings was more resistant. The emergence of the Revolutionary Council gave hope for new initiatives, and the Constitution of 1791 proposed bold changes. Yet, within the Revolutionary Council, the Jacobins and the Mountain could not agree on an educational agenda, nor did they believe they could spare resources. And so word was not accompanied by deed. Napoleon manifested considerable interest in education, and, just as with the writing of the Civil Code, he devised an entirely new framework for the organization and administration of education called The University. Within The University academies were to be established in each region with colleges in each department leading down to the community schools of each canton. But Napoleon's grand plan was accompanied by minimal action except at the secondary level where a number of excellent *lycées* were either rehabilitated or newly established and several *grandes écoles* were strengthened.

In England there were many advocates for greater public responsibility in education, but well into the nineteenth century England relied on the voluntary principle. Only with the Education Act of 1870 did England open up a substantial role for the public sector, and even so this role initially was 'voluntary'. The English aristocracy had long been comfortable with their own network of public schools such as Winchester, Harrow, Eton and Rugby. With industrialization and the expansion of the bourgeoisie, numerous day schools known as grammar schools were established to provide a somewhat equivalent education for those with sufficient means. While some leaders saw advantages in educating the 'backward' classes, most felt this would lead the poor to become too uppity. An early compromise was the establishment of Sunday schools to provide a minimum level of literacy for the poor. Only as the franchise was expanded to include members of the working class did Parliament begin to give serious attention to popular education as a responsibility of the state, and parallel with Parliament's new interest in popular education, it found ways to provide substantial subsidies to schools managed by local education authorities that served the common people.

The American colonies from their earliest days evidenced much interest in popular education, as did the other late developers. What is of special interest in the American case is the peculiar fascination with higher education. The founding of Harvard College is generally agreed to have been in 1636, only sixteen years after the Pilgrims arrived at Plymouth Rock, when the General Court of Massachusetts provided four hundred pounds 'towards a schoale or college' (Boorstin, 1958, p. 174). Soon thereafter William and Mary and Yale College were founded. By the time of the revolutionary war, as many as eighty like institutions had been established (Boorstin, 1958, p. 79) – which seems all the more remarkable when we recall that England at that time had only two degree-granting institutions, Oxford and Cambridge. As Daniel Boorstin observes, 'Americans came to believe that no community was complete without its own college' (1958, p. 181). Thus, both the Land Ordinance of 1785 and the Northwest Ordinance of 1787 included provisions for an educational land fund, long before the Morill Act of 1862 that is widely remembered as the instigator of America's highly regarded 'land-grant' universities.

Turning to the two late developers, we find that both gave a high priority to popular education from virtually the first days of their emergence. The Meiji revolutionaries recognized that the nation was desperately behind in modern technology and so they expressed a keen interest in the Charter Oath of 1869, seeking knowledge throughout the world. An important first step in this endeavour was to provide Japanese young people with the essential intellectual tools, and this was promised in the Fundamental Code of Education issued in 1872, only four years after the formation of the new government. Similarly, in Russia following the Bolshevik Revolution the new socialist education was given strong emphasis from the very beginning.

The Purposes of Education

Chapter 2 has identified the major demands stimulating modernity. While all of these demands were experienced in some degree by each of the core societies, Reisner (1923) argues that the salience of these factors varied by setting, with Germany stressing nationalism, the USA favouring democratization, and England industrialization. While Reisner focused mainly on the factors of nationalism, democratization and industrialization, to this list might be added religious development, public health, scientific inquiry, and other concerns.

In Germany, the earliest inspiration for popular education was to enable all to have a better understanding of God's word. As the German states increased their autonomy and thereby became more vulnerable to attacks from their neighbours, there was a steady drift to bring the various German states together in a larger nation. And so over time there was an increasing nationalistic tone in education alongside the theme of religious devotion. Napolean's defeat of the German states in 1804 led to the oppressive terms of the Treaty of Tilsit. In response, German intellectuals such as Johann Gotlieb Fichte came to articulate a strong case for German unity. The nationalistic theme was to remain prominent in discussions of educational purpose thereafter, and some have suggested it even began to take on racist tones by the end of the nineteenth century. An example of the new nationalism was the historic address of Kaiser William II at the Conference on Secondary School Reform in 1890:

> The foundation of our gymnasium must be German. It is our duty to educate young Germans, not young Greeks or Romans ... We must make German the basis, and German composition must be the center around which everything else revolves ... There is another point which I should like to see more developed with us; that is the 'National' in questions of history, geography, and heroic tradition. (Cited in Reisner, 1923, p. 211)

Only from the second half of the nineteenth century does Germany begin to emphasize vocational skills for industrialization, and democratization comes to be stressed only after the Second World War.

In sharp contrast to Germany is the USA, which was born as a democratic society and turned to education as a vehicle for ensuring that democracy would be sound; Horace Mann, who played a major role in developing the Common School, had this to say about civic education:

> Now as a republican government represents all interests, whether social or military, the necessity of a degree of intelligence adequate to the due

> *administration of them all, is so self-evident, that a bare statement is the*
> *best argument ... In a republican government, legislators are a mirror*
> *reflecting the moral countenance of their constituents. And hence it is,*
> *that the establishment of a republican government, without self-*
> *appointed and efficient means for the universal education of the people,*
> *is the most rash and foolhardy experiment ever tried by man. (Quoted*
> *in Thayer, 1965, p. 96)*

Only towards the end of the nineteenth century did Americans come to view education as a vehicle for advancing the industrial revolution (Bowles & Gintis, 1976). And nationalism, while always a prominent concern, did not come to the forefront of American educational rhetoric until the Second World War.

France can be portrayed as vacillating between the themes of democratization and nationalism. Condorcet in his report to the Legislative Assembly of 21 April 1792 expressed the following hopes for national education:

> *To offer all individuals of the human race the means of providing for*
> *their wants, of insuring their welfare, of knowing and exercising their*
> *rights, of knowing and fulfilling their duties;*
> *To assure each one the opportunity of making himself more efficient in*
> *his industry, of making himself more capable of performing social*
> *functions to which he may be called, of developing to the fullest extent*
> *the talents which he has received from nature; and by that means to*
> *establish among the citizens an equality in fact, making real the*
> *political equality recognized by the law;*
> *Such ought to be the first aim of national education.*
> *(Cited in Reisner, 1923, p. 18)*

While Condorcet outlined the type of structures he felt would be needed to realize this purpose, the Assembly could not decide on a course of action. Over the ensuing months, the struggle between the major factions of the Revolution intensified until the Mountain prevailed over the Girondists during the Reign of Terror. Robespierre revived Condorcet's ideas and especially the theme that the National Schools should build the new citizen. These schools were to be boarding schools and all parents would be expected to send their children 'to suck Republican milk'. The object of instruction was 'to strengthen the bodies of the children and to develop them through gymnastic exercises, to accustom them to hard work, to harden them against every kind of fatigue, to bend them to the yoke of salutary discipline, to form their minds and hearts by means of suitable lessons, and to give them that information which is necessary to every citizen whatever may be his calling in life'.

But the effort of developing the new democracy left France weak and exposed. And so by the conclusion of the eighteenth century the Republican government was looking for a strong leader who could rally the nation and mount its defence. Napoleon answered the call, and he promoted a sharp shift towards nationalism, with every fabric of French society under his control. In the field of education he insisted that no school, no establishment of instruction whatsoever, could be set up outside the Imperial University and without the authorization of its head. A decree of 1808 states:

> All schools of the Imperial University shall take as the basis of their instruction: a) the precepts of the Catholic religion; b) fidelity to the Emperor and the Imperial Monarchy, which is the trustee of the welfare of the people, and to the Napoleonic dynasty, which is the conservator of the unity of France and of all the ideas proclaimed by the Constitution; and c) obedience to the statutes of the teaching corporation, which have as their object uniformity of instruction and which tend to the production for the state of citizens attached to their religion, to their country, and to their families. (Cited in Reisner, 1923, p. 37)

Napoleon was concerned to build a strong France that also excelled in science and technology and so he strengthened the scientific emphasis in secondary education and encouraged the development of the *école polytechnique* and related institutions. Following Napoleon, the nationalistic tone of French education was mollified and greater efforts were made to promote popular education and especially to increase opportunities for vocational and technical education for the common citizen. And so in France, there seems to be a continuing accommodation between nationalism and democracy. But reflecting Napoleon's concern for technological supremacy, there is also a clear bias towards the sciences and to technical competence.

English ideas about education go back a long way and have an aristocratic flair to them. John Locke, in his reflection on 'the Conduct of the Understanding' wrote:

> The best aid to professional and scientific study, and [that] educated men can do what illiterate cannot; and the man who has learned to think and to reason and to compare and to discriminate and to analyse, who has refined his taste, and formed his judgment, and sharpened his mental vision, will not indeed at once be [whatever he intends to be professionally], but he will be placed in that state of intellect in which he can take up any one of the sciences or callings ... with an ease, a grace, a versatility, and a success, to which another is a stranger. (Cited in Tristram, 1952, p. 32)

This ideal was later referred to by Cardinal Newman as a liberal education. Newman distinguishes between a useful education that 'teaches some mechanical art or some physical secret', and a liberal education that develops the whole man (Newman in *Discourse V*, pp. 88-109). Sir William Hamilton elaborated on the concept of a liberal education:

> *An education in which the individual is cultivated, not as an*
> *instrument towards some ulterior end, but as an end unto himself alone;*
> *in other words, an education, in which his absolute perfection as a man,*
> *and not merely his relative dexterity as a professional man, is the scope*
> *immediately in view. (Cited in Tristram, 1952, p. 32)*

Implicit in these statements is the assumption that only a select group needs and is capable of a liberal education. For the rest, it would certainly be a waste of time. The question for England, then, was should the nation bother with educating the rest or not, a question that was finally and reluctantly answered in the affirmative in the second half of the nineteenth century. Forster presented the argument for the Elementary Education Act to Parliament as follows:

> *We must not delay. Upon the speedy provision of elementary education*
> *depends our industrial prosperity. It is of no use trying to give technical*
> *teaching to our artisans without elementary education; uneducated*
> *labourers – and many of our labourers are utterly uneducated – are for*
> *the most part, unskilled labourers, and if we leave our workfolk any*
> *longer unskilled, notwithstanding their strong sinews and determined*
> *energy, they will become over-matched in the competition of the world.*
> *If we are to hold our position among men of our own race or among the*
> *nations of the world we must make up the smallness of our numbers by*
> *increasing the intellectual force of the individual. (Quoted in Young,*
> *1958, p. 34)*

Just as England was debating the issues of educational reform, a coalition of reformers decided to deliver Japan from over 250 years of feudal life under the Tokugawa family. These reformers first travelled widely in the West and hastily drafted proposals for a new institutional framework that had a Western face. Foreign consultants were invited to help the new government develop a banking system, modern factories, a transportation system, an electrical power grid, and a new educational system. With rapid Westernization under way, the Meiji leaders began to evaluate their handiwork. By the mid-1880s they had devised a new constitution that was far more conservative than the earlier reforms. They also reviewed education with the thought of finally setting it on a Japanese course. Mori Arinori, who had been appointed Minister of Education and who is certainly regarded as one of the most important shapers of modern Japanese education, offered the following reflections in a paper he presented to the Japanese cabinet:

> *Civilization is gradually spreading as can be seen by the progressive*
> *changes in the objects we use for our daily activities. Is the spirit of our*
> *people sufficiently hardened and trained that they may withstand*
> *adversity, bear up and endure under pain, and shoulder the heavy*
> *burdens of the long road ahead? This must be doubted. Since the Middle*
> *Ages, in our country only the warriors* (bushi) *have performed civil and*
> *military* (bunbu) *duties. Now, as a result, only one portion of the*

people adequately understands and supports the modernization of the state. In contrast, the great majority are confused and may lack those qualities of strong character essential for guaranteeing the independence of the state … We have identified those general moral principles which we hope the educational system will instil in the people, but what is the detailed educational programme that will realize these principles? Consider for a moment. Our country has never been subject to indignity from a foreign nation thanks to the authority of the imperial throne which has been occupied by an unbroken line of Emperors from ancient times. The people's traditional spirit of defending the fatherland and of total loyalty to the Emperor still remains firm. This is the essential foundation for national wealth and strength. If this is made the goal of education and the character of the people is advanced according to this spirit, there will be no need for fear. The people will feel a strong sense of loyalty to the throne (chukon) *and love for their country* (aikoku); *they will have strong character, and be pure in thought. We must establish through education the principle of abhorring those who are insulting and evil. If we are successful, there is no doubt that the people will be able to endure much difficulty and will be prepared to strive together to carry out their tasks … This vitality if channelled into productive labour will develop the national wealth. There is not one element in advancing the fate of this vital spirit. The elderly pass this vital spirit to the young. Fathers and ancestors pass this vital spirit to posterity. From person to person and household, all are made the same according to this vital spirit. The vital spirit of our nation becomes fixed, and the nation naturally becomes something of great strength. (cited in Ministry of Education, 1980, pp. 94-95)*

Mori seems to be urging his fellow Ministers to support an educational system that provides Western science while strengthening the will of the Japanese people to work together to build a strong nation and empire. His ideas were later reflected in the Imperial Rescript on Education.

Turning finally to Russia, the People's Commissariat of Education was formed in 1918 with A.V. Lunacharsky as the first commissioner. In his first annual report, Lunacharsky set out the principles for Soviet education which continue down to the present day:

In place of schools of all varieties and kinds – which formerly were sharply divided into a lower school for the plain people, and the middle school for the privileged classes and the well-to-do people, and divided further into schools for boys and those for girls, into technical and classical secondary schools, general and special school institutions – the Commissariat has introduced the Unified Workers' School, covering the entire length of the course of instruction.

The unity of this school should be understood in two ways: first, that the class divisions are abolished and the school adopts a continuous grade system. In principle, every child of the Russian Republic enters a school of an identical type and has the same chances as every other to complete the higher education. Second, that up to the age of 16, all specialization is omitted. It is self-understood that this does not hinder the adoption of the principle of individual attention and of the greatest possible variety of forms inside each school. But specialization in the full meaning of the word is permitted only after the attaining of the age of 16, and upon the foundation of a general and polytechnical education acquired already. The school is declared an absolutely lay institution; diplomas in their character of certificates granting special rights are abolished. The classical languages are declared nonobligatory. (Quoted in Bereday et al, 1960, pp. 51-52)

Over time, the Russian school experienced reforms including an upgrading of academic content. But the principles of accessibility, practicality, and the emphasis on socialist principles were a continuing concern.

Education for All?

Prior to the modern age, a clear distinction was drawn between those who ruled and those who were ruled. The former group, modest in size, was composed of the political head, who may have achieved prominence through military supremacy and/or appointment by the Pope, couriers, major landowners, the clergy, officials, and powerful merchants. The progeny of the rulers were likely to receive education in classical and religious texts either by tutors or through attendance at school. Some went as far as the university where they obtained degrees signifying their learned accomplishments. While the rulers were expected to achieve some learning, the common folk were generally neglected. Indeed, many in the ruling class felt that the spread of literacy to the common people might contribute to social disorder.

The ideological, political and economic forces unleashed in the modern period brought about significant changes in the composition and structuration of social classes. These social changes prompted major reviews of the value of literacy and learning. A certain level of intellectual competence came to be seen as valuable for religious worship, for effectiveness in armed conflict, for efficient work, and for thoughtful participation in civic affairs. The extent of these changes in educational assumptions varied from place to place and decade to decade. In the locales where change had been less abrupt, while rulers came to believe it important for the common people to gain a certain level of learning, they were careful to preserve a distinction between the intellectual opportunities open to the ruled relative to those available to the rulers.

This separation was most evident in England where there were very few opportunities extended to the working class until 1870, and even thereafter the quality of public education was much inferior to that available to the ruling class in their exclusive school system. France on several occasions following the French Revolution proposed bold plans to establish and expand public schools for the common people, but did not back these up in a decisive way until 1870, following its disastrous defeat by Germany. On the continent, Germany did the most to provide popular education, but these schools did not readily lead to further education; in contrast, the German urban middle classes and the ruling elite had access to the *Gymnasiums*, which had virtually an exclusive monopoly on access to the universities. King Frederick William II of Prussia once commented on the dangers of overeducating the common people:

> *In respect to the loud and ever louder demand for popular education by means of improved schools, I find myself in a disagreeable position which causes me considerable uneasiness. It must be granted that popular education is the foundation upon which the welfare of the people must rest. A neglected, uncouth, illiterate people can be neither a good nor a happy people. Therefore I have given the good-schools interest a free hand and supported it as far as the economic condition of the state allowed. I have also been pleased to hear the many reports of progress in the Prussian territories. I have also had satisfaction in hearing the comparison made between my own land, in which the great majority of the children receive instruction, and other lands of Europe in which no schools whatever exist.*

> *But just where educational conditions are most advanced, all kinds of doubts and forebodings force themselves upon me. May one ask himself regarding popular education whether or not it has its limits. If it has no bounds, then we are not justified in interfering with, hindering, or restricting its development, but must let it take its natural course. That, however, I cannot approve without reservations. The answer becomes still more difficult when one wishes to set up limitations and then tries to say where they are to be and whether or not they can be established.*

> *We do not confer upon the individual or upon society any benefit when we educate him beyond the bounds of his social class and vocation, give him a cultivation which he cannot make use of, and awaken in him pretensions and needs which his lot in life does not allow him to satisfy. (Cited in Reisner, 1923, pp. 143-144)*

Baron von Altenstein in proclaiming the General Order for Education lists several goals and concludes:

> *According to these principles, I regard popular education as truly something more than a scanty instruction in the bare instrumentalities of culture – reading, writing, and arithmetic. On the other hand I do not think that the principles enunciated will raise the common people out of the sphere designated for them by God and human society. I think rather that they are able to make the common man's lot agreeable and profitable to him. (Cited in Reisner, 1923, p. 145)*

In contrast, in both Japan and Russia following the modernizing revolutions that brought in the Meiji oligarchy on the one hand and the Bolshevik regime on the other, rapid steps were taken to establish a new educational system that would include all. As already noted, Japan's Fundamental Code of Education of 1872 declared:

> *There shall, in the future, be no community with an illiterate family, nor a family with an illiterate person. Every guardian, acting in accordance with this, shall bring up his children with tender care, never failing to have them attend school. (Passin, 1966, pp. 209-211)*

Similarly, in Russia, the Congress of the Communist Party in March 1919, stated:

> *Our school will be in fact accessible to all. To attain this end, not only are all tuition fees abolished, but the children are provided with gratuitous hot food, and the poorest children with shoes and clothing. It goes without saying that all school manuals are offered to the children free of charge by the school. (From Bereday et al, 1960, p. 52)*

This same pledge was reiterated in Article 121 of the 1936 Stalin Constitution:

> *Citizens of the USSR have the right to education. This right is ensured by universal and compulsory education; by free education up to and including the seventh grade; by a system of state stipends for students of higher educational establishments who excel in their studies; by instruction in schools being conducted in the native language, and by the organization in the factories, state farms, machine and tractor stations, and collective farms of free vocational, technical and agronomic training for the working people. (From Bereday et al, 1960, p. 69)*

The American experience perhaps stands in between these two extremes. The American sentiment was clearly in favour of inclusiveness from the earliest decades of the new republic, and this soon became manifest in the common school movement. Charles Fenton Mercer, a Virginia Federalist, gave eloquent expression to this egalitarian sentiment in a speech he delivered in 1826:

> *Intellectual and moral worth constitute in America our only nobility; and this high distinction is placed by the laws, and should be brought in fact, within the reach of every citizen.*
>
> *Where distinct ranks exist in a society, it may be plausibly objected to the intellectual improvement of the lower classes of the community, that it will invert the public sentiment, or impose on the privileged orders the necessity of proportional exertion to protect themselves from the scorn of their inferiors. But the equality on which our institutions are founded, cannot be too intimately interwoven in the habits of thinking among our*

youth, and it is obvious that it would be greatly promoted by their continuance together, for the longest possible period, in the same schools of juvenile instruction; to sit upon the same forms; engage in the same competitions, partake of the same recreations and amusements, and pursue the same studies, in connexion with each other; under the same discipline, and in obedience to the same authority. (Cited in Cremin, 1951, p. 57)

Still the various states of the United States made specific provisions to protect the independence of private schools serving particular religions and class groups. Similarly, at the collegiate level, institutions were given the right to set their own admissions policies without any regulations to guarantee against exclusiveness.

The First Schools

The new thinking about education was accompanied by efforts to establish new schools. In the case of France and Japan, the modern reformers laid out a grand design and then proceeded to establish new schools in accordance with this design. In the other nations, the first schools were more likely to emerge from local initiatives. It might be said that the first schools established a precedent for later schools. Thus, a review of the first schools tells us much about what follows. We will create portraits of these first schools through borrowing from the work of recent pioneers of the history of education who have shifted the focus of that field from national to local histories. Our sketches will necessarily be selective, given the broader concerns of this book.

Germany's Primary School or Folk School

The Reformation stressed popular education initially for religious knowledge, and so local churches provided the financial base for school establishment through the tithes they solicited from their worshippers. Mary Jo Maynes (1985) has provided a survey of the early folk schools in Baden, a state that includes the towns of Mannheim and Heidelberg. The river Rhine goes along the western side of this state, opening it up for trade with other areas. Therefore it has always been a relatively prosperous state, albeit with an exceptionally diverse population.

Prosperity was accompanied by generous tithing to the church, that in turn led to solid support for the local folk schools. By 1770, nine of the ten communities had schools, and by the turn of the century all had schools. Each of these schools had a building that included space for a single large classroom and for the residence of the teacher and his family (Maynes, 1985, p. 38). The teachers received reasonable compensation from a variety of sources, including their right to farm communal land. The report on enrolments by grade for the Heidelberg Reformed School, which had seventy-five boys and forty-seven girls in 1728, is described as somewhat typical (see Table 3.1).

Ordnung (class)	Number of pupils	Age range	Length of time enrolled	Subjects
V	14	4½-7	¼-½ year	ABCs
IV	23	5½-9	¾-1¼ years	Spelling
III	20	6½-11	1-4½ years	Reading in psalter
II	28	5½-14	2-5 years	Memorizing, reading in New Testament, most also writing
I	38	9-14	½-5¾ years	Reading Old and New Testaments and letters, writing

Table 3.1. Class organization, Heidelberg Reformed School, 1728.

Table 3.1 summarizes the enrolments by grade and the curriculum. The main focus was on literacy and Bible reading, in keeping with the spirit of the Reformation. Arithmetic, while not specified as a separate subject, was introduced in the upper grades in response to local demand. Singing and prayers were the only activities where all of the pupils joined together. For the other subjects, the teacher (one teacher for 123 pupils) focused on one group while the other pupils were asked to engage in self-study. All of the activities were coeducational.

The German state's interest in popular education picked up after Germany's defeat by Napoleon in the early 1800s. In an increasing number of states, school attendance was made obligatory (Maynes, 1985, p. 56), and the state began to share in the subsidies provided by the local churches. Accordingly, the curriculum came to place greater emphasis on civics and 'loyalty to the Grand Duke'. The curriculum also became somewhat more demanding. But the main features of the modern system were already in place by the close of the eighteenth century – high access, relatively small local schools, coeducation, and a curriculum of limited scope with a focus on reading, religious content and some attention to the modern subject of arithmetic (but no science at that time). The teachers were adequately compensated and competent.

The French Lycée

France was not known for its primary schools, either before or after the Revolution. French primary schools were not as well funded nor were they as accessible as the German folk school. And the second cycle of primary education in the *écoles primaires supérieures* was characterized by a tough curriculum designed to weed out the average student, leaving only a small number eligible for secondary education. But for those who were successful, secondary education was a refreshing change.

Secondary education was conducted in residential institutions called colleges that, compared to French primary schools, were comparatively well funded and stimulating. During the Revolution they were renamed *lycées* and given a special push by Napoleon (Palmer, 1975, pp. 194ff.) Napoleon was said to favour these schools as a way of pleasing his social base, the bourgeoisie. At first, these new institutions had the position of an advanced tier for secondary education above the *Gymnasiums*, but by the 1820s the term of *lycée* came to be used for all upper secondary schools of the academic track, and that practice has continued to the present.

Robert Palmer has provided a detailed documentary history of the Collège of Louis-Le-Grand, one of the most distinguished of the French *lycées*, as it evolved during the revolutionary period. It was originally established as a Jesuit College attached to the University of Paris and traces its origins to the seventeenth century. Students tended to enter at the seventh or sixth level, complete secondary education and stay on for three years of professional education – and so might stay for as many as twelve years. Most students (about 600, or more than the total number enrolled in Oxford and Cambridge at that time) were boarders. Most had their tuition fees waived and received a scholarship to cover room and board on the premises of the college. The curriculum mainly consisted of Latin classics (Cicero, Livy, Tacitus, etc.) with some exposure to Greek, as Latin was viewed as an important tool for advanced studies in theology, law and medicine.

From 1762 to 1764, long before the French Revolution, the Jesuits were expelled from all colleges in France – though Catholicism as such was not rejected. However, this was accompanied by a new era of national education. A major goal was to prepare men as social beings, effective and participating members of a modern society, and not as religious devotees preparing for the afterlife. This trend was accelerated during the Revolution.

With the Revolution the most evident change in the curriculum was the moderate introduction of mathematics and modern science.[1] College enrolments declined during the early days of the Revolution due to the turmoil. Later, the College's endowment was expropriated by the state, thus depriving the College of the possibility of offering scholarships to needy students. But with the emergence of Napoleon as First Consul, new measures were taken to strengthen secondary education. First, the College was made an advanced secondary school and renamed the Imperial Lycée. Later, it was joined with other academic upper secondary schools, all of which came to be named *lycée*, differing in their relative status and size. The Imperial Lycée became one of the top institutions and received relatively generous allocations from the state as well as more scholarship students (now paid for directly by the state).

Palmer concludes his study of the Collège of Louis-le-Grand (renamed the Imperial Lycée) as follows:

> *In 1814, when the Napoleonic empire came to an end, the Imperial Lycée was in many ways very different from what the Collège of Louis-le-Grand had been in the generation before the Revolution. Mathematics and Science were taught to a higher level. Religion was less pervasive. The students were more mixed; not all were scholarship students, as they had been until 1800. The students were also younger, for the lycée had become a 'secondary' school; there were no longer those who went out to professional schools for their studies, as there had been at the old Louis-le-Grand (and like institutes). Resident students were in uniform. Drums beat every hour or so. The classes were invaded by several hundred day pupils from satellite boarding schools. All told, there were about a thousand students, twice as many as before the Revolution. Classrooms were overcrowded.*

> *In other ways the lack of change is surprising, considering all that had happened. In physical accommodation the school was larger, having annexed the buildings of Plessis College, but all buildings were inherited from the Old Regime. Teaching methods had changed very little; the old scholastic disputation was not revived, but supervised study, recitation, declamation, and written and oral examinations went on as before. The same spirit of competitive achievement prevailed. Pupils moved forward in graded annual classes. The daily schedule of getting up, eating, studying, reciting, mingling in the courtyards, and going to bed was much the same in 1814 as in 1774. (1975, pp. 232-233)*

In accounting for this continuity, Palmer observes that the basic professorial staff remained remarkably stable. For example, among the faculty before the Revolution was Jean-François Champagne, who was born in 1751 in Burgundy. He attended the College on a scholarship and became a member of the clergy, received a *maîtrise ès arts* in 1774, and became professor in 1778. With the Revolution, he joined the reform committee in 1790, and was made principal in 1791. He gave up his religious orders in 1793 and married. Champagne stayed on as principal until 1810. He was one of several staff who persevered through the ups and downs of this transition to recreate this representative school. Thus, in France the first modern school was much like the last pre-modern school. *Plus ça change.*

The English Public School

The first school of the English educational revolution has certain parallels to the French *lycée*. From medieval times, the Church had supported a number of schools across England to provide the highest quality education for the various learned professions associated with managing the affairs of the Church and the nation. Occupying the top tier were the famous universities of Oxford and Cambridge that provided advanced preparation for the fields of theology, law and medicine. But to prepare for Oxford, the Church supported several public schools, including Winchester, Harrow, Eton, Rugby, Westminster, Charterhouse and Shrewsbury. Admission to these schools was a privilege guarded by the respective schools. Aspirants were typically recommended by people of importance in their communities, and following a recommendation they might be expected to travel to the public school for an interview. Those who could demonstrate both academic promise and good character were considered for admission. Coming from a family of proper breeding was also an explicit consideration; the children of former students were given favourable consideration. As the scholars accepted at the public schools had to travel from distant homes, all were residential institutions.[2]

The curriculum for the public schools adhered to much the same pattern as that of the classical French college or the German *Gymnasium*. The main focus was on the Greek and Latin classics in the original languages. By the nineteenth century the curriculum had broadened somewhat to include some attention to European art and literature as well as the new fields of mathematics and the sciences. But these were generally considered frivolous extras which the teaching staff might indulge in as a complement to their attention to the core curriculum of the classics.

Compared with the French *lycée*, the English public school was far more attentive to religious studies. The chapel was typically the most prominent building and students were expected to attend chapel every day. One of the daily core courses for all students was theology, and prayers were routinely offered before every meal. While education in France was secularized by the French Revolution, most English thinkers viewed this as a grave mistake.

To develop the total faculties of their pupils, the English public schools believed that the co-curriculum was equal in importance to the core curriculum. At the conclusion of classes every day in the mid-afternoon, the pupils were expected to participate in the various co-curricular activities ongoing at the school. Each member of the academic staff had the additional responsibility for supervising some area of the co-curriculum. Included in the array of opportunities were drama, debate, music, and various forms of athletics ranging from archery to rowing. Following an afternoon of co-curricular activities, pupils were expected to sit for dinner in the common dining room and then study (usually in the official study hall) until lights out.

To foster order in the life of the schools, the masters and their academic staff appointed prefects from among the senior pupils to supervise events such as chapel, common meals, study halls, and athletic events. To establish the environment for this discipline, new pupils to the public schools underwent a period where they were subjected to various humiliating tasks at the discretion of seniors, such as polishing shoes, cleaning rooms, and engaging in strenuous physical feats. Prefects were even allowed to use stern disciplinary measures, including flogging junior boys they deemed out of line (Weinberg, 1967, p. 47).

Most of the members of the English parliament of the early nineteenth century had attended a public school, and they could see little use in any other form of education.[3] And as this was an elite education, they therefore saw little use in providing publicly supported modern education for the working classes. Over the course of the nineteenth century, the ruling class was gradually persuaded of the benefits of some form of publicly supported popular education so that England could become more competitive. They also were persuaded that some changes might be required in the public schools. Gradually, the curriculum was reformed to give greater attention to new fields such as the social and natural sciences, but keeping to the ideal that a good mind should mainly apply itself to the classical texts, students were encouraged to focus on a few specialities rather than to cover everything.[4]

Meanwhile, the state school system was developing secondary schools of its own, and the graduates of these institutions sought an equal chance to gain entrance to the English universities. Thus, Ordinary and Advanced level tests were devised to determine the degree of preparation of young people for admission to the universities, and advanced students of the elite public schools came to sit for these tests alongside their fellow countrymen from the state schools. Preserving the public school belief that students should not spread themselves too thinly, students were only expected to sit for examinations in a small number of subjects. Performance in these tests was shared with the universities as one criterion for selection. But the universities retained their independent right to admissions and it was not unknown for a student from a public school with average grades to be admitted whereas a student from a state school with superior grades was denied admission. The presumption was that the public school student was better educated even though lacking in examination proficiency. The public school ideal of a balanced education has continued to command attention in England over the course of the modern transformation.

The American College

The first ships travelling to New England had an exceptionally well-educated passenger list for that era, and much the same could be said of the ships to follow. The new settlers were products of the Reformation who viewed America, the new land, as the place to build God's kingdom on earth. Every new community built their church and every church needed a pastor. Partly to respond to this demand, Harvard College was established in 1636, only sixteen years after the Pilgrims had landed on Plymouth Rock. Soon thereafter Yale College was established, and by the time of the revolutionary war as many as nine colleges had been established across the thirteen colonies. By the time of the Civil War, one report indicates that there were over 600 colleges in the USA. Daniel Boorstin (1958), reflecting on the American proclivity for establishing colleges, notes that most of these institutions bypassed the English requirement of seeking charters from the crown. Also, it seems that American communities felt more complete when they had their own college, much as they desire sports teams in the modern era.

This abundance of colleges is to be compared with England where there were only two degree-granting institutions up to 1800 and only three by 1850. The American fascination with colleges is also to be compared with the relatively sparse number of lesser institutions available in America for college preparation. During the colonial period, most aspirants prepared through self-study and tutorials or at local dame schools. While public school systems slowly evolved over the course of the nineteenth century, it would have to be said that the representative American educational institution was the liberal arts college.

The American colleges initially patterned their instructional programme after their English forebears, with an emphasis on classical studies taught in Greek and Latin. This practice was continued at most colleges well into the nineteenth century. But there were several important characteristics of the new land that led to change. First, as the American colleges lacked the generous resources that the Church provided to European colleges, they created lay boards to ensure their financial stability. The lay boards were at least as concerned with increasing financial revenues as they were with academic tradition, and this made them open to innovative approaches that might be responsive to student needs. Thus, from relatively early in the nineteenth century, many American colleges were providing unorthodox optional courses in such areas as commercial studies, legal studies, and technology. Boorstin (1958, p. 180) argues that the geographic spread of the USA and the tendency of most colleges to serve local interests as contrasted to a broader national public interest also fostered innovativeness; despite many initiatives over the nineteenth century, the various American colleges shied away from the formation of any national body that would define the purpose of higher education or the necessary standards. This tendency towards new approaches was accelerated by the Morill Act of 1862, which offered the several American states large grants of land providing these states established specialized institutions focusing on the 'agricultural and the mechanical arts ... in order to promote the liberal education of the industrial classes'; over the latter half of the century, state after state founded its land-grant college dedicated to these practical studies.

In this context, President Charles W. Eliot of America's first college, Harvard, decided to introduce a radical curricular reform known as the 'free elective' principle. Whereas students before had been expected to follow a prescribed set of courses leading to their chosen degree, whether in law, theology, medicine, or other specialization, the elective principle totally abandoned the concept of prescribing course sequences. Henceforth, at least in the initial reform proposed by Eliot, students could elect any sequence of courses they desired. All that was required for graduation was that they complete a sufficient number of courses and that they be able to demonstrate that the combination they had chosen fitted their needs (Boorstin, 1974, p. 493). Among Eliot's various arguments for the elective principle was that, in a democratic society, young people were mature enough to make their own choices. After all, their education was their preparation for life, and thus it would be inappropriate for the college to tell them what they had to do.

Eliot's Harvard at the turn of the twentieth century was a relatively modest sized institution with slightly over 1500 students and some eighty faculty. The main thrust of the curriculum was focused on the classical professions of theology, law and medicine. The introduction of the elective principle enabled Eliot and his successors to add appointments in such experimental fields as science and psychology. And in the early 1920s Harvard became the first 'Ivy League' institution to add a Faculty of Education. Over time, other specialisms were added and so it has been said that it became a place 'for any person, any study'. This breadth of opportunities, combined with the responsibility placed on the individual to make the wise choice, is perhaps the fundamental feature of the American curriculum.

Most Harvard students at the turn of the century came from nearby communities, but the commute home was lengthy and, moreover, Cambridge was an interesting place. Therefore nearly all students elected to reside in one of the college's houses. Some of their classes took place on the actual premises of their houses whereas for others they had to walk to other houses or central classrooms. The college also encouraged extra-curricular activities, including debate, drama and athletics.

The curricular reforms introduced by Eliot at Harvard, while controversial, were soon adopted at other colleges across the USA. Later, Eliot was to make the same arguments for greater choice for the American high school student that he had made for the college student, thus leading to the diffusion of the elective principle to the lower levels of American education.

The Japanese Elementary School

While in all of the aforementioned Western cases modern education might be said to have evolved, in Japan it was catapulted out of the bold shift embodied in the Meiji Revolution, which sought to 'restore the Emperor' and rekindle 'Eastern morality' on the one hand, and to 'foster Western science' so as to withstand the imperial designs of Western nations on the other hand. Among the bold changes proposed were the abolition of feudalism and the uplifting of the common people. Thus, the Charter Oath of 1872 declared that every child should become literate, and the Education System Order of that same year devoted its early sections to the provisions necessary for the establishment of a universal system of elementary education. The preamble to the Order stressed 'the necessity for individual self-improvement and the fruits that could be expected from regular school attendance' regardless of family background or gender (Ministry of Education, 1980, p. 35). Among the provisions of this Order was the division of the nation into eight university districts; within each there was to be a university, thirty-two middle schools, and 210 elementary schools (according to the design there were to be 53,760 elementary schools). The original expectation was that local communities would finance the construction of these new schools as well as pay for a portion of the operating costs. This Order also authorized the establishment of normal schools, which was certainly a novel idea in Japan as most professional training up to that point had been by apprenticeship.

Remarkably, within just a few years as many as 25,000 new schools had been founded and most were operational.[5] According to the Course of Study for Elementary Schools published in 1872, students were to attend every day except Sunday for five hours a day. The first semester included reading, calligraphy, dictation, vocabulary, arithmetic, and physical education; in later semesters, geography, including the study of the globe, Japanese and world history, and composition were added. The first texts used in these new schools were mainly translations of American texts, but by the late 1870s Japanese authors had developed acceptable indigenous texts. However, the public expressed much discontent with the impracticality of these new schools, and these complaints led the Emperor to order a comprehensive review. As a result of this review, the national government decided to place more emphasis on traditional morality (*shushin*), to strengthen the practical side of the curriculum [6], and to assume full responsibility for funding the primary schools as well as for providing the curriculum, texts, staff and other essentials. Also, children were required to attend for no more than sixteen weeks out of the year (the number of weeks was gradually increased to forty by the turn of the century).

With the strong encouragement of the Meiji government, elementary schools were rapidly constructed throughout Japan. A typical school had an external wall around a playing field, with the school prominently visible from the front gate. Whereas the Tokugawa *terakoya* were of wooden construction, the new elementary school was a two-storey frame building of brick construction covered over with plaster and with hard wood floors.[7] Students were expected to proceed down the pathway from the front gate to the front entrance of the school, at which point they would take off their shoes, step up to the main floor of the school, and put on their slippers. Proceeding down the hall, there were two classrooms on each side and at the back there was one room for the principal and a second for the teachers, and on the first floor there were additional classrooms. Rather than allow the children to sit on mats as in the *terakoya*, the classrooms provided wooden desks for each child. Outside were separate latrines for boys and girls. Each day of school, the young students were expected to line up outside in the playground to hear some words of inspiration and guidance from their principal as well as to learn about forthcoming activities. (After 1890, they were also expected to recite the Imperial Rescript on Education.) Then they proceeded to their classrooms to begin their day of studies. At Mitsuke school, boys and girls sat in the same classroom but on different sides. All six of the teachers at Mitsuke had at least a middle school education and two had also graduated from the recently established Tokyo normal school. The headteacher or principal assumed a normal teaching load along with his staff. The teachers received good salaries and other benefits and those who came from other communities were provided with free rooms.

On the recommendation of American consultants, the academic programme was divided into grades, with students having to pass a test in each subject in order to move forward. In the back of each classroom, there was a board to hang each student's name plaque in the order of their current rank in the testing programme. Usually, a teacher began with a first grade class, teaching them in all subjects for the first four semesters before turning them over to a new teacher. Students who excelled in the tests were sometimes allowed to skip grades and slow students were held back. But most students stayed with their cohort and completed at least the first cycle of primary education. To fail to complete the programme was considered shameful.

During the first two decades of the Meiji period testing was strict, relying on examinations provided by regional authorities. Average scores were computed for each school, and the reputations of teachers were associated with the academic performance of their students. Partly for this reason, teachers developed a habit of teaching to the test. And schools were known to recruit outstanding pupils from nearby schools so as to boost their averages. The pernicious effects of this competition came to be viewed as unhealthy, and so the responsibility for grade-level testing was shifted to the staff of each school (Amano, 1990, p. 67). Generally speaking, schools came to follow the practice of automatic promotion.

Japan's modern elementary school provided courses covering subjects as diverse as physical and moral education and science and world geography. Teachers were respected, comparatively well paid, and had big jobs requiring them to teach all subjects over two or more grades. The elementary schools were beacons of modernity, with their European architecture, their expectation that children sit on chairs at desks, and that all young people regardless of class or gender should study together in a common classroom. Whereas early Meiji education stressed individual development through competition, these themes were gradually muted, with increasing emphasis on hard work as part of a team effort, filial piety, and loyalty to the Emperor.

The Russian General School

Tsarist education was virtually a carbon copy of nineteenth-century German education. Peter the Great was enamoured of Germany and thus invited many experts to help him with his efforts to modernize Russia. Among them was a group that drew up the overall design for Russian education, which not unsurprisingly had contours much like the German system of that time. This made sense as German education had a good reputation and was reputed to have helped Germany catch up with her European neighbours. But education made slow progress in Russia after Peter. During the reign of Alexander II there was a window of liberalism, but this was again followed by stagnation through the remainder of the nineteenth century. Education in tsarist Russia was essentially elitist, but even the elites were not notably desirous of education.

The revolution brought on a new spirit of innovation. During the first few years there were many progressive ideas. Even Lenin's wife, Nadezhda Krupskaya, threw her energies into educational reform. As the battles with the White Russians subsided, Lenin took steps to provide shape to modern education. The first focus was on the Unified Workers' School that, in principle, was to cover the full length of pre-tertiary education.

While the ideal was to establish schools covering all grades, in many settings the primary grades were broken off as a separate unit. But even so, these separate primary schools retained the important principles of accessibility, practicality and the emphasis on socialist principles.

The Unified School of that time was a neighbourhood school. It was usually modest in size, having one or two entering classes. Given the poverty of the times, classes were relatively large, consisting of 40-50 students who were from all social backgrounds and both genders. As in the Japanese school, a first grade teacher would welcome a cohort and then stay with them through at least the second grade, if not longer. The curriculum was of modest scope, emphasizing literacy and numeracy, with some attention to science. It was also strong on political and moral education, while religious education was completely abandoned. Music and art education were also included and considerable emphasis was placed on physical education to strengthen the youngsters' bodies to withstand the harsh Russian winter. Each school had, along with individual classrooms, a large general room that could be used for physical education, assemblies, and other common events. The Unified School retained the same principle of a common curriculum through the last years of secondary education (ten years) before the graduates proceeded either to an academic institution or a polytechnic.

Over time, the Russian school experienced reforms, including an upgrading of academic content. Under Stalin, the pedagogue Anton S. Makarenko, who emphasized the value of collectivist educational principles to provide support for all pupils and also as a way of building a socialist consciousness, gained favour. Thus, the Soviet classroom came to place more stress on cooperative learning, and, moreover, collectivist links were established between grades as well as with supporting collectives in the world of work (Bronfenbrenner, 1970).

As with the other first schools discussed above, despite many changes in Russia over the turbulent twentieth century, the main characteristics of the Soviet Unified School are still very much alive in post-Soviet Russia.

Conclusion

In this chapter we have reviewed many of the new ideas about education that were articulated in the early decades of the modern period and have provided a snapshot of several representative schools of this period. Our review has necessarily been selective, emphasizing those views that carried the day. In all of the cases we have reviewed there was much debate about the future of education. The more progressive voices seemed to have the most influence in the later developing societies of the USA, Japan and Russia. Conservatism prevailed in England. Germany allowed much change while seeming to preserve old traditions. And France preserved many old traditions while seeming to champion change. In the next chapter, we will see how these initial changes were built on as the first modern nations moved beyond their initial experiments to structure a new system for the advancement of modern education.

Notes

[1] The functions of the former college were divided into two levels, to be provided by *Gymnasiums* for lower secondary education and the *lycées* for upper secondary education. Concerning the *Gymnasium*, a proposal for its curriculum begins as follows: 'Public instruction will be divided into three courses embracing all knowledge necessary to prepare young men for the functions needed by society'. The first course, extending over three years, was to include instruction in French language, Greek, Latin, religion, morals, the constitution, arithmetic, algebra, geometry, mythology, geography, ancient and modern history, and ideas on the arts and commerce of France. The second and third courses, for a combined period of three years, were to develop the above subjects as well as to cover logic, natural history, mathematics and experimental physics, and the Constitutional Degrees of the National Assembly. In sum, the *Gymnasium* had an encyclopaedic curriculum. Graduates were to enter one of four colleges that were specialized respectively in language and philosophy, the physical sciences, the biological sciences, and the arts. Louis-le-Grand was to focus on the first specialization.

[2] Indeed, at some 'public schools', especially those created in the nineteenth century near large urban centres, such as Merchant Taylor's and St Paul's, many students were day students; but the schools that accepted day students were generally considered the most prestigious (Weinberg, 1967, p. x).

[3] Boyd (1973) indicates that over the twentieth century at least three-quarters of the English 'elite' in the civil service, the foreign service, the judiciary, the Church of England, and the financial sector attended a public school.

[4] At one of the most prestigious public schools, as late as 1917 the typical fifth form student spent twenty-seven hours a week studying the classics, six hours on mathematics, three on history, three on English, and none on geography and science (cited in Weinberg, 1967, p. 41 from Seymour Bryant [1917] *The Public School System in Relation to the Coming Conflict for National Supremacy*, p. 24. London: Longmans, Green).

[5] A report of 1875 indicates that 40 per cent of the structures were leased from Buddhist temples (e.g. former *terakoya*) and 30 per cent were leased from private individuals (Ministry of Education, 1980, p. 49), and the majority had only one or two teachers and from forty to fifty pupils; however, over the next decade most obtained their own structures and expanded their enrolments and staff.

[6] Natural history and physics were added to the intermediate cycle, economics for boys, and sewing and home economics for girls. Singing was added for all students.

[7] This is a description of Mitsuke Elementary School, constructed in 1875 and featured in the Ministry of Education's *History* (1980). This Western-style construction was more than most local districts could afford, and so the majority of new construction during the Meiji period was, in fact, wood frame with the traditional sliding doors and windows.

CHAPTER 4

The Systematization and Expansion of Modern Education

In Prussia every child is taught, and must be taught, for a penalty is inflicted on parents who neglect to send their children to school ... In Prussia, the Minister of Instruction is one of the most important ministers of the state. The Department of Instruction is organized as carefully as that of war or of the treasury, and is intended to act on every district and family in the kingdom. In New England, it is no man's business to watch over public education. (William Ellery Channing. Christian Examiner, 1833)

Modern Education is one among several projects launched by the modernizing state. It is essentially a new venture and at least for the first states embarking on the project, there was no clear design or master plan. How many different types of schools would be required? What should be the mix of academic and technical training? Who should be allowed to attend these schools? Who should pay for them – the state, the students, or private benefactors? These were some of the design issues for which there were no ready answers. And so in the early years, especially for the first modernizing societies, there was much trial and error.

The First Steps

In the previous chapter, we suggested that the first steps focused on the design of a particular 'representative' school that best reflected the most pressing needs of the modernizers. Building on this first venture, these same modernizers and their successors added other schools to respond to other needs – for different skills, regions, and interested groups. As new schools were established, the elites had to make decisions about the relations between the respective schools. The decisions they made led gradually to an overall design for the emerging modern educational system. Germany was the pioneer in these endeavours and France followed in Germany's footsteps; Victor Cousin, for example, prepared a detailed report on German education which played a critical role in the reforms of the 1830s promoted by Guizot. Numerous Americans travelled to Germany and France in the 1830s and

101

1840s to gather the insights that were later expressed in the US Common Schools Movement. And, following the Meiji Revolution of 1868, Japan sent several missions to observe educational practice on the European continent, and in Great Britain and the USA. Those states that began later drew extensively from the lessons learned by the pioneers, and this helped the latecomers to complete their task of systematization in a briefer time span. Thus, Japan completed its major systemic decisions within the first two decades of the Meiji Revolution and the Bolsheviks took less than fifteen years to draw up the decisive educational law of 1931.

In this chapter, we compare these emerging systems in terms of two dimensions: the differentiation/integration of various educational opportunities both through vertical and horizontal divisions, and the segregation/inclusion of different social groups in the various educational opportunities, primarily through horizontal segmentation/tracking. We will suggest that there are distinctive differences both in the structure of the respective systems and in the means the respective states relied on to establish direction. Among the means available to the state for influencing direction were establishment standards, accreditation, finance, admissions and examinations.

Once the state is satisfied with the direction of modern education, it may delegate most educational decisions to boards or other decision-making bodies composed primarily of educators. But now and again the state is likely to intervene with a new wave of reform in an apparent effort to get education back on track. These waves of reform symbolize the reality that the processes of systematization and expansion are never complete. Yet while these later reforms generate much interest and concern, some observers suggest that they amount at most to fine-tuning. Ravitch (1983) finds that later reform often involves a mere recycling of old practices and thus only creates the illusion of reform.

The Political and Administrative Setting

In Chapter 2 we explored major differences in the structure of modern states; in particular, we noted that some are more centralized than others and that some are more inclusive or 'democratic'. In centralized systems, according to Margaret Archer (1977), the flow of educational decisions is likely to reflect the pattern for other sectors such as the judiciary, the police, and public health. In decentralized societies, educational decision-making may vary between locales. Thus, in the United Kingdom, local educational authorities were established that often had no overlap with other government offices. In the USA, some states decided to assume a primary role in educational decision-making while others left this task to local communities.

To the extent that a polity is more inclusive, it is likely that a greater array of stakeholders will be offered a role in the systematizing decisions. It is common in the USA and the United Kingdom, when considering major educational reforms, to create consultative bodies that include representatives from the various political parties, the different levels of education, and the different working groups involved in educational practice such as the principals' association and the teachers' union. Where the polity is more narrowly constituted, it is more likely that the state will consult with a small group of interests such as corporate leaders, the military and religious elites.

The priority that the polities of the core societies assigned to their educational project also varied. Especially from the early nineteenth century, Prussia/Germany became concerned with its national identity and increased its emphasis on the educational project. The educational project also received exceptionally high priority in the late developing cases of Meiji Japan and Bolshevik Russia as both of these centralized states were determined to make radical departures from their immediate past and looked to education as a prime asset for the new nation-building agenda. In the USA, the federal government was constituted in such a manner that it could not assume responsibility for education; however, in several of the US states, local governments came to stress the importance of education as a means for cultivating an informed citizenry. In the other core nations, education was assigned a lower priority.

Vertical Differentiation

The first modern schools were established for a specific need that was high on the agenda of the modernizing elite. Tracing a couple of examples may suggest the way the architects approached the establishment of the first schools and how those first steps then shaped second steps and so on.

In the long-established nations of Germany, France and the United Kingdom there was already a precedent of schools that the children of aristocratic and middle-class families had become familiar with. Early education was often provided in the homes by tutors and parents. When a child had reached a certain level of competence, they entered appropriate preparatory schools, and thereafter in France gained entrance to the *lycée*, in Germany to the *Gymnasium*, and in the United Kingdom either to public schools or grammar schools. Thus, in these societies a system was already partially established, and what remained was to develop a more formal approach to the primary level for the children from ordinary homes whose parents lacked the cultural or financial resources to provide tutors and home schooling. Also, in both France and Germany, the modernizing educational leaders took steps to transform the structure and curriculum of higher education. In France the *grandes écoles* were diversified and strengthened. In Germany, new support was provided to the universities and new rigour introduced to the process of selecting students.

While a system was already in place in these long-established societies, there was ample room for clarification. One of Napoleon's many notable administrative accomplishments was the drafting of the law of the university.

While the term university normally refers to a tertiary-level institution, Napoleon used the concept in its literal sense as the organization for the promotion of all learning. For him this meant learning from infancy to adulthood. Thus, his university specified that there be several vertically differentiated levels of education, the *école primaire*, the lower secondary boarding schools, the colleges and *lycées*, and the *grandes écoles*; and that these respective levels of schools be provided by the corresponding administrative units of the commune, department, academy and university. Each administrative level was to provide the physical plant for the schools at the respective educational levels while the academic programme was to be the responsibility of the University Rector. The Rector was to be appointed by the Emperor, as were the members of the Oversight Board; those responsible for administering, operating and supervising lower levels of the system were to be appointed by the Rector or his delegates. This law was exceptional for its administrative clarity and has had a major influence on much subsequent thinking in the field of educational administration.

In Japan the Meiji elite had no prior experience with an elaborate multilevel education system; samurai simply came to fief schools that consisted of several grades with a provision for further individual tutelage. The Meiji leaders were keenly aware of their technological backwardness and thus declared their intent 'to seek knowledge throughout the world'. To gain access to this knowledge, they recognized that their emissaries would require a command of foreign languages and thus one of their earliest acts was to establish a translation bureau that was essentially a small college. Given their technical focus, they also established several engineering schools. Several of these early colleges later were consolidated in Tokyo University, which was recognized as the first Imperial University in 1886. At the same time, the Meiji elites declared their intention of developing a new post-feudal social structure that would enable the entire population to contribute to national development. Moreover, they established a national army that would be staffed by conscripts from all social groups, including the offspring not only of the former samurai class but also those from the peasant and commercial classes. To prepare youth for their roles both in national development and national defence, they looked to the primary school as an important agent of initial socialization. Thus, in early Meiji Japan both the primary school and the university were given high priority in the first decade of the design period.

The first recruits for the early Japanese 'universities' were the legions of bright samurai who had received a Confucian education in the old feudal system that they balanced with self-education in foreign languages and books. But once this cohort had entered the new higher educational institutions, the Meiji leaders had to decide what would be required to prepare the new wave of primary school students for tertiary education. Their first step was to establish several middle schools to provide further training for the primary school graduates. In the late 1870s, there was only one place in the middle schools for every twenty graduates of the primary schools. Yet the curriculum they formulated for the middle school did not provide sufficient preparation for the new higher educational institutions. To fill this gap, numerous private specialized schools (*senmon gakko*) were rapidly established, specializing in foreign languages and the study of selected foreign books. The government response was slower, depending on the discussion in various official committees. Finally, in 1886, with the establishment of the Imperial University, the central government decided to establish a number of higher schools, modelled on the German *Gymnasium* and the French *lycée*, to complete the transition from the middle school to the university. Reflecting the orderly thinking of that era, these higher schools were given the names 'No. 1 Higher School', 'No. 2 Higher School', and so on. Meanwhile, the government decided to distinguish between higher educational institutions focused on higher learning on the one hand and those focused on specialized learning on the other. With this distinction various new regulations were issued outlining the types of the post-primary (or secondary) level experiences appropriate for the respective higher educational courses.[1] As will be noted below, these regulations initially had the effect of devaluing the merits of enrolment in the now extensive private sector of post-primary specialized schools.

In decentralized systems, the process of filling the gaps between different levels of the system was less uniform. The United Kingdom system was highly segmented, reflecting class distinctions, and prominent educators were reluctant to introduce refinements out of concern that they might lower the barriers between the established classes. In the USA, first there were many colleges and underneath these was a patchwork of preparatory institutions. Most notable were the grammar schools to get most youth started in their schooling, but often lacking was an intermediary institution to bridge the gap between the grammar schools and the colleges. Partly to address this issue, grammar schools tended to have many grades, sometimes as many as ten. Then students might go to an independent preparatory school or even a preparatory school attached to one of the colleges. Over time, various intermediary arrangements were introduced, the most common being the four-year high school. From the mid-twentieth century it became more popular to have a five- or six-year primary school, a three- or four-year middle school, and a three-year high school.

Comparing these approaches to vertical differentiation, it can be said that they reflect several different approaches to the 'serious' business of education. In the continental systems and to some degree in England this serious business was carried out at the secondary level in schools that were originally intended for aristocratic and middle-class families – the *Gymnasium* in Germany, the *lycée* in France, the public school in England. In contrast, in the USA, serious education began in the college. And in Japan and Russia, where modern education was established to break down old aristocratic traditions, serious education for all began in the primary schools. These differences in tradition are reflected in such diverse aspects as the quality of educational materials, the workload expected of educational personnel and the compensation provided to them, and finally, the pace of student learning. Simply put, *things get better in each system at the level where that system gets serious.* Empirical evidence on these generalizations will be presented in the third part of this study.

Horizontal Differentiation of Segments and Tracks

Studies of educational structure make a distinction between two principles for accommodating group differences:

Tracking (or streaming) occurs when two more or less distinctive curriculums are offered and young people are placed in the respective curriculum based on some form of testing of their motivation and/or ability. Tracking may occur as early as the primary grades when students are placed into parallel tracks or streams that are more or less difficult; for example, the A stream in Malaysia for the top third-graders, the B stream for the runners up, the C stream for the average student, and so on. At later stages in the progression of grades, the curriculums for the different tracks may become qualitatively different, as, for example, between an academic track which prepares students for tertiary education and a vocational/technical track which prepares students for a manual labour role in the labour force.

Segmentation is said to take place when the members of the two groups are clearly identified and explicitly routed into separate schools; these separate schools may have ostensibly similar features, as was the claim for the separate but equal schools many American states provided for white and black children, or they may vary in certain respects, as was the case for the schools in the British colonies provided for members of the colonial government, on the one hand, that taught a rigorous academic curriculum in the English language, and for the natives, on the other hand, that taught a more practical curriculum in the vernacular languages.

Tracking tends to be introduced as a strategy for optimizing human resource development. With limited resources, the state asserts that it has a responsibility to provide preparation for sufficient numbers in the different spheres of the modern workplace. While tracking was evident even in the primary grades in the early modern period, most systems subsequently abandoned this practice, concluding that it was difficult at that early age to truly evaluate aptitude and that the process of attempting to make these judgements placed too much pressure on young people. Hence, most systems came to introduce tracking following the primary grades, with the track assignment based primarily on academic performance during the primary years and/or a primary school leaving examination. Typically, the academically more proficient were tracked to the academic schools and the less proficient were tracked to the vocational schools. This form of tracking at the secondary level was accepted in most of the early modernizing societies, though the extent of its elaboration seems to have been determined by the

106

relative prominence of the business class in operations of the state. In Germany and France, where the business classes were most prominent, the diversity of vocational/technical tracks seems to have been most extensive, whereas in the USA and Russia there were fewer tracks.[2] Indeed, in many US school systems, there were essentially no opportunities provided for vocational and technical training.

The relative centralization of a system also appears to have favoured tracking. In centralized systems authorities had responsibility for the entirety of the national labour force and thus were inclined to carry out systematic studies of labour force needs. These studies naturally led to conclusions about vocational/technical areas that were both over- and under-supplied. From these inferences, the central government authorities then might propose new policies for alterations in the composition of vocational/technical education to address future needs. Decentralized governments, lacking such an overarching perspective, were less likely to make such recommendations.

In the actual practice of tracking, certain social groups – e.g. minorities or children from the lower classes – are more likely to end up in the less esteemed track, but this is said to be a function of meritocratic selection. In some cases, societies have strong feelings about the need to preserve ascriptive differences: girls should receive a different education from boys, aristocrats should not mix with commoners, whites and blacks should not mix. Where these sentiments have prevailed, the respective groups may be segregated in horizontally segmented educational systems that may begin from the first day of schooling. We will have more to say about segmentation below.

Horizontal Segmentation to Serve Different Groups

All of the modernizing societies were composed of young people with diverse backgrounds and gender differences. Marxist reinterpretations tend to suggest the major issue confronting the modern reformers was equality. While equality was an important issue, far more pronounced at the early stages of the modern transformation was the concern to build a new national identity that superseded separate religions, ethnicities and racial identities. Equality of social classes was initially a lesser theme and tended to increase in salience over time. Gender equity was rarely considered – a woman's place was to help her husband. While national integration was a major concern, there was always the question of how far to go in bringing people together. The other side of this question was to ask whether the members of these diverse groups wished to mix with each other.

Religion

The German states launched the modern transformation with the Reformation. While many states broke with the Church, others did not. For many decades, wars took place to force a common policy. Ultimately, a truce was negotiated which allowed each state to go the way of its prince. These differences were preserved as the German states consolidated (Lamberti, 1989), and religious differences were allowed to persist according to locality, and were reflected in the religious areas of the school curriculum. Integration was achieved in other subjects. It should be noted that the German solution recognized two major religious groupings – Catholicism and Protestantism. Other religions were not acknowledged – notably Judaism.

France rejected the German solution by separating Church and State, and this was followed in the USA as well as in Japan and Russia. Of course, in each setting there were subtleties. While Church and State formally separated in the USA, many schools featured religion until well into the twentieth century, and, as Bellah (1975) notes, the American schools featured the civil religion. In Japan, the public schools were religiously secular except that they allowed emperor worship, and in Soviet Russia, the schools were also religiously secular but celebrated Soviet heroes.

However, in all of these 'secular' cases, powerful religious groups were discontented – and they continuously lobbied for an independent educational system. In the USA and elsewhere, this was ultimately allowed, with the conditions that religious schools could receive no support from state funds and that they would conform to basic establishment standards for the secular subjects. And so in the USA parallel systems emerged, with the main public system supported by the state, the second independent.

Major schools in England had always been religiously based, and the English leaders rejected the continental theory that the Church and State could or should be separated. Influential in this debate was Edmund Burke's commentary on the disastrous French Revolution. In earlier times, the English aristocracy and their schools conformed to the Catholic Church. Henry VIII replaced Catholic orthodoxy with the Anglican Church; after an awkward period, both the nation and its schools accommodated. And so England preserved the role of religion in the schools. Most schools included a chapel along with classrooms. By the mid-nineteenth century England became more relaxed about these matters, allowing different Protestant sects to practise. Similarly, it allowed different schools to feature different religions.

Class.

An emerging theme of the modern revolution was the promotion of equality. Class differences clearly troubled the German leaders, but they chose to use the education system to preserve class differences (Mueller, 1984). In

England some mobility took place through allowing able commoners to buy a position in the upper class. But especially in France there was much tension as the bourgeoisie were largely excluded from the royal court, and the imperial government levied exceptionally heavy taxes on the commercial and peasant classes in order to carry out its policies of national defence and conquest. And so the concern with equality was increasingly articulated and became a clarion call of the French Revolution. But, as soon became evident, the revolutionaries were interested in limited equality – for the bourgeoisie but not for the workers or peasants – and the educational reforms that followed mainly focused on opening up new opportunities for those resident in the cities and towns.

The entry-level schools in the urban areas were generally of superior quality in Germany and France, and so in this way the upper classes gained an advantage.[3] In England the upper classes were unwilling to leave their destiny to chance – and so they retained a system of independent public schools that preserved the right to select their students based on such criteria as lineage and upbringing. The USA was essentially a rural nation and so these issues were less salient. But ultimately it followed the continental pattern by instituting the norm of neighbourhood schools. Residential class segregation led to class segregation in educational access.

Japan was somewhat unique in recognizing the threat of class segregation. The new leaders, who were themselves from relatively peripheral fiefs, were determined to give commoners a decent chance, especially those from peripheral rural areas, and so they set up schools throughout the nation, including rural areas, and they put in place financial regulations requiring the government to actually spend more on rural than on urban schools. Moreover, within an area they set up a hierarchy of middle schools and high schools and enforced strict meritocratic criteria for entrance to the best schools. As it turned out, the former samurai did better on average, but many commoners also succeeded.

Russia also was concerned about class equality. Indeed, in the earlier stages, the revolutionary general schools actually favoured children from worker families over those from upper- and middle-class good families.

Ethnicity and Race

All of the modernizing states were formed through bringing together people of diverse cultural backgrounds. This was perhaps most notable in the USA, which is often depicted as a nation of immigrants. But in the European states there was also much diversity as the new nation states were composed of numerous principalities with their distinct traditions. Similarly, Soviet Russia was composed of many nations, languages and religions. Even in supposedly homogeneous Japan, the Tokugawa system spanned a far-flung archipelago, and there had been such diverse developments of the supposedly common Japanese language that natives of the island of Kyushu in the south were unable to understand natives of central Kyoto, not to speak of those from the north-eastern areas of Tohoku and Hokkaido. For most of the modernizing states, modern education was seen as a mechanism for blending ethnic differences. As long as children could do well in the official language of the state, they were included in the common school.

The USA was somewhat unique in its unwillingness to include one subgroup, the Negroes, in its conception of equality. This reluctance varied by region, but in most Southern states the Negroes were held as slaves and provided with no social rights, including the right to education. After the Civil War the Negroes (later to refer to themselves as Blacks and African Americans) obtained citizenship and became eligible for equal education. But the response in many states was to provide 'separate but equal' education. Race was not an official consideration in the other core societies – except possibly for Japan, where a separate system was set up to provide education for certain 'immigrant' groups (notably Koreans).[4]

Groups/Nations	Religion	Class	Race & Ethnicity	Gender
Germany	Protestantism and Catholicism allowed by locality	Tracking	Equal as long as able in national language	Equality but implicit tracking from upper elementary
France	No religion in schools	Tracking with urban bias in school location	Equal as long as able in national language	Equality but implicit tracking from upper elementary
UK	Anglican religion featured in all schools	Elite schools use ascriptive criteria for admissions	Equal as long as able in national language	Equality but implicit tracking from upper elementary
US	No religion in public schools, but independent Catholic segment allowed	None, except Neighbourhood admission principle	"Separate but equal" segmented schools systems for whites and blacks	Equality but implicit tracking from upper elementary
Japan	No religion in public schools, but independent private schools allowed to include religious instruction	Resources favour periphery schools	Equal as long as able in national language	Explicit girls' track after the primary grades
Russia	No religion in schools	Admissions may discriminate against descendents of old ruling class	Equal, and local languages allowed in primary schools	Gender equality

Table 4.1.Segmentation principle for different groups.

110

Gender

Finally, in virtually all of the core societies, gender was treated in a special way. German laws discuss girls in the same breath as boys, but a somewhat distinct curriculum was prepared for the two sexes. Japan was explicit about separation; girls were to become good wives and wise mothers while boys were to become productive members of the economy. And so, especially after the primary school, distinct tracks were established for Japanese boys and girls; until the Second World War girls were not admitted to the imperial universities. Only in Bolshevik Russia was there no separate formal provision for boys and girls.

Summary

Different patterns of tracking/segmentation were thus established to provide for the preservation of religious, class, racial and gender differences, as outlined in Table 4.1.

Vertical Integration of Levels

Rules are created to build links between the different types of schools. The most significant are those relating to student admissions and passage from one grade or level to the next.

Perhaps the most dramatic initiative of modern education was to declare that all children had the right to education. The various German states made this assertion from the middle to the end of the eighteenth century. The Revolutionary Council of France made its declaration on the right to education in 1794. England debated this question for several decades, but did not actually issue a formal declaration until 1902. Both Japan and Russia asserted every child's right to education within a few years of their respective revolutions. The declaration of the right to education placed a responsibility on the state to provide educational opportunities for all and on parents to send their children to school (or otherwise provide for the educational needs of their children).

Whereas schools might in the past have been able to select new students from a larger group, now they were expected to accept all who applied. In some systems, this new obligation led schools to attempt to design a school atmosphere that adjusted to the needs of all of the children, regardless of their sociocultural background. In others, notably France, the approach was to accept all students but to place stiff barriers in front of those who did not adjust to the school routine. In the early modern French primary schools, children were given academic tests at the middle and end of each academic year in each subject, and those children who failed even one test were expected to take the school year over again. Thus, the early French system was characterized by high repetition rates, leading to frequent drop-outs. In contrast, the Japanese and Russian systems from early on adopted a

111

philosophy of automatic promotion that placed considerable pressure on the schools to find ways to reach out to their slow learners.

While the approaches for the early years varied, most systems developed procedures for measuring the academic potential of their primary school graduates. In the continental schools, summative examinations tended to be exclusively relied on. In contrast, in the USA, Japan and Russia, the schools tended to combine course grades with summative examinations as the basis for determining academic potential. In chapter 9, we will go into greater detail on the examination procedures of the different systems.

As these decisions were being made, another highly contentious issue was the assignment of formal responsibility for decisions on admissions and promotion for those school levels beyond compulsory education. In that the state was paying either some or all of the bill for public education, the argument was advanced that it should have this responsibility. On the other hand, educators were inclined to assert that academic matters were their responsibility. In the more centralized systems, the state tended to win out in these debates. Thus, in France, the examinations came to be prepared by the centre. In contrast, in the USA, in most cases the teachers of the respective schools came to assume responsibility for the examinations. In the other systems, the responsibility varied depending on the level. To the extent that evaluation was the responsibility of front-line educators there was a tendency for multiple criteria to be used (and in the US case written summative examinations might be excluded from these criteria) whereas when the responsibility rested with the state the hard criteria of performance in a national examination was relied on.

In the cases of Germany and Japan (Ringer, 1974; Amano, 1990) schools and universities were initially invested with the responsibility for examinations. But after some time, the respective states sought to insert their authority in the process. Among the various reasons put forth was the argument that the educational institutions were training future civil servants and thus the state needed to be involved. The university counter-argued that in certain fields, such as medicine, the state lacked the competence to manage sensible examinations. The actual responsibility for different examinations seesawed back and forth. Eventually both ran their respective examinations.

In England, a variant of the examination system known as 'payment by results' was introduced in the 1870s (Reisner, 1923, p. 282) to allow individual schools considerable autonomy in the conduct of their programmes but to subject their students to an annual performance test. Schools that did well in these examinations were provided with increased resources whereas those who did poorly had their allocations cut. Once schools came to understand the impact of this system, they began to dismiss low-performing students and at the same time to recruit superior students from nearby schools. The result was so disruptive of the lives of young people that it was discarded within a few years. The reader may appreciate the similarity of the English 'payment by results' approach and recent reforms proposed for the USA.

As the objective of these measures was to ensure quality control, some systems also considered alternative approaches such as supervision or accreditation. In most of the centralized systems, inspectors were appointed to visit schools and evaluate their educational programmes. Where these inspection systems were well staffed and considered reliable, the process of inspection of the whole school could substitute for an evaluation based on the examination performance of each student in the school. Recognizing the possibility of the external imposition of quality control measures, educators in the USA from the late 1800s devised an alternative approach of voluntary evaluation where several educational institutions joined in an educational association, set their own standards, and carried out their own evaluation exercises (Selden, 1960). The evaluation involved a statement of institutional mission and a report on the resources available to realize that mission. If peer institutions felt the resources were appropriate for the mission, the institution was accredited. In this way, the schools and universities of the decentralized American system sought to forestall opportunities for the state to intervene in their autonomous educational activities. Accreditation came to be widely practised in the USA.

Vertical Integration of School and Economy

An important factor thought to influence equality of opportunity is the way the different systems link to the labour market. A major goal of modern education is to provide human resources for the various positions that are available in the economy. The salience of this goal varies across the societies. In late-developing societies such as Japan and Russia, one of the strongest arguments advanced for the establishment of particular institutions was their vital importance in preparing elites or cadres for particular jobs of national importance. Indeed, in Japan it was said that vocational schools were set up first and factories followed as the first cohort of graduates finished their commencement ceremonies. While the rhetoric was more muted, England looked to its top universities for recruits to join both the civil and colonial services.

In chapter 2, it was argued that the economies of the core societies varied considerably in terms of their 'work systems', with some economies having a greater prevalence of daily wage and entrepreneurial opportunities, some an emphasis on organizational jobs, and yet others an emphasis on professional jobs. Where the former types of job are prevalent, employers are more likely to stress the importance of vocational-technical education and where the latter jobs are prevalent the stress will be on academic training preparing young people for first and second degrees in the higher educational system. Distinct from the demands of the labour market is the overall philosophy concerning the role of the state in preparing young people for work. In all of the core societies, lip service is given to job preparation. But in socialist societies, the state tends to guarantee every school graduate a specific job, and in corporatist societies there tends to be a relatively close alliance between employers and the educational system both at a policy level and through personnel connections. Thus, every Japanese secondary school and higher educational institution has a network of employers that it works with for the placement of graduates, and these educational institutions consider it to be their responsibility to place every one of their graduates who seeks employment.

	Philosophy	School Education	Secondary Education	Human Resource Training Programmes	Job Search
USA	Market	General	Mainly general	Pre-hire, mainly at training schools, public funding	Individual responsibility
England	Market	General, but with tracking	Mainly general but with voc-tech tracks	Pre-hire, mainly at work sites, public funding	Individual responsibility
France	Market and corporatist	General, but with tracking	Half general and half voc-tech	Pre-hire, mainly at work sites, public funding	Individual responsibility
Germany	Corporatist	General, but with tracking	Half general and half voc-tech	Pre-hire, all at work sites, corporate funding	Individual responsibility
Japan	Corporatist	General	Half general and half voc-tech	Post-hire, all at work sites, corporate funding	Schools help
Russia	Socialist	General	More voc-tech than general	Post-hire, all at work sites, public funding	State guarantees

Table 4.2. The links of schooling with human resource training programmes.

In the socialist and corporatist systems, the educational system is expected to prepare youth for work. Therefore, these systems have a well-developed vocational/technical education system for blue-collar workers. And even in their academic system, the various programmes tend to be relatively specialized in nature (e.g. three-year professional first degrees) as contrasted with the liberal arts degree prized in the USA or England. Thus, in the socialist as well as the Japanese systems, young people move directly from schools into jobs and receive all of their training on-site and fully funded by their employers. In Germany, training is offered on-site and largely funded by employers. Ironically, the more democratic systems build the sharpest division between schools and employers. Since these links are weaker, the public sector there spends relatively more on post-school training programmes. In England training may be on the premises of (prospective) employers, but the state provides large subsidies for this training. In the USA, training is more typically provided in job training centres managed by and paid for by the state with no or minimal support from employers. Participation in these centres provides limited connections with employers and no guarantee of actual employment. The several patterns are depicted in Table 4.2.

Administrative Efficiency/Autonomy

Margaret Archer (1977), who provided one of the most thought-provoking studies of the role of states in systematizing education, drew a clear distinction between centralized and decentralized systems of education, and viewed Germany, France, Japan and Russia as in the former camp with England and the USA in the latter. Archer argued that the pattern of reform in the former camp was more top–down and episodic or replicative, whereas in the latter camp it was more bottom–up and imitative.

In fact, finer distinctions may be preferable. For example, among the so-called centralized systems, Germany invested considerable authority in the several states that joined to form the German nation. Through most of the nineteenth century, these states were totally independent and even after they joined in the German union they had their own ministers of education. In France, while the central ministry of education coordinated a grand design for all of education in France, it looked to local governments to provide half of the funds necessary to carry out the actual operations. Only in Japan and Russia did the central government shoulder the full burden of financial responsibility. And while the centre provided much direction for the Russian educational revolution, the vast size of the nation and the many languages in which basic education was conducted inevitably led to the investment of much authority in the educational officers appointed to the numerous oblasts. Thus, the degree of centralization varied widely.

Similarly, concerning the two 'decentralized' systems, the USA can be viewed as far more complex than the UK. In the USA, the primary responsibility for education first came to be assumed by local communities. By the turn of the twentieth century there were over 100,000 school districts representing the then constituted communities (Tyack, 1974; Fuller, 1982). In certain states such as New York and Massachusetts the state assumed a somewhat stronger role in coordinating these communities whereas in others the state was more benign. Above the state was, of course, the federal government, which assumed a minor role in educational policy. Nevertheless, it is worth noting that there were three distinctive levels of responsibility above the actual schools. In contrast, in the UK there was only the central government and local educational authorities, of which at the turn of the twentieth century there were only slightly over 100. And in the UK, in sharp contrast to the USA, the central government always assumed that it had an important role to play in establishing national educational policy.

And so, comparing these six systems, it might be said that they can be grouped with Japan, France and Russia towards the centralized side, Germany and the UK in the middle, and the USA towards the decentralized side.[5] While these different administrative systems naturally evolved in accord with the laws and administrative traditions of the respective nations, in more recent times it has become common to speculate on the relative merits of these different administrative traditions. Some of the arguments advanced are as follows.

Centralized systems are administratively more efficient. They can make more decisions at the highest level, thus reducing the number of decisions that need to be made at the multiple lower levels. Centralized systems are more likely to develop uniform procedures for school buildings, teacher recruitment and training, salary scales for educational personnel, and for curricular standards. In decentralized systems, many of these decisions are made at lower levels, either at the regional or district level.

Centralized systems are better able to develop and implement common standards. In most centralized systems there is a single set of curricular goals established, and all of the sub-units throughout the nation are expected to follow those goals. In most centralized systems, the central ministry also plays a prominent role in screening textbooks to ensure that they conform to the common standards. Additionally, the centre monitors critical resources such as teachers, inspectors, school buildings and instructional materials to ensure that they are distributed to all of the regions and to all of the schools within these regions. In decentralized systems, lower level units are responsible for these areas, resulting in a variety of approaches. The diverse approaches enabled by the decentralized approach have the advantage of being more responsive to local interests and needs, but they result in a diversity of standards, a topic that will be given more detailed consideration in chapter 6.

As centralized systems leave fewer decisions for the lower levels, it also can be expected that centralized systems require fewer administrative personnel. While historical data on this issue are not available, the recent cross-national studies of the Organization for Economic Cooperation and Development (OECD, 1995b, 2001) provide considerable support for this proposition. In the highly decentralized US system, as indicated in Table 4.3, nearly one out of every two individuals employed in education is engaged in an administrative or support position. In contrast, in the highly centralized Japanese system, only one out of every five educational employees is engaged in a similar capacity.[7] Of course, the US system is really an aggregation of many systems, and these apparently vary widely in terms of their administrative intensity. Those educational districts towards the mountain states have a much lower level of administrative intensity than those on the east coast (Ornstein, 1988). When one moves between regions in centralized systems, there is far less variation in terms of administrative intensity.

	Per cent of labour force in education	Per cent of labour force who are teachers	Per cent of educational personnel who are not teachers
UK	3.9	3.5	10
France	6.0	3.7	38
Germany	3.3	2.7	18
Japan	3.2	2.4	25
USA	6.4	3.3	48

Table 4.3 Educational labour force and its responsibilities.[6]
Source: OECD, 2001; German figures are from OECD, 1995b.

As decentralized systems leave more decisions to lower levels it is often assumed that this leads to more discretion at the lowest levels of the educational system. But it appears that an important distinction needs to made between the lower and the lowest levels, for in decentralized systems the available evidence suggests that the level above schools exercises most of the discretion and schools are left relatively powerless (OECD, 2000). Table 4.4 indicates who has the primary decision-making responsibility for the curriculum at the lower secondary level. In all systems except the 'decentralized' USA, at least one of the decision-making areas is left to the schools. The chief administrators of schools in decentralized systems are said to spend much of their time in external relations and as cheer leaders striving to motivate their academic staff. In contrast, the chief administrators of schools in centralized systems spend much of their time running their schools according to procedures established by officials and committees at higher levels.

While decentralization may not result in as much discretion for public school administrators as might be expected, privatization does lead to considerable discretion at the school level (OECD, 2000). Most private schools stand alone.[8] Of course, some private schools belong to large school systems such as the Catholic Church or Edison Schools (Murphy, 1988). Where private schools are participants in a large private school system, the degree of school-level autonomy may be no greater than is the case for state schools.

	Range of subjects taught	Definition of course content	Selection of programmes offered	Choice of textbooks
GERMANY	SCHOOL	STATE	STATE	SCHOOL
FRANCE	CENTRAL	CENTRAL	CENTRAL	SCHOOL
ENGLAND	CENTRAL	CENTRAL	SCHOOL	SCHOOL
USA	LOCAL	LOCAL	LOCAL	LOCAL
JAPAN	CENTRAL	CENTRAL	LOCAL	SCHOOL
RUSSIA	CENTRAL	LOCAL	SCHOOL	SCHOOL

Table 4.4. Decision-making about the curriculum at the lower secondary level. Source: OECD, 2000, p. 242.

Systems and Equity

While equity may have been a secondary concern in the early stages of the modern educational revolution, it later emerged as an important issue. In that public education was funded from tax revenues, should not all of the people gain the benefits? Also, to the extent that public education neglected one group relative to others, was not the nation depriving itself of the potential contributions that might be provided by the neglected groups? Often the neglected groups, lacking education, placed a greater burden on other public resources such as social welfare and even health services, and they tended to become more involved in crime and other social pathologies. And so the concern for equity was stimulated both by ideological and practical reasons. But what are the systemic conditions most supportive of equity?

Educational systems tend to allocate resources equally among schools of a common level or category – all primary schools or all academic high schools are funded equally. Earlier, we have suggested that centralized systems are somewhat more inclined to elaborate the vertical and horizontal differentiation of their systems. To the extent that there is differentiation, it opens up the possibility for the differential funding of different subgroups of institutions. Thus, elite high schools receive more than high schools specializing in secretarial skills, or full universities receive more funds than junior colleges.

On the other hand, in centralized systems there is likely to be a smaller number of geographically based administrative units compared to decentralized systems. And in centralized systems these units are likely to receive a large proportion of their funds from the centre according to general formulae that are equally generous to each of these units. Thus, centralized funding is likely to lead to geographical equity. In contrast, in decentralized systems, each local geographical unit is likely to depend for the great majority of its revenues on local services. To the extent that the revenue-generating capacity of local units varies, there may be wide disparities in the resource base for the support of public schools.

These two broad and contrasting principles make it difficult to predict a priori whether a centralized or decentralized system favours equity. However, recent experience certainly suggests that the latter principle has the greatest impact. In modern societies, there are wide discrepancies by region and subregion in their economic capacity and hence in the revenues that their local governments can hope to collect for the support of public services. Across a modern society of average scale, the per capita income of the most affluent local district is likely to be at least ten times more than that of the poorest district. These disparities in income are directly proportionate to the tax capacity of the respective districts. State subsidies may be used to reduce these inequities – if that is the policy – but until recently, at least in the USA, there were wide disparities between and within states. But even where the state decides to reduce these disparities through state equalizing subsidies, it is rarely prepared to insist on perfect parity. Indeed, to the extent that the state does strive for perfect parity, it is not uncommon for the parents in the most affluent areas to take their children out of public schools and into the private sector. The public sector of Japan or France provides an interesting contrast; in these nations there is a single national formula for the finance of each type of school as a well as a single national salary scale for the payment of educational staff. By virtue of these uniform scales and equalizing formulae to provide assistance to local areas with weak revenue capacity, schools are essentially equally funded. And as will be suggested in a later chapter, educational outcomes are comparatively more equal than in the USA.

Private Sector or Not

In the pre-modern educational systems, most schools were private and usually associated with religious organizations. Germany's folk schools were supported by local churches and communities, France's schools were provided by the Catholic Church, and most schools in England were affiliated with the Anglican Church until the 1870 Education Act.

The modern education project is normally thought of as an initiative of the new nation state, and in this initiative the state may absorb prior private initiatives in order to realize its self-proclaimed mission. Indeed, in France, the Revolutionary Council sought to nationalize the Catholic educational system. Also, whereas the private system played a major role in Japanese and Russian education both prior to the respective revolutions as well as in the early years after the revolution, the new states were determined to launch major educational initiatives aimed at eliminating the private sector. In the Soviet case, all private schools were eventually closed, and in the Japanese case the state at one point indicated that no young person who had received training in a non-state school need apply for a position in the national civil service, a regulation that had the potential for severely undermining the demand for private schools.

But even in these instances, private educators played an important role. Fukuza Yukichi's Keio Juku is generally regarded as the first modern school in Japan, having been established in 1855, thirteen years before the Meiji Revolution. There were important revolutionary private initiatives in the first days of the Russian Revolution. And while the French revolutionaries threw out the Catholic schools, they rehired the former teachers who abandoned their monastic robes to assume positions in the new revolutionary schools. In England, the private sector provided the only response to popular needs for education, while the parliament procrastinated. Similarly, in the early decades of the American experience all educational opportunities were provided by private institutions.

While the private sector made important contributions, it nevertheless was viewed as a threat by most states. These states questioned the advisability of allowing private education. A prominent theory argues that these states were persuaded to permit private schools as they became convinced that private schools had the capability of responding to special needs that important sectors of the public wanted but that the state, with its limited resources, did not consider essential. Indeed, Estelle James (1987) has identified two distinctive ways in which private schools can serve special needs: (a) through responding to the differentiated demands or needs of particular class, religious, or gender interests that are not prioritized by the state; and (b) through responding to the excess demand for educational opportunities over and above that which the state is prepared to meet. According to this theory, private education will accordingly have two patterns – a set of differentiated schools from grade 1 to higher education for key interest groups such as the Catholics in the USA, and a set of excess schools to meet the popular demand for secondary and higher education in societies where educational expansion is still in its early stages, as in nineteenth-century Japan or a contemporary developing society.

While this theory is interesting, it turns out that there are numerous exceptional cases. For example, there are a number of contemporary societies where the entire educational system is provided by the private sector (Cummings & Riddell, 1994). There are several societies in Africa and Latin America where the private sector is prominent at the elementary school level but less so at the secondary level. These exceptions suggest a simpler explanation for the prevalence of private schools than that proposed by the above theory. From the institutional perspective, the several core nations develop unique political solutions for the recognition of private educational institutions; later, these solutions are imitated by the newly emerging societies as they draw on the models of the core nations to develop their respective systems.

The solutions of the core nations were as follows.

- In Germany, the states were in control, but depended on local/private support for folk schools.
- In France, private schools were initially disallowed. But France did not have sufficient resources to develop a public system, and so it allowed the Church to play a major role in primary education in the early years. Later, when the state was able to collect more resources, the state policy towards Catholic schools vacillated.
- In England the private sector prevailed – the so-called public and independent schools that start from the lowest grades and go through college. These schools were firmly entrenched and the state never considered the option of disbanding these institutions or interfering in their operations.
- The USA as it approached independence was increasingly influenced by French thought, which placed a strong emphasis on the separation of Church and State. This thinking was embodied in the US Constitution and over time had a profound impact on private education in the USA. During the early decades of the nineteenth century, young children were not allowed to attend religiously founded schools. But from the second half of the nineteenth century, religious schools were allowed so long as they provided the curriculum of public schools and independently secured adequate financial resources. These changes led to the opening of a prominent Catholic school sector at all grade levels. Private institutions also thrived at the tertiary level.
- In Japan, private schools were initially allowed without restraint, and thus many were created at all levels, but especially at the secondary and tertiary levels. But the state became nervous – perceiving some private schools as politically too liberal – and was shocked that the Christian schools taught that there was a god other than the Emperor. These concerns peaked in the 1880s with the proclamation of the new constitution and various educational laws that included much stiffer rules for the founding and operation of private schools. While these regulations were later relaxed, the private sector had been dealt a blow. Subsequently, private schools were able to regain an important foothold at the secondary and tertiary levels but they were not able to re-establish their prominence at the primary level.
- In Russia, private schools were closed soon after the commencement of the Revolution and they were not tolerated through the period of Soviet rule.

And so the private sector is restrained in every system, but the pattern varies. The above 'systemic' solutions were first practised in the core societies and then later exported around the world. Thus, when Cummings & Riddell (1994) reviewed the prevalence of private education in 129 countries, they found that most of the countries had developed a public–private educational mix that resembled one or the other of the above patterns practised by the core nations.

Systems with a modest private sector are able to accommodate the demands of certain interest groups without significantly jeopardizing core policy objectives. In contrast, in systems with large private sectors, such as Japan, where over half the places in secondary and higher education are in private schools [9], it is difficult to preserve certain policy objectives. In particular, the principles of uniform quality and equal access may be compromised.

	Germany	France	England	USA	Japan	Russia
Speed of Systemizing	Slow and deliberate	Quick on grand design but slow in implementing	Slow and episodic	Begins slow and depends on each state's initiative	Two decades	One decade
Vertical Differentiation	Initially 4 levels	Initially 4 levels	Initially 2-3 levels	Initially 3 levels	Initially 3 levels starting with a 4 year primary school	Initially 3 levels starting with a 10 year general school
Horizontal Differentiation	Segmented by religion; implicit tracking by class	Implicit tracking by class, gender	Segmented by class; implicit tracking by class, gender	Segmented by race, implicit tracking by gender	Tracking at secondary level by ability and gender	Tracking at secondary level
Vertical Integration	Summative examinations at conclusion of levels	Summative examinations at conclusion of grades and levels	Summative examinations at conclusion of levels	School-based tests and school-based summative examinations	School-based tests and centralized summative examinations	School-based tests and school-based summative examinations
School Workforce Link	Industry provides internships	Schools designed to feed particular workplaces	Market-based, with an old boy system	Market-based	Schools use connections to place graduates	State guarantees work
Centralization	Centralized but local level shares in funding	Centralized but local level shares in funding	Centralized system, local administration	Decentralized to local level	Centralized	Centralized with local implementation
Privatization	Moderate	Very limited	Moderate with some state subsidies	Moderate	Extensive	Not permitted

Table 4.5. Systemic features of education in the core societies after the foundation period.

Conclusion

This chapter has focused on three areas where the state has sought to shape education: through establishment and finance; through examinations; and through employment. Through working in these three areas, the several states have established distinctive systems. These systems vary in their complexity, as indicated by their different degrees of vertical and horizontal differentiation as well as by the extent and locus of their integration. It is apparent that some systems took all levels of their educational systems seriously whereas others put particular emphasis on one level or another. Similarly, some systems put more effort into monitoring and/or smoothing the transition from one level or segment to another, whereas others allowed these differentiated parts to stand as obstacles or challenges for the young people going through the systems. While the several states devoted most of their effort to influencing these three levers of control, they evidenced less interest in other matters, such as the recruitment of teachers or framing the pedagogy – all to be taken up in the second major section of this study.

This chapter has considered several dimensions of systematization. Several of the main contrasts of the foundation period of the core systems are summarized in Table 4.5. Of course, the systems were in continuous development and so some of these features were later revised, though in most cases the revisions amounted to fine-tuning rather than drastic alterations.

Notes

[1] The Ministry of Education's (1980) *Japan's Modern Educational System* provides an excellent summary of the various regulations.

[2] While there were relatively fewer tracks differentiated in the Soviet Russian system, at least during the early decades, the proportions of general school graduates channelled to these tracks were perhaps as large as was the case in continental Europe. In these systems, a smaller proportion went on to the academic track. In the USA, the proportion sent to the vocational-technical track was always comparatively modest.

[3] Mueller (1984, pp. 143ff.) argues that the Prussian King William III, following Napoleon's defeat in 1806 of the German states, intentionally favoured the urban schools so as to improve the prospects for the recruitment of the urban middle classes into the Prussian civil and military services. The King felt that aristocratic nepotism had weakened the quality of these services, and, moreover, he doubted the loyalty of many of the aristocrats.

[4] Nations that favoured segmented education at home, such as the United Kingdom and the USA, replicated this pattern in their empires. The British set up separate schools in English for the colonial officers and in the vernacular for the 'natives'. While the French and the Japanese 'welcomed' everyone in the colonies to a single school system, these schools set such high linguistic (classes were only in the language of the colonial administration) and academic standards that most locals failed.

[5] The administration and finance of Japanese education was significantly altered after the Second World War to strengthen the role of local governments.

[6] Over time, the percentages reported in the OECD reports show some fluctuations. For example, in 1995, the French 'percent of educational personnel who are not teachers' was only 25. However, the US percentage is consistently close to 50.

[7] In the Korean system only one in ten educational employees is involved in administration and support work.

[8] The 1998 edition of the OECD's *Education at a Glance* presents an extensive survey of these issues, showing that private schools have more autonomy than

public schools; it also confirms the pattern presented in Table 4.4 of less autonomy at the school level in the US system than for the other systems. The US system concentrates more of the decisions at the local level, whereas in the other systems it is spread across levels according to decision-making area.

[9] See William K. Cummings, 'Private Education in Asia', in Cummings & Altbach (1996) for an explanation for the very large private sectors in the educational systems of Eastern Asia.

CHAPTER 5

Expansion and the Worldwide Diffusion of Educational InstitutionS

If a nation expects to be ignorant and free, in a state of civilization, it expects what never was and never will be. (Thomas Jefferson)

The poorer classes who formerly could in no way be constrained to uninterrupted school attendance now attend for the most part regularly, and not only receive instruction sufficient for their future occupations, but also an appropriate religious and moral training. (French School Inspector, 1831)

Prior to the introduction of modern education, few young people were in schools. Today nearly all attend primary schools and large numbers go on to secondary and tertiary education. This shift is commonly referred to as expansion, a concept that has important implications both for policy and practice. In this chapter we will review the nature and dynamics of expansion with special attention to the role of the institutions of education in influencing the patterns of expansion experienced in different settings.

Access Expansion Contrasted to Enrolment Expansion

Before turning to actual experience with expansion, it is important to distinguish between two different meanings of this concept. *Enrolment expansion* refers to an increase in the number of students who are enrolled in schools. More students lead to a need for more building space, teachers, textbooks and other resources; hence, more students mean a greater financial burden for the sponsors of education. *Access expansion* refers to the increase in the proportion of an age cohort attending school.

The usual formula for computing this proportion takes the following form: the number of students at a given level divided by the number of young people in the age cohort normally expected to attend schools of the given level. For example, in most countries primary school is for six years and welcomes children who are six years old; thus, the gross enrolment rate

(GER) for primary school students is usually computed with the cohort aged 6-12. This measure can lead to certain distortions: where there are many repeaters, or overaged children attending school, a nation can have very high enrolment ratios for a certain period, typically early in the development of the system. Later, the numbers attributable to these reasons decline, and there may be a downward turn in the GER even though more children seem to be in school. To correct for this distortion, educational planners prefer to use the net enrolment ratio (NER), which is the number of children of a particular age group who are in school divided by the number of children of that age group. Unfortunately, it is usually difficult to collect the necessary data to compute the NER.

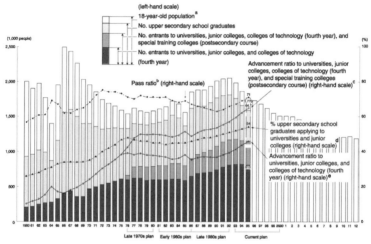

a : No. lower secondary school graduates three years earlier
b : [No. entrants to universities and junior colleges (including graduates from earlier years)] ÷ [Total no. applicants (including graduates from earlier years)] x 100
c : [No. entrants to universities, junior colleges, colleges of technology (fourth year), and special training colleges (postsecondary course)] ÷ [No. lower secondary school graduates three years earlier] x 100
d : [No. upper secondary school graduates applying to universities and junior colleges] ÷ [Total no. upper secondary school graduates] x 100
e : [No. entrants to universities, junior colleges, and colleges technology (forth year)] ÷ [No. lower secondary school graduates three years earlier] x 100

Figure 5.1. Recent trends in the size of the college-aged cohort in Japan.

Under 'normal' circumstances, the two forms of expansion are positively related. But there can be circumstances when access expansion goes up but the number of students stays the same. Such special circumstances include the baby drought that there is currently in Japan and several European countries. Figure 5.1 traces the size of the college cohort in contemporary Japan (Japanese Government Policies in Education, 1995). Over the coming years, the actual number in this cohort is expected to decrease by 40 per cent. Therefore, even if Japanese higher education approaches near universal access, it is unlikely that the actual number of students enrolled in higher education will increase. In all probability, many universities and colleges will go bankrupt owing to a shortage of students. At the school level in Japan, the shortage of students has the ironic result that class sizes are currently decreasing. In the near future, many schools will be closed and there will be a sharp decline in the number of new positions available for prospective teachers.

Alternatively, in France immediately following the Second World War the soldiers came home and began building their families; thus, the number of children enrolled in primary schools increased by 40 per cent between 1951 and 1956. But so did the total number of children of school age. And so there was no access expansion, but much enrolment expansion. And a great need for new schools and teachers.

When there is a large baby boom, as in post-war France or the other major nations involved in the Second World War, it is often followed by a drop-off in births. And then, as the baby-boomers grow up, they form families, and so there is a new wave of babies. This is illustrated for post-war Japan in Figure 5.1. Access expansion and enrolment expansion are independent concepts.

Theories of Expansion

Craig (1981) has reviewed various theories that have proposed explanations for expansion – functional, conflict, social differentiation, legitimation, status competition – and he concludes that none are very successful. While expansion according to these theories is often explained as an outcome of positive socio-economic and technological developments, there is, for example, the anomaly that secondary expansion occurred most rapidly in the USA during the Great Depression (Trow, 1961). During this same period and later during the Second World War, Japan experienced its most rapid years of tertiary expansion (Kaneko, 1987). Social crises seem to be an important factor, spurring activities to relieve the hardships faced by youth and the broader society. These crises and the ensuing expansion are more typical during bad than good economic times. None of the standard theories anticipates this anomaly.

Institutional theory proposes that different systems have different goals, and hence different prospective levels of expansion. The modern educational revolution is associated with a steady increase in access expansion to basic education followed by increases at the upper levels. But across countries, the speed with which this access expansion occurs is expected to vary. Institutional theory anticipates that expansion would be exceptionally fast in Soviet Russia owing to the commitment of the Bolshevik Revolution to addressing the needs of the working class, whereas it was very slow in Victorian England owing to the considerable indifference there to the workers. Even today, there are interesting differences across countries –

higher education is exceptionally inclusive in the USA and somewhat restrictive in France.

Easterlin (1981) has compiled several series of historical data on expansion, and these indicate that latecomers have the most rapid rates of primary education expansion. Figure 5.2 compares the pattern of primary education expansion of the six core societies. Already by the turn of the nineteenth century, expansion had achieved a high level in Germany. French and English expansion was gradual, that in the USA somewhat more rapid, and that in Japan and post-tsarist Russia very fast. InstitutionS Theory is distinguished from other theories of social change by its emphasis on these differences in the 'slope' of change. Concerning post-primary expansion, InstitutionS Theory would hypothesize that France is exceptional in secondary-level expansion, the USA in tertiary expansion, and the Soviet system is notable for youth education and adult education. The available data generally support these predictions.

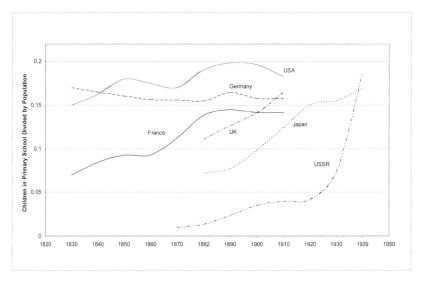

Figure 5.2. The expansion of primary education in the six core societies.

Two Laws of Expansion

While the mainline social science theories do not have a very good track record in accounting for expansion, there are a couple of 'common-sense' generalizations to be noted. The first is what might be called the basic law of expansion, which says that expansion always follows the Z-curve. Starting from 0, expansion will start slowly, speed up in the intermediate levels, and then slow down as full participation is approached. This common-sense approach assumes that it takes some time to get basic policies clarified in the early stages of expansion and that it is also difficult to reach out to the more peripheral areas of national landscape in the latter stages of expansion. This same Z-curve pattern of expansion has been observed for many other social phenomena, such as the increase in the probability of infant survival.

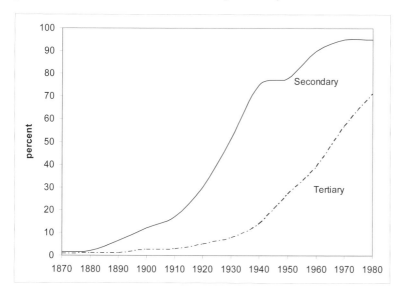

Figure 5.3. The expansion of secondary education in the USA.
Source: adapted from Trow (1961).

A second law is that primary expansion is a necessary condition for secondary expansion, and secondary expansion is a necessary condition for tertiary expansion. The curves may be 'parallel', but the curves for secondary and tertiary enrolment rates do not reach as high a percentage before levelling off. Martin Trow (1961) has provided an interesting discussion of the US experience, observing that secondary expansion accelerated during the Great Depression (see Figure 5.3). He also noted that the rate of secondary expansion may be affected by the relative prevalence of tracking, a practice common in the United Kingdom and continental Europe; the greater the incidence of tracking, the slower the pace of expansion. Trow (1974) subsequently focused on higher education, noting the gradual shift from elite to mass to universal higher education in the USA, with the implication that this same trend was likely to be replicated in other nations. He argued that over the course of expansion, unit costs would go down, higher education would become more student-centred, and the range of programmes would diversify. Actually, despite Trow's bullish prediction, no system thus far has realized universal higher education.

Expansion as Replication or Imitation

Archer (1977), in her study of systematization, made a major distinction between centralized and decentralized systems. In more centralized systems, the centre is likely to devise a plan for expansion that specifies how many new schools will be established per year and where. In addition, the centre sets clear guidelines for the construction of schools. And so the later schools are essentially replications of the first schools. They may even have the same architectural design and student intake. Among the centralized societies, Russia and Japan were notable for their urgency in replicating these new schools throughout the nation, whereas France proceeded at a more leisurely pace.

In decentralized systems, in contrast, there may be no grand plan. For example, in England each local education authority enjoyed the freedom to design and build its own schools at its own pace. Some were very energetic while others took no action. Moreover, among those which took steps to open new schools, each acted independently, resulting in considerable variety in the nature of schools across the English landscape.

Essentially, the same story was repeated in the USA where the authority for building new schools rested with local school districts. Fuller (1982) provides an account of the early American primary schools that were authorized by the Northwest Ordinance. He observes that each community, as it faced its decision to open up a new school, reviewed the practices of neighbouring communities. Each community drew some lessons from its neighbours but then introduced small differences. In discussing the incidence of expansion, Fuller suggested the principle of contagion. An important spur for a community to set up a school was that a nearby community had already done so. In general, those communities that were along major thoroughfares, both of road and rail, were the most likely to set up new schools first. In contrast, communities in the hinterlands, lacking neighbouring schools to imitate, were slower to build their first schools. Veysey (1965), in discussing the spread of the American college, describes a similar pattern of collegiate 'contagion'. Colleges spread west essentially along the lines of the major railroads.

The Worldwide Diffusion/Expansion of Modern Education

Our attention thus far has focused on the core patterns as they were implemented in their original settings. However, one reason for our focus on these six examples is that, in each instance, the nation state responsible for building a modern educational system also decided to build an empire. And as the respective nations expanded their empires and systematized their offices for colonial administration, they saw fit to include an educational dimension in their portfolios of colonial public services (Williams, 1997). The imperial nations differed in their enthusiasm for sponsoring colonial education, with the Americans and Japanese being the most enthusiastic and

130

the French possibly the least so. But in their devotion to exporting their respective indigenous models to the colonies they were all alike.

There are today a number of excellent studies of colonial education. Carnoy (1974) focuses on the transplant of the English system to India and Jamaica. Kelly (1982) examines the French assimilationist approach in French Indo-China. Ashby (1966) highlights both the English and French impact on higher education in India and Africa. Tsurumi (1977) looks at the Japanese approach in Taiwan, and Hong (1992) follows up with a thoughtful study of Korea. Drawing on this literature, it is possible to create a family tree of educational systems that begins with two grandparents, the continental and English models, then leads to several children, to some intermarriage, and cosmetic surgery (the Japanese system experienced dramatic change after the Second World War under the US-led Occupation), and then finally to the present range of educational systems. These developments can be illustrated by a focus on Eastern Asia.

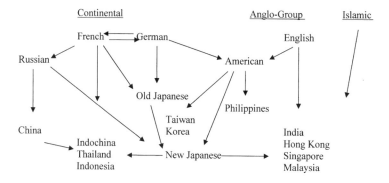

Figure 5.4. Main models and their impact.

In Eastern Asia, the Japanese system combines the influence of both the continental and Anglo-American traditions, while other systems get their primary influence from one or the other of these traditions. All Asian systems are in some degree influenced by Japan, though obviously the Japanese impact on Korea and Taiwan is greatest (see Figure 5.4). The diagram also recognizes the presence of Islamic education, which was suppressed during the colonial period but has since re-emerged to exert a powerful influence on Malaysia and Indonesia, and on parts of Thailand, the Philippines, and China. Japan has been the central figure in Asian education for over a century, and as can be seen from Figure 5.4, Japan has profited from most of the other traditions. The Japanese stream is in the middle at least in terms of structure.

It is no accident that there are major differences in the systems depicted in Figure 5.4. Those to the left are more likely to be managed from the top down, in contrast with a high level of community involvement of those to the right. Those to the left rely more on political signals for the allocation of resources while those on the right look to markets. Those to the left stress planning, whereas those to the right invoke the language of choice. And those to the left tend to favour a more formal and standardized approach to schooling whereas those to the right are open to non-formal approaches.

In terms of this diagram, Japan has carved a path down the middle. On decentralization, it once was centralized but now has moved halfway toward decentralization. On public–private, it has many public schools, especially at the basic educational level, but at the secondary and tertiary levels there are many privately established institutions as well as a vigorous proprietary sector providing supplementary education. Several others of the Eastern Asian states also tend to be in the middle.

Extending our discussion of the family tree, in Africa virtually all of the educational systems there were initiated during the colonial period where France was a prominent colonizer in West Africa and Great Britain was prominent elsewhere. Most Latin American nations gained their independence in the early decades of the nineteenth century, but already the imprint of the continental education system was evident. Education in Latin America has thus tended to follow the European pattern, with a modest degree of influence from education in North America. These different heritages seem to have had an influence on the degree of expansion of education.

Cross-national Pattern of Expansions

While our interest here is in expansion over relatively long periods, in fact truly comparable data for most countries are only available for the last few decades and much of the research on expansion has focused on these short-term data to make generalizations that are generally understood to apply for longer periods. There is, obviously, a concern that some of these generalizations may not be confirmed when better historical data become available. However, with these caveats, some findings from recent cross-sectional studies follow.

One of the first such studies was by Harbison & Myers (1964). They identified a strong positive correlation between the level of access of national educational systems (both to primary and secondary education) and the nation's economic level as measured by per capita income. They argued that education played a major role in fostering economic growth, and hence that educational expansion should be more widely promoted. Some subsequent studies suggested the relation might be the opposite, that economic growth promotes expansion. Wheeler (1984) decided to take a more careful look at these relations through introducing time lags – this enabled an examination of the possibility that educational growth in a certain period might be associated with economic growth at a later point. Wheeler's research led to a qualified conclusion that educational expansion does contribute to economic growth.

While the above studies focus on the role of economic growth in educational expansion, they do not devote much attention to the determinants of educational expansion. According to the arguments presented earlier in this study, institutional factors might be expected to have an impact. Cummings (in Nielsen & Cummings, 1997, p. 15) compiled data on the gross enrolment ratios for primary and secondary education of some 129 nations for the mid-1980s and then related the differences in these ratios to several possible determinants. As illustrated in Table 5.1, this analysis suggests that:

- centralized systems are less expansionary than decentralized systems;
- systems with a francophone heritage are least expansionary;
- systems with an anglophone heritage are average in terms of expansion.

Correlate	Primary enrolment ratio	Secondary enrolment ratio
GNP per capita	0.29	0.67
Population	0.16	0.04
Population density	0.10	0.20
Urbanization	0.52	0.81
Ethnic complexity	-0.36	-0.45
Centralized government	-0.37	-0.53
Centralized finance	-0.20	-0.40
English tradition	-0.09	-0.04
French tradition	-0.30	-0.46

Table 5.1. The cross-national correlates of gross enrolment ratios, 1985.
Source: PIE database.

While the number of cases is too few to justify statistical analysis, it can be noted that systems that were heavily influenced by the US, Japanese and Russian models are more inclined to achieve higher levels of expansion. Specifically, the Philippines, a former American colony, led South-east Asia in terms of enrolment ratios for several decades until it was surpassed in the 1980s by Singapore, one of the 'Asian Tigers'. Taiwan and Korea, which were Japanese colonies for several decades, achieved universal primary enrolment by the 1950s, and they also tend to be among the region's leaders in terms of secondary and tertiary enrolment ratios. Vietnam, after gaining independence from France, began to expand its enrolment rate at the primary level; and later, under Soviet influence, North Vietnam made rapid gains in primary education relative to South Korea. In sum, the models nations have adopted seem to influence their approach to realizing education for all.

Expansion and Equality of Opportunity

Expansion is often assumed to promote greater equality of opportunity for the labour force. Expansion is seen as opening up educational opportunities to young people from a wider range of class backgrounds and thus enabling them to compete on an equal basis for jobs in the modern occupational sector. To the extent that these jobs are meritocratically recruited, it stands to reason that children from ordinary homes will be as advantaged in obtaining attractive jobs as those from privileged homes. During periods of rapid expansion it appears that expansion may be associated with more equal educational and employment opportunities. Accounts of the United Kingdom in the early Industrial Revolution suggest extensive mobility. Similarly, during the period of rapid economic and educational expansion of post-war Japan, educational attainment was a very strong predictor of occupational attainment (Cummings & Naoi, 1974), whereas parental socio-economic status was not so influential. However, as economies slow down and the occupational structure becomes more stable and structured, educational expansion may do little to promote equality of opportunity in the labour market. For example, Ushiogi (1986) reports for societies with highly expanded higher educational systems that relatively larger proportions of higher education graduates end up in blue-collar jobs.

An important distinction also needs to be drawn between access to secondary and higher education as a whole and access to the top tier. Fritz Ringer (1979) reminds us that enrolment expansion alone is insufficient to open up greater opportunity. In the 1630s, Oxford and Cambridge admitted nearly 1000 students a year, or nearly 1 per cent of the age group appropriate for university admissions. This age group gradually increased so that by the end of the nineteenth century it was five times as large, but the entering class to Oxbridge only doubled; thus, in the 1890s these famous universities only had spaces for 0.3 per cent of the age cohort (Ringer, 1979, p. 226). According to Ringer (p. 239), the upper and the upper middle classes monopolized admission to these precious places, so that in the 1890s no more than 1 per cent of the admitted students had working-class backgrounds. Turning to more recent times, Neave (1985b) finds that the post-war massification of higher education in England has not been accompanied by increased access for children from the working class – partly because they seem less likely to be in the school tracks that prepare them for the elite track. Similarly, in recent years in Japan nearly 80 per cent of the entering students at the prestigious University of Tokyo, a public institution that is the major supplier of employees in the national civil service, come from upper- to upper middle-class homes. And so highly expanded systems may be no more egalitarian than systems with more restricted educational opportunities (Boudon, 1973a).

Conclusion

Educational systems vary widely in both the scale of opportunities they provide and the groups that take advantage of these opportunities. Among the first modern systems that we have reviewed, those in Scandinavia and Germany appeared to have expanded most rapidly whereas those in other parts of Europe, including the United Kingdom, were slower to open up opportunities. The latecomers, Japan and especially Soviet Russia, achieved the highest rates of expansion. These same proclivities for expansion appear to have been exported around the world through colonial administrations and national emulation. There is much discussion of the role of expansion in promoting economic growth as well as social equity, but it is difficult to reach firm conclusions in these areas. Where an economy is experiencing rapid growth and occupational upgrading, educational expansion may contribute to greater social equity. However, in all systems there appears to be an elite track that benefits children who come from the most advantaged homes.

PART THREE

The Delivery of Modern Education

CHAPTER 6

Creating Curriculums
for Modern Schools

Through the teaching of reading and writing and arithmetic [the
proposed curriculum] provides for the most essential necessities of life;
through teaching the legal system of weights and measures and of the
French language [it] implants everywhere, enhances and extends the
spirit and unity of the French nation; through moral and religious
instruction it provides for another order of needs every bit as real ... for
the dignity of human life and the protection of the social order.
(François Guizot, 1833)

Education in pre-modern times involved the holistic development of human capacity. Young people learned to sing and dance, to compete in community athletic events, to develop practical skills, and to worship God. Those who showed a penchant for book learning might receive encouragement if someone was available to help them. Those who enjoyed singing were encouraged. Most education was conducted in the families and communities, with more specialized education provided by the churches, crafts, and guilds. Much of this education was through apprenticeship. Only a minority of the population attended specialized institutions intended for the specific purpose of teaching a prescribed area of knowledge. There was no central body concerned with defining what everyone should know, though there were occasionally efforts by rulers or church authorities to discourage people from accepting certain ideas, deemed heretical, that these authorities did not like.

With the modern revolution, the approach to education gradually changed. Intellectuals and statesmen emerged to advance new theories about how people should be educated and what they should be taught. While some proposed a natural theory of education, with the emergence of the modern state it became increasingly popular to propose the 'unnatural' environment of the school as the proper setting for this new modern education. The education programme of the modern school came to be referred to as the curriculum. The root meaning of curriculum is 'to run a (race) course' involving completing (or learning) a sequence of steps (or learning experiences) (Schmidt et al, 2001, p. 2). In this chapter, we will consider how different modern systems have organized their races.

The Stakeholders for the Modern Curriculum

In the early stages of the modern transition, there were many views on what should be taught in schools. Homes and communities were responsible for 'educating' their children in the skills necessary for life. Religious organizations were responsible for formal education. Guilds provided apprenticeships to teach vocational skills. Into this mix the modern state sought to provide new direction. Figure 6.1 identifies the key stakeholders concerned to influence the modern curriculum.[1]

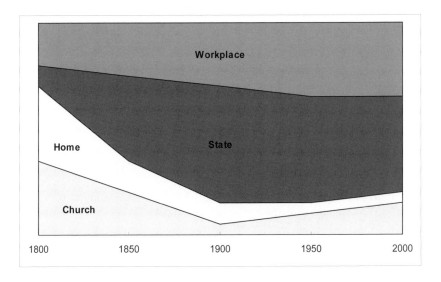

Figure 6.1 Relative influence of key stakeholders.

Over the course of the early modern shift, the weight of influence of the various stakeholders on the curriculum shifted. In most settings, the relative influence of the Church and the home declined relative to that of the state and the workplace. At the peak of the French Revolution, Danton insisted that families turn their young over to the Republican schools so that they could drink the milk of the revolution. In the French schools religious materials were thoroughly excised from the approved texts and teachers were expected to resign their former positions as priests. Later, however, Napoleon made some concessions to the Church and it regained a limited presence in public education. Also, in most modernizing societies, enrolment in public schools was made compulsory with the related implication that parents who did not send their children to school might be subject to arrest.

And so at least in some settings the role of religious authorities as well as that of the home in education was significantly challenged by modern education. But it was both impossible and undesirable totally to eliminate their influence. After all, children spent their formative years at home, and even after reaching school age and commencing attendance at school, most children returned to their homes after school to spend time with their family and friends. Similarly, they were free to attend religious services and otherwise participate in religious life if that was their family custom.

In the early stages of modern education, employers were mainly concerned with the quality of graduates from the universities and the vocational-technical schools. Thus, in Germany there was a constant battle between universities and outside groups over the content of academic programmes as well as the procedures for assessing graduates. But by the middle of the nineteenth century employers were also voicing concerns about the content of basic education. French authorities identified a connection between the quality of basic education and the effectiveness of the French military. And in both Germany and England, industrialists were beginning to express their preference for a better educated and hence more productive labour force in their new and more technologically advanced factories. By the middle of the nineteenth century, employers were seeking to influence decisions concerning all levels of the educational system.

In England, in the absence of a strong state initiative for modern education, religious organizations were among the prime sponsors for new schools for the working classes. And in the American colonies and later in the several United States of America, churches in collaboration with community associations were the principal founders of new schools across the ever-moving frontier. In these new settings, the federal government had no obvious role except that of possibly granting land for school sites. Similarly, there were no major employers to voice their concerns about the new curriculum. Thus, especially in the USA during the foundation era of modern education, the influence of religious groups and parents was quite prominent.

Over time, certain curricular ideas came to assume more weight in particular national settings. In the more centralized societies, such as France and Japan, the move to consolidation was relatively swift and led to an essentially monolithic national curriculum (with some legitimate dissension). In France, the curriculum extended down to the time in each day for teaching each subject; also, the French state selected a specific text for each subject. And there was an exceptionally high level of uniformity in the French system. This was also the case in the Japanese system. The German and Soviet systems, while also centralized, allowed for local adaptation in terms of religious preference in the former and language of instruction in the latter. In the more decentralized societies, the process of consolidation was slower and the consensus less stable, though even in the decentralized systems it can be said that a main trend emerged. For example, in the USA, despite the lack of a central curricular policy, local school systems felt it important to achieve a certain degree of uniformity with other systems so that children moving between school districts would not suffer.

Despite these changes over time, it would appear that these early precedents of stakeholder involvement have largely persisted. Robin Alexander (2001), in his recent comparative review of culture and pedagogy, argues that the home and especially the local community have a relatively large influence in the USA, followed by England, and he finds the influence of the workplace to be especially notable in Germany and Russia.

What is Curriculum?

There are many views on the curriculum in a given national system and even in a particular school. Ralph Tyler (1949) has outlined the variety of thinking prevalent in the USA. It is for this very reason that educational systems seek at different times to reach a consensus. This consensus may be formed through discussions hosted by a national ministry, a professional society of teachers, a local school board, or some other group. In most contemporary systems, these discussions are reconvened from time to time in order to update the curriculum.

Recognizing that various stakeholders have an interest in schools, we will define the curriculum as the consensus among stakeholders concerning what should be taught, why, how and where. This consensus covers not only the lessons conveyed in the formal subjects but also those conveyed through the co-curriculum and the entire routine of the modern school. For example, contemporary researchers have 'discovered' the hidden curriculum where young people are tracked into groups of high flyers as contrasted with the slow but steady, or into racially segregated groups. Such groups are created with the intent of conveying lessons to young children about the school's view of their potential, and hence are said to be another face of the curriculum. The curriculum also gets expressed in the architectural design of educational places: Mitsuke elementary school in Kanagawa, Japan selected the European style for its school building in order to convey to the local community and its students that their school was going to bring traditional Japan into the modern era of strong, outward-looking nation states. The prominence of the chapel in the English public school and its absence in the post-revolutionary French *lyceé* emphasizes the relative stress on religious education in these two traditions.

Some Highlights of Curricular
Discussions at the Dawn of Modernity

Brian Holmes & Martin MacLean (1989), in their comparative historical survey of curricula, argue that four distinctive approaches emerged over the modern transition. In medieval Europe the prevailing essentialist theory stressed the mastery of the core classical texts that built on Platonic and Aristotelian assumptions. Students normally studied these texts in the original Greek and Latin. The essentialist approach was supported by the

Catholic Church and later by the Anglican Church in England and thus had a major impact across all of Western Europe and later in the USA. However, in the latter settings there was more attention to balancing book learning with the development of physical skills as well as some practical skills.

The essentialist theory was challenged by Comenius, who marvelled at the advances in knowledge on various fronts during the Enlightenment and argued that the modern school should prepare young minds to appreciate as wide an array of this new knowledge as possible. Comenius engaged in a gigantic project to record all of the prevailing knowledge in a project known as the Encyclopaedia, and this project was expected to serve as a resource for educators. This approach, referred to as the encyclopaedic approach, had its greatest impact on France.

With the rise of socialism, educators expressed a growing concern to provide an educational experience more directly relevant to the modern industrializing economy. One outcome was a heightened stress on basic education, with the inclusion of mathematics and the sciences, as these subjects were viewed as the backbone of modern technology. Also, practical skills in such areas as industrial arts and homemaking were mixed in with the academic courses. Hence, Holmes & Maclean refer to this approach as the polytechnic theory. This approach was initiated in West Germany but most extensively developed by Soviet Russia.

A final theory highlighted by Holmes & Maclean is pragmatism, as articulated in the USA by John Dewey. Dewey argued that education should prepare young people for their lives as adults and thus there should be a rich interaction between the principal institutions of adult society and the schools. Dewey also stressed the role of schools in helping young people to mature socially and get along with each other; thus, academic lessons needed to be integrated with social content. Where democracy was prevalent, young people should learn about and practise democracy. Similarly, young people should become engaged in community affairs and gain knowledge about workplaces through internships and related experiences.

While Holmes & MacLean provided a useful summary of Western curricular experience, and this experience had a profound impact on the development of the educational systems that were established by the late developing societies, there are a few cases where the late developing societies devised their own distinctive approach, Japan being the most notable example. At the dawn of the Meiji era, several Japanese educators visited Western countries, and these visits were followed by the appointment of several Western consultants to help in the establishment of the new educational system, including the creation of a new Westernized curriculum. Yet, as Shigeru Nakayama observes, there was already a long-standing educational approach in Asia based on Confucian precepts and pedagogy. This approach stressed mastery of the key Confucian texts and a requirement that mastery be demonstrated through written exposition. Nakayama (1984) describes this as a documentary tradition, as it stresses the ability to argue in writing through reference to the original documents. In contrast, he notes that the stress in the European traditions of that time, essentialism and encyclopaedism, was on the ability to develop a logical oral argument. Nakayama refers to the European approach as rhetoric. Indeed, as will be pointed out at various points in this chapter, the documentary tradition provides some profound contrasts with the rhetorical tradition. Thus, it is important to add the Confucian documentary tradition as a fifth curricular approach.

Curriculum in the First Schools

The discussion of the first schools in chapter 3 illustrated considerable variety in the way that the early modern schools in different settings organized their curriculums. Here, it will be helpful to review some of the findings about the curriculums of these first schools. Systemic national approaches to the curriculum tended to undergo frequent revision during the first years of each modernizing experience, and these local initiatives played an important role in shaping the national approach.

As Holmes & McLean (1989) suggest, essentialism was the predominant pattern across Western Europe prior to the modern era. This approach continued to characterize secondary education in Germany through the early decades of the nineteenth century. Meanwhile, the folk schools created for the common people were forging a major departure. Both boys and girls were welcome at these schools, which were located within walking distance of their homes. The curriculum focused on basic literacy and Bible studies, with some attention to arithmetic and practical skills. And whereas the secondary schools emphasized study of classical texts in Greek and Latin, the folk schools conducted their classes in the local dialects of the German language.

In France, the main focus of the secondary schools was also on the classics. But over the eighteenth century under the influence of Comenius a number of new subjects were added, and this trend was accelerated by the French Revolution. Thus, at the Imperial Lyceum, along with the classics students were now expected to study French literature and culture, natural history, other science subjects and mathematics. The revolution initiated the shift from an essentialist to an encyclopaedic curriculum.

The English public schools were much slower to change than their continental counterparts, retaining their firm attachment to the classical curriculum until the 1860s after which they slowly began to introduce more modern subjects. However, relative to the French *lyceé*, the public schools placed far more emphasis on developing a well-rounded gentleman through their insistence that students would participate in a rich co-curriculum as well as join daily in religious services (Weinberg, 1967, pp. 44ff.)

The American college also initially focused on the classical curriculum to prepare young people for the traditional professions of religion, medicine and the law. But many of the core documents in these professional fields were no longer in the classical languages but, rather, in English – such as the King James Bible and English common law – and so it was natural to question the value of extensive study in the dead languages. Also, the changing circumstances of the dynamic American setting, especially commercialization and industrialization, led these colleges to add many practical subjects to their curriculum. By the end of the nineteenth century, most American colleges had essentially abandoned serious study of the classics. President Charles Eliot's decision to introduce the elective system at Harvard symbolized this change. It can be said that America was a pragmatic nation. In the early decades of the twentieth century it was to give birth to several pragmatic philosophers.

The Japanese primary school combined elements from several traditions. From its Confucian antecedents it borrowed the strong emphasis on moral (not religious) education, from France it borrowed the emphasis on the modern academic subjects of science and mathematics, and from Germany it added attention to physical and aesthetic development. At first the Japanese primary school curriculum was demanding and fostered keen competition between students (Amano, 1990), but by the 1880s this tendency was modified. The schools came to place more emphasis on a good start, with gradual acceleration of the pace in the upper grades. From early on, Japanese educators recognized that the public school could not do everything. Children were given extensive homework and urged to study hard. Also, the Japanese primary school was supplemented by informal schools known as *juku* set up in their neighbourhoods and at community centres.

The Soviet Russian unified workers' school had many of the characteristics of the Japanese primary school, with a modern secular curriculum, a graded progression of study with a gradual acceleration of pace, and attention to physical and aesthetic development. However, the Soviet school was more inclusive – for example, gender differences were not stressed and local languages were allowed to be used for instruction. In principle, primary schools were on the same premises as secondary schools, so that older children could help their juniors. In this and other ways, the Soviet school sought to model collective responsibility. Unlike Japan, the private sector was absolutely forbidden, so that children from all social backgrounds had no choice but to attend the same schools.

Later Developments

The first modern schools led to modest interventions in the way young people matured and became educated: these first schools received only a fraction of all eligible youth and kept them engaged for less than half the year. However, from these modest beginnings not only did the number of young people attending schools steadily increase but so did the amount of time they were expected to devote to their studies. Both the number of years required for completing education as well as the number of days per year increased. The curriculum was becoming more demanding.

These changes are illustrated in the Common School Movement (Glenn, 1988) that swept across Western Europe in the early nineteenth century and then caught the imagination of American educators such as Horace Mann and Henry Barnard, who introduced the common school to the progressive states of Massachusetts and New York. Prior to the promotion of the common school, there were no clear expectations for basic education in the USA. Many communities established primary or grammar schools, but the requirements varied from place to place. In many communities young people attended these schools for no more than sixteen weeks a year over a four- or five-year period. The common school when first introduced in Massachusetts in the 1830s set forth the expectation that every child should go to school for a minimum of twenty-five weeks per year over six continuous years; by the end of the nineteenth century, these expectations were increased to thirty-six weeks over eight years. While European societies established academic calendars of a similar length, in the late-developing societies of Japan and Russia, which were anxious to catch up with the leading Western societies, the academic calendars tended to be longer. In the early Meiji period Japan had prescribed only sixteen weeks per year; by 1902, this had increased to thirty-six weeks; and by 1912 it had increased to forty-two weeks with five and a half days of school per week or 240 days of school per year compared to approximately 180 days in Western Europe and the USA.

The increased time at school was recommended in order to cover an expanded range of subjects. Kamens & Benavot (1992) indicate that mathematics was introduced as a new subject in the primary school over the first half of the nineteenth century and in most settings science became respectable over the second half. Of course, in settings such as England and certain US states where fundamentalist religious groups were prevalent, science encountered stiff resistance – of particular note was the controversy between the biblical story of the creation of the earth and the scientific theory of evolution. In these settings it took more time for science to be included in the curriculum. Whereas mathematics and science were slow to enter the curriculum of the core societies of Western Europe, by the mid-nineteenth century these subjects had come to be viewed as central to the modern drive for industrialization and national strength and thus were included in the curriculum of the Japanese and Russian late developers on virtually the dawn of their revolutions. Over the course of the twentieth century, as will be noted below, the social sciences became more prominent in school curriculums.

The Decline of Values Education, especially in the USA

Values education, especially with an emphasis on religious principles, was an important emphasis in the pre-modern schools. The Reformation challenged religious orthodoxy and the Enlightenment challenged the foundations of religious belief. Thus, in France the revolutionary state sought to distance itself from the Catholic Church, and the American constitution established the principle of separation of Church and State.

These secularizing tendencies led schools continually to re-evaluate the approach they took to values education. By the early twentieth century, religious education was significantly curtailed in the American school (Nord, 1998). How could religion be taught in a society that practised so many different religions (and sects within these religions)? In contrast, religion seemed to experience a revival in England, at least in the public schools, towards the end of the nineteenth century.

The Japanese and Russian states also took a strong position against the teaching of the doctrines of the prevailing religious orthodoxy. However, in both cases the state took bold steps to introduce the new orthodoxy of their respective state religions, emperor worship in the Japanese case and communism in the Russian Soviet case. In the Japanese case, the state religion was conveyed through such courses as Japanese language, Japanese history, moral education, and the co-curriculum. In the Soviet school, the aim of the 'all-round development of the communist personality' was broadly diffused through the curriculum and co-curriculum, including the involvement of young children in physical labour (Muckle, 1988, p. 15). Of course, all of the modernizing states were concerned to advance their distinctive versions of nationalism. Thus, Bellah (1975) details the rising prominence of America's civil religion over the nineteenth century and Reisner (1923) stresses the prominence of nationalism in imperial Germany.

While the different systems approached religion and nationalism in their distinctive ways, all came to place greater importance on the social sciences. Geography had for some time been featured in the primary school curriculum and certain historical subjects were taken up at the secondary level. Increasing attention came to be devoted to these subjects, while, in addition, new consideration was given to the social science subjects of psychology, sociology, economics and international affairs. Meyer et al (1992) suggest that these subjects began to appear in the curriculum at the turn of the century, but the complicated international tensions leading up to the Second World War, as well as the determination in the aftermath of the First World War to build new and better societies, gave a critical impetus to social studies. Thus, as illustrated in Table 6.1, social studies became particularly prominent from the 1950s on. These subjects were introduced in the hope that they would prepare young people for citizenship as well as to help youth make good decisions about their personal life in an increasingly complex world. The rise in social studies appears to have been accompanied

147

by a slight decline in the 'related' subjects of civics, moral education, and religion – though there are obvious variations by region.[2]

Region/ Subject/Period	Sub- Saharan Africa	Mideast/ N. Africa	Asia	Latin America	Carib- bean	Eastern Europe	The West
Moral Education							
1920-44	0.0 (1)	0.3 (6)	3.4 (7)	0.3 (4)	0.0 (2)	0.0 (5)	0.5 (20)
1945-69	0.6 (17)	0.5 (14)	3.4 (17)	1.1 (12)	0.6 (6)	0.0 (10)	0.0 (20)
1970-86	0.8 (29)	0.6 (13)	2.9 (17)	1.0 (16)	0.4 (10)	0.0 (9)	0.2 (20)
Religion							
1920-44	0.0 (2)	14.0 (7)	0.0 (10)	1.0 (6)	1.2 (3)	5.5 (5)	5.5 (20)
1945-69	5,2 (17)	12.6 (13)	2.4 (20)	2.0 (12)	3.2 (6)	0.0 (9)	7.1 (20)
1970-86	3.8 (29)	11.8 (15)	3.0 (18)	2.2 (14)	2.2 (9)	0.0 (9)	4.7 (18)
Civics							
1920-44	0.0 (2)	1.1 (7)	0.4 (10)	0.3 (4)	1.1 (2)	1.2 (5)	1.7 (20)
1945-69	1.8 (17)	1.3 (14)	1.0 (20)	0.9 (12)	0.7 (6)	0.0 (10)	1.4 (20)
1970-86	1.5 (291)	0.6 (15)	1.3 (18)	1.0 (16)	0.4 (10)	0.2 (9)	0.7 (20)
Social Studies							
1920-44	0.0 (2)	0.0 (8)	0.3 (10)	3.9 (4)	0.3 (3)	0.3 (5)	0.6 (20)
1945-69	1.2 (1)	0.2 (1)	5.3 (1)	6.9 (1)	3.7 (1)	0.0 (1)	1.3 (20)
1970-86	3.3 (29)	3.8 (15)	6.0 (18)	8.7 (15)	7.2 (9)	0.0 (9)	5.0 (21)

Table 6.1. Mean percentages of curricular time devoted to moral education, religion, civics and social studies in primary curricula by world region (number of cases in parentheses). Source: Meyer et al (1992, p. 149).

As already discussed in chapter 4, the core societies differed in their determination to provide a common or consistent values education to all students. In general, the systems that were founded first showed a greater tendency to differentiate tracks or segments for children from different social backgrounds as well as of different gender. The German *Gymnasiums*, the French *lyceés*, and the English public schools mainly received male children from the elite classes and provided a different values curriculum from the parallel segments intended for the working classes. In contrast, there was less differentiation in the American common school and the Soviet general school – both strove to receive children from all social backgrounds and of both genders. The Japanese primary school was as inclusive as the American and

Soviet examples, but it was more explicit in conveying distinctive values to young boys and girls; and following primary school, while Japanese secondary education differentiated children into different tracks ostensibly on the basis of merit, social background also had a strong influence on placement.

The Contemporary Curricula

Curricula undergo changes over time. For example, the Japanese Ministry of Education tends to foster a curricular review every ten years; in other systems, a review may be precipitated by a change in government or a perception of a new 'crisis'. These changes are partially a reflection of common pressures, including global competition, the increasing recognition of human rights and especially the rights of children, and new developments in pedagogical theory. Thus, there are some common features of the curricula developed in most societies: they tend to stress the affective and to evaluate sides of personality development in the early years, while the pace of cognitive development accelerates in later years. Also, all curricula focus on the common subjects of national language, reading and writing, arithmetic, science and social studies.

While there are many similarities across societies, equally striking are the many differences in national curricular practice that can be illustrated at all levels from kindergarten to postgraduate education. Here the focus will be on several examples of important differences in the early stages where the curricula are less differentiated and hence easier to compare. The differences that are highlighted reflect the continuity of the respective national traditions.

We will draw on recognized comparative sources such as the International Association for the Evaluation of Educational Achievement (IEA) and the Organisation for Economic Cooperation and Development (OECD) as well as the recent study of Robin Alexander (2001). Each of these sources has its limitations. The IEA work includes most of the countries that we are interested in, but it focuses primarily on the subjects of mathematics and science, which are perhaps the most culturally neutral subjects; if differences are found in the way different countries organize these neutral subjects, all the more reason to expect differences in the other subjects. The OECD leans heavily on national reports and sometimes uses questionable procedures for interpreting these reports, so at several points we will be moved to question OECD findings. Alexander's research was based on a small sample of schools in each country, and so some may question whether he accurately portrays the national picture. Also, his research did not include Japan. It is interesting that all of these studies ended up stressing the differences across countries. As Schmidt et al (2001) observe for eighth grade mathematics:

In the world according to TIMSS [Third International Mathematics and Science Study], the central topics of eighth grade mathematics are most consistently perimeter, area, and volume and equations and formulas. This is true regardless of the way in which curriculum is made visible for examination and is true with great consistency across the TIMSS countries. How few topics meet these criteria certainly emphasizes that 'mathematics is not mathematics is not mathematics' in the terms of the eighth grade curriculum. (p. 110)

For eighth grade science, Schmidt and his team only found the large topical area of human biology to be shared across most countries, but within biology and three other science areas there was essentially no consensus on subtopics (2001, pp. 145-146).

In the discussion that follows we will mainly focus on the most recent data. This is somewhat problematic as nations frequently alter their curriculums. For example, England introduced a national curriculum in 1988, Japan considerably simplified its curriculum in the mid-1990s, and post-glasnost Russia introduced major reforms of the former Soviet curriculum. Where appropriate, data from earlier periods will be included to provide a more stable account for each system.

Comparing Scope

The discussion thus far has indicated some clear contrasts in the scope of the curricula. France is exceptional for its cognitive emphasis and neglect of most other areas. England emphasizes a balanced education, but as the focus is on the proper education of the gentleman, the 'feminine' pursuits of art and music are somewhat neglected. Japan and Russia stress whole person education that leads to a significant emphasis on all of the subject areas. These differences are summarized in Table 6.2.

	Germany	France	England	USA	Japan	Russia
Cognitive	xx	xxxx	xx	xx	xxx	xxx
Moral/religious	xx		xxx	x	xxx	xx
Civic/national	xx	xx	x	xxx	xx	xxx
Physical	x		xx	x	xx	xx
Aesthetic	x	x	x	x	xx	xx
Musical	x		x	x	xx	xx

Table 6.2. Relative stress on different subject areas of the core societies (each x represents increasing degree of stress).

Comparing Number of Subjects and Content (and Extent of Choice)

Clearly, the Japanese and Russian curriculums are the most ambitious in terms of scope and the French the least ambitious. To implement the ambitious scope of their curriculum, the Japanese and Russian curriculum authorities make several interesting compromises.

They limit the number of distinctive academic subjects (relative to the French) through integrating academic content across subjects. Whereas the primary curriculum in a French school has eight academic subjects, that in Japan and Russia has only five or so. The several sciences are integrated in a general science course, and at the lowest grades this subject may also be integrated with social studies. Similarly, the various areas of mathematics are integrated in a common subject. This integration enables the provision of separate courses for art and music.

In Japan and Russia, the content for most courses is broken into fewer units. Schmidt et al (2001, p. 92 for mathematics; p. 136 for science) report that Japan and Russia (as well as Germany) stand out for breaking their primary-level texts of each grade level into fewer topics (typically 20-25 per year), with considerably more space devoted to each topic. In contrast, the US and French texts specify nearly twice as many topics, with less space per topic; while the Schmidt report did not report the pattern for England, it can be noted that the neighbouring countries of Ireland and Scotland follow a practice close to that of the USA.

The Japanese and Russian curriculums require all children to master the same content. As Muckle (1988, p. 187) observes for Russia, 'The curriculum of the Soviet school is standard: all the subjects in a very substantial "core" are offered to every child. All children receive a balanced programme of study, and though a little specialization is possible through the options, no one is allowed to drop basic subjects until he leaves school' (p. 187). In the USA and England there is some choice allowed as different elementary schools serving the same community feature distinctive curricular emphases; also, within the elementary schools, there is some streaming even in the lower grades of the elementary education cycle. In the USA the range of choice broadens from the lower secondary level; for example, a student preferring the humanities might take only two sciences courses at the junior high level along with a revisit of basic mathematics whereas a student favouring the sciences would certainly take three years of science and a rigorous mathematics programme that would include exposure to pre-calculus, geometry, and possibly trigonometry. The Japanese and Russian middle schools do not encourage choice.

Comparing Length of Units in Syllabi and Their Repetition

The TIMSS analysis also illustrates different strategies for the coverage of particular topics. McKnight et al (1987) looked at the sequence of content development over several grades and found that the US texts favoured the spiral concept of briefly presenting a concept in one year and then coming back to it several times over the ensuing years. American educators are apparently concerned not to pressure children to achieve mastery of a new concept on first exposure as this might be too challenging and lead to disappointment; thus, the concept is presented in one year and revisited over successive years. Another reason American texts repeat the same topic in successive years is that educators are concerned that children will forget concepts over the vacation periods (which are generally longer than the vacation periods of other systems). The spiral approach helps explain why US texts take up more topics in a given year but give them less space. In contrast, the Russian and Japanese approach seems to involve a more intensive treatment at a given time, with less revisiting. The assumption in these systems is that an early topic naturally serves as a foundation for later topics and hence will be automatically invoked when necessary at the later stages.

Comparing Pace or Pattern of Development (and the Point of Acceleration)

There are major differences across the several systems in terms of pace. The French system starts off at a fast pace from grade 1. In Germany there is a somewhat relaxed pace at the primary level with a quick pick-up from the lower secondary level. In the USA, for the mainstream student there is a slow start with little acceleration until college (though high school students in honours or advanced placement courses experience a more demanding curriculum which is comparable to that in some of the other countries). Japan and Russia also begin with a slow start but the pace picks up from the latter months of grade 3. Schmidt et al (2001) find that the Japanese curriculum in both mathematics and science is one grade ahead of the USA by grade 8. Alexander (2001) reports the same for Russia. And by grade 12, Rohlen (1983) suggests the Japanese curriculum is at least two grades ahead of the US curriculum. Recent concern that the Japanese curriculum is too demanding has led to a certain degree of simplification, including fewer required days at school and the coverage of fewer topics. Even so, there remains a substantial gap between the learning objectives across these several societies, with the US goals being the least demanding.

Comparing Time

Clearly, the curriculums vary. The Japanese curriculum is perhaps the most demanding due to its wide scope and the acceleration of its pace from the fourth grade of the primary school until the completion of high school. The Russian curriculum is also demanding in terms of both scope and acceleration. The French curriculum is mainly demanding in terms of number of academic subjects and pace, but the scope is narrower.

One might expect that the time allocated for learning would be in proportion to these demands, but the 'reported' data on this subject lead to somewhat ambiguous conclusions. Indeed, if the comparison was made twenty years ago this expectation would have been confirmed. Across the systems, the number of hours children spend at a primary school on a typical day is about the same – typically from 8.30 to 2.30, or six hours a day. Thus, the major differentiator is the number of days per year in school. Twenty years ago, there was considerable variation: 240 days in Japan compared to 210 in France and Germany and 180 in the USA and England.[3] However, from the early 1990s, Japan decided to shift from a six-day school week to five days of school a week, and so currently Japanese children attend school for about as many days as their European counterparts, about 210 days a year, or only thirty more days than US or English children.

Children in the six nations spend about the same number of hours in school each day, and so the number of days is a major differentiator in their exposure to the total school experience of curricular and co-curricular activities. Thus, one might say that the Japanese and European schools are more central in the life of their children and the US and English schools are less central.

However, the number of hours children spend in school can be used in various ways – in instructional time, breaks between instructional periods, assemblies, lunch periods, and club activities. According to OECD statisticians, children in US schools have longer class periods and less break time per day. So, based on these assumptions, the OECD concludes that US students spend the most time in school in class each year across the six countries under discussion, and Japanese children spend the least time in school-based instruction (OECD, 2002, p. 283).[4]

Distinct from the number of hours children spend on instruction in schools is the time they spend after school on instruction-related tasks. US, English and German schools tend to de-emphasise homework for the primary grades whereas homework is expected in the other systems. All of the systems encourage homework for secondary school, but again the differences tend to follow the pattern for the primary grades. Surveys of schoolchildren in the mid-1990s conducted by the National Assessment of Educational Progress (NAEP) suggested that American children spend relatively few hours per week on homework (Lapointe et al, 1989). Surprisingly, according to the recent OECD study that provides comparative information for fifteen year-olds in some twenty countries, Japanese children are said to spend only 2.9 hours on homework a week compared to 5.6 in England, 4.9 in France, 4.5 in Germany, and 4.6 in the USA (see Table 6.3).[5] This same report also compares the likelihood of children in these countries attending a supplementary school either for enrichment or remedial education. Such schools, known in Japan as *juku* and *yobiko*, are shown to be very popular. Many contemporary Russian children are also reported to be attending these schools. In the other countries, about one in every four students attends a supplementary school (OECD, 2002, p. 286).[6]

	Total intended annual instruction time for students (hours per year)	Estimated mean numbers of hours spent on homework per day	Percentage of students who attend supplementary schools
France	979	4.9	n.d.
Germany	921	4.5	10
Japan	875	2.9	71
Russia	945	–	45
UK	940	5.4	20
USA	980	4.6	25

Table 6.3. Several indicators of student involvement in learning at age 14-15. Source: OECD, 2001, 2002.

Some Characteristics of the Co-Curriculum

The curriculum is usually viewed as the vehicle for outlining the core content of the modern school. The subjects outlined in the curriculum are those which the state promises to provide as its public responsibility to its citizens. However, educators and other stakeholders associated with the educational endeavour often believe that there are other lessons for young people that are not adequately captured in the curriculum. Where this conviction prevails, they are likely to add educational opportunities that may or may not be obligatory and may or may not be associated with the formal schooling process. Some of these additional opportunities are provided through the co-curriculum in the English, Japanese and Russian schools or the extra-curriculum in US schools. The distinction between 'co' and 'extra' seems to signify the relative importance the respective systems give to these activities. The German system does not have a specific word for these opportunities though the concern is there. In France, these opportunities are largely provided by community associations and not by the school.

In the English public school tradition, classroom education concludes in the early afternoon and then most students are expected to engage in co-curricular activities for the remainder of the afternoon. Teachers and prefects are expected to supervise these activities as part of their normal job. Participation in these activities is generally regarded as a privilege, and students who are being disciplined for bad behaviour or poor grades are deprived of this privilege.[7]

In the American primary school there is a limited range of extra-curricular activities, such as participation in the school band or choir. These activities are voluntary and some practices are held during school (children are excused from their normal class work) while other practices are held after school. Children may be charged a small fee for participation. Distinct from these extra-curricular activities, many American youngsters also participate in athletic teams run by local civic organizations. These events are organized seasonally so that a young person can play football or soccer in the autumn, basketball in the winter, and so on. From the secondary level, some of these athletic events become part of the school extra-curriculum; again they are voluntary and participants are expected to pay a fee.

In the Japanese and Russian systems, virtually all of the co-curricular activities are associated with the school. Music and art are part of the core curriculum, and all students are expected to participate in these subject areas; however, those who want more exposure are encouraged to join a related club. Clubs are also established for athletic development and in such areas as history, drama, industrial arts and cooking. Typically, clubs meet at the conclusion of the school day, and it is normally the responsibility of teachers to supervise the activities. Because all clubs meet at a common time, a child normally can only belong to one club. Thus, a child who elects for soccer has to forego participation in baseball. Club activity begins with the upper grades of primary school and continues through middle school and high school.

The Intended, Implemented, and Achieved Curricula

Our discussion thus far has focused on the formal curriculum that is set by educational authorities in central or local offices. This 'intended' curriculum is approved through a political process where certain stakeholders are represented. However, the actual presentation of this curriculum depends on the cooperation of teachers and students.

Teachers have their own ideas about what children need to learn as well as their own understanding of what they are capable of teaching. Often teachers decide that they cannot teach all of the intended curriculum to the particular class(es) they are working with. What teachers actually teach is sometimes referred to as the 'implemented' curriculum.

Children cannot learn curricular material unless they are exposed to it, and in most systems teachers (both through their instruction and the homework they assign) are viewed as the major gatekeepers for determining what children are exposed to. However, as noted earlier, children may also have lessons in supplementary schools and through the co-curriculum. And, of course, parents, friends, and the media may expose children to new ideas. Some of the recent research studies on 'the opportunity to learn' have compared the material that teachers say they teach with the material children say they have been exposed to. In most cases children report that they have been exposed to somewhat less material than teachers say they have taught. However, in one study it was reported that Japanese children reported exposure to a wider range of material, suggesting that the additional educational opportunities provided by that system beyond the classroom teacher have an impact in expanding the implemented curriculum (Livingstone, 1986).

Of course, the ultimate objective of the curriculum is to promote the development of children. The IEA studies refer to the cognitive gains of children as the achieved curriculum. Other areas of child growth are in the social, moral, aesthetic and physical realms.

After reviewing the role of teachers in chapter 7, we will focus our attention in chapter 8 on what children actually learn from the school and these other teachers. It has already been indicated in this chapter that the intentions of the several systems vary, with some having a more ambitious intended curriculum than others. Interestingly, some of those systems with the most ambitious intended curriculums also excel in their levels of implementation and achievement (Livingstone, 1986; Schmidt et al, 2001); additionally, centralized systems seem to implement more of their intended curriculum than do decentralized systems (Stevenson & Baker, 1991). This implies that children have a great untapped capacity for learning. Perhaps the greatest challenge to modern education remains that of identifying the best ways to help children realize their potential.

Conclusion: how similar are the late modern curricula?

Some would argue (Meyer et al, 1992) that virtually everywhere in the modern world a common curriculum emerged. In so far as this argument asserts that the focus of thinking about education shifted to schools, to the neglect of other educational settings, the preceding discussion concurs. But the evidence presented in this chapter points to serious flaws in the contention that schools in all modern settings follow a common curriculum.[8] Rather, it has been shown that several distinctive curricula emerged, and that these persist.

Another charge against modern education has been its supposed singular focus on cognitive education to the neglect of other sensitivities (Gardner & Hatch, 1989). This charge can be levelled against the contemporary French pattern (and I would also say the American approach), but it should be apparent from the preceding discussion that most modern systems are more holistic in their educational objectives. The Russian and Japanese curriculums have the broadest scope, with the arrangement of the other core societies falling between the two extremes. Another salient issue is the flexibility of curriculums in allowing individual students to focus on the objectives they prefer as contrasted to the objectives the system sanctions. In this latter respect, the systems that are more successful in delivering their intended curriculum seem to be less responsive to individual preferences. Thus, a future challenge is to open up ways to accommodate the collective and individual needs of pupils.

Notes

[1] The diagram presents my estimates of the shifts in relative influence of the respective stakeholders, recognizing that there were major differences between the core societies both in the relative influence of different stakeholders and

the timeline for change. The 'educational establishment', including local school officials, schools of education, and teacher associations became over time an increasingly influential stakeholder, and in the diagram all of these groups are included as a component of state influence.

[2] In a related analysis, Meyer et al (1992, p. 150) observe that new nations that were formerly English colonies are more likely to feature religious studies in the curriculum whereas those that were former Spanish or Portuguese colonies are more likely to stress social studies, and those that were former French colonies are somewhat more likely to stress civics.

[3] What explains the differences in days? One could argue that the greater number of days in Japan reflects a determination to catch up with the West through hard effort. The greater number of days on the continent reflects the challenge of covering the encyclopaedic curriculum. The modest number of days in England reflects the assumption that exceptional students learn as much on their own as in school and so there is no need to overdo schooling; also, children need relief from the life as a boarder to spend some time with their families. In the case of the USA it is worth noting that the average number of days in school has steadily increased since the nineteenth century when America was an agrarian society and children were needed to help on the farm, and currently, at 180 days per year, is at its peak. From this historical perspective, which indicates for the USA a steady increase in the number of days in schools since the mid-nineteenth century, the long US summer vacation does not seem sacrosanct; indeed, a projection of the US historical trend suggests year-round schooling calendars may gain greater favour in the near future.

[4] The assignments of minutes per class made by the OECD, of course, are based on the official reports of the participating countries, but they do not accurately reflect actual instructional time. The US reports apparently indicate US schools have a shorter break time between classes, but observational studies indicate that US classes tend to spend relatively more time getting classes started as children straggle in and teachers get organized for the period whereas Russian and Japanese classrooms start promptly with the sound of the bell.

[5] No data were reported for Russia.

[6] No data were reported for France.

[7] In the English maintained sector the situation is different.

[8] The work of Meyer et al (1992) focuses on the distribution of nominal subjects featured in different curricula, which is a useful but somewhat rough indicator of curricular emphases. The analysis in this chapter suggests that the big differences become evident when such features as relative scope of the curricula are considered as well as the actual contents of particular subjects at particular grade levels.

CHAPTER 7

Modern Teachers

Over and over again the Prussians proved that elementary education
couldn't be fully attained without purposely-prepared teachers. They
deem these seminaries of priceless value; and declare them, in all their
reports and laws, to be the fountains of all their success ... we are
confident that teachers thoroughly prepared, as they are in Prussia,
would put a new face on elementary education, and produce through
our State an era of light and of love. (Charles Brooks, 1837)

Teachers are the front line of education. In the pre-modern period, most teachers either taught on a temporary basis or as an extension of other professional activities. They learned how to teach through apprenticeship. Once recognized as master teachers, the pre-modern teachers enjoyed much autonomy and responsibility, and modest rewards.

Modern education sought to align education with the goals of the nation state. Education was both systematized and expanded. The state expressed its goals through a new curriculum and selective examinations, and the public school became the agent. To expand, the new school system needed many teachers to replicate delivery of the modern curriculum in settings throughout the nation. And so a special training programme was conceived to mould a common teacher for the common school. Prussia pioneered with first training schools, though it was perhaps the French who pushed the new model to its most extreme limits with a nationwide system of *écoles normales*. Other settings followed these pacesetters.

The first section of this chapter presents a general model of the forces shaping the evolution of the new position of schoolteacher across the several core societies. It goes on to consider the unique adaptations as each setting defined its teacher need, and sought to expand the supply of teachers to serve the whole nation. Several distinctive outcomes will be highlighted.

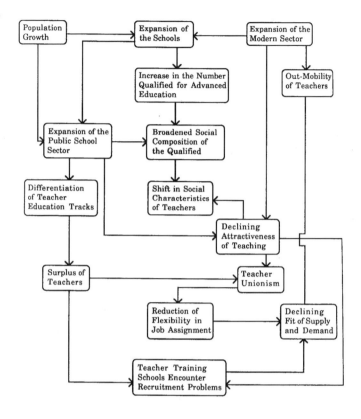

Figure 7.1. Variables influencing the historical shift in teacher characteristics.
Source: Cummings (1990a).

The 'Iron Law' of Teacher Status

One of the great ironies of modern education is the belief, despite all the efforts and resources devoted to expanding and improving the schools system, that 'today's' teachers are not like they used to be. Observers recall an earlier golden age when teachers came from more exalted social backgrounds, they worked harder, and they were more effective as teachers. Indeed, over the course of developing modern education, a variety of factors have influenced the status of teachers and hence who becomes a teacher (summarized in Figure 7.1). Cummings, in Rust & Dalin's (1990) review of the changing social characteristics of teachers, identified several broad trends that apply to a greater or lesser degree across the core systems.

Teaching initially was a moderate to high status job that competed with other jobs requiring advanced education, and thus the early recruits tended to come from middle-class backgrounds similar to those of their pupils.

With the expansion of educational demand, the state took steps to expand the public school system and hence the training of teachers. One related measure was the differentiation of teacher training institutes from other higher educational institutions.

- The expansion of schools broadened the social base of pupils and, correspondingly, the social base of those young people qualified to enter teacher education institutions.

- Teacher education institutions were expanded rapidly to meet the rising educational demand, but when this demand began to fall off the capacity of teacher education institutions did not, resulting in an excess supply of teacher candidates.

- The surplus of teacher candidates created a 'buyer's market' and teachers' pay thus began to decline relative to the pay for positions requiring similar educational qualifications.

- The declining conditions of teaching encouraged teachers to form associations to struggle for improvements.

- Among the unanticipated outcomes of these struggles was the formalization of work rules that tended to reduce the flexibility of teaching and the assignment of teachers and hence contributed to teacher dissatisfaction.

- These various trends certainly led to changes in the social characteristics of new teachers; essentially, teachers over time became more diverse, just as did the pupils they met in their classrooms.

- These trends, at least in certain settings, create obstacles for improving the academic quality of new applicants to the profession.

The analysis that follows argues that educational systems such as the US system, that are continually expanding, are more subject to the challenge of maintaining the status of the teaching profession relative to European systems with more stable populations. Of the six systems considered here, it would appear that the Japanese system has devoted the most consistent attention to maintaining teacher status. Several times over the modern period, the central Japanese government that sets the national pay schedule for teachers substantially increased the average pay of teachers; also, the government took steps to upgrade the setting for teacher training.[1] The reform of teacher training and the improvement of teacher status has also been an important concern in Western Europe (Popkewitz, 1993; Judge et al, 1994).

Pre-modern Education

In pre-modern society, most learning was through apprenticeship. Young people learned a trade through apprenticeship. Similarly, they learned law through clerking at a reputable firm while studying in their spare time and, when adequately prepared, taking the bar examination. As preparation for the period of apprenticeship in fields such as law, medicine, and the clergy required book learning, young people often sought the guidance of tutors who came to their homes. Some would go to a village school where they would receive instruction from a learned adult who might appoint selected older students to guide the newcomers.

Even the larger educational organizations such as the medieval universities relied heavily on apprenticeship. Lectures were used to convey substance, but these were to groups of apprentices who received individual instruction either directly from the master or from his senior apprentices. The master alone would provide the certifying examination for a particular course (Durkheim, 1969). Groups of masters would administer a comprehensive examination as a condition for the apprentice to gain recognition as a master. The organization of this education varied; for example, in Italy apprentices were said to pay their fees directly to their master whereas in Germany tuition was collected by the guilds of the masters who combined to form the university (Metzger, 1955).

Dore (1965) describes a similar pattern of apprenticeship in Tokugawa education. But, of course, there were important differences in etiquette when compared to the Western examples. In the Tokugawa schools, the students were of different hereditary rank in the samurai class and the teachers were under some pressure to protect the dignity of the students destined for high-rank positions. Thus, meritocratic evaluation was de-emphasized; all students were expected to work hard and succeed in their studies. Also, the curriculum was based on Confucian principles of law and science rather than Western knowledge.

While the apprentice model had the advantage of ensuring continuity in a professional group, it had the limitation that each master could only work with a small number of students. Also, the masters enjoyed 'autonomy' in their guidance of their apprentices while the modern state sought control over schooling.

The Original Patterns of Teacher
Job Definition and Preparation[2]

Prussia

The first major break with the apprentice model is often attributed to eighteenth-century Prussia. Martin Luther (1483-1546) was a strong advocate of popular education:

> *Since we are all required, and especially the magistrates, above all other things, to educate the youth who are born and growing up among us, and to train them up in the fear of God and in the ways of virtue, it is needful that we have schools and preachers and pastors. If the parents*

will not reform, they must go their way to ruin, but if the young are
neglected, and left without education, it is the fault of the state; and the
effect will be that the country will swarm with vile and lawless people, so
that our safety, no less than the command of God requireth us to foresee
and ward off the evil. (Barnard, 1851, p. 17, quoted from Dr Sears,
Life of Martin Luther)

Luther urged the local rulers of the various German states to provide education for the new generation, and during his time there was much progress in popular education.

The Thirty Years War (starting in 1618) interrupted this trend, but thereafter popular education spread rapidly. The typical German school, combining religious and practical education, was substantially subsidized by the local ruler, and hence extolled virtues of respect and loyalty to the local patron. The spread of local schools led some local rulers to develop more systematic rules for the organization of schools and the training of teachers. Prussia was a leader in this regard, establishing a normal school *circa* 1735. Frederick the Great, who became King of Prussia in 1763, took further steps to advance popular and professional education. During his time there were important new developments in pedagogical theory leading to a new stress on active teaching and learning.

In the period following Germany's defeat by Napoleon (1807 on), Prussia and the neighbouring states took the boldest steps towards systematizing their educational systems. In Prussia, a central curriculum was devised and to ensure its effective delivery the Prussian state elaborated central requirements for teacher preparation. Other states followed the Prussian lead, and it is said that these collaborative endeavours helped smooth the way for the eventual unification of Germany.

By the mid-nineteenth century, when Henry Barnard, Superintendent of Schools in Connecticut, visited Europe, easily half a dozen variations on the normal school had evolved (Barnard, 1851, pp. 5-8). Barnard noted that the initial concept of a 'normal' school was the provision of ideal schools that apprentice teachers might visit to observe recommended classroom procedures. These teachers concurrently received courses of lectures on educational theory and subject matter. The combination of observation and study was one mode of teacher preparation. A second mode involved attendance at teacher seminaries organized by local governments. Other modes included experienced teachers moving between the schools of a local area to provide on-site guidance, the formation of teacher associations, and the development of examinations as a basis for certifying teachers. Barnard (pp. 34-35) reports that Prussia by this time had fifty-one normal schools, with the other German states having between one and ten apiece. Barnard also reflected on the high status of the German teacher. According to him, they were respected, had many opportunities for training, were carefully selected (and if they exhibited bad conduct expelled), had good salaries, opportunities for promotion, opportunities to go to conferences, and various other benefits.

As popular education advanced, there were parallel developments at the secondary level where two distinctive tracks were available, the highly practical *Realschule* and the academic *Gymnasium*. The former was supported by employers and provided young people with a combination of academic education and on-the-job training in industry and commerce. In contrast, the *Gymnasiums* were supported by the universities and provided the preparation necessary for further study at the universities. While the teaching in the former included much practical application and was often provided by technical specialists in the sponsoring workplaces, teaching in the *Gymnasiums* was of high academic quality. Many of the *Gymnasium* teachers who were university graduates saw their teaching there as the first step on a career ladder which could lead to a position as professor at a university. The teachers enjoyed much freedom in the selection of materials for their lectures and the evaluation of their students.

And so, on the one hand, the Prussian system was characterized by a bureaucratically dominated primary school and, on the other hand, by relatively independent *Gymnasiums* that provided a select group of young people with a liberal education prior to their entry into a professional faculty of the university.

France

France and Germany shared a somewhat similar intellectual heritage, but the Catholic Church had been more prominent in France, where Catholic schools were widely established. Owing to the Church's role in education, the French monarchy was reluctant to become involved in popular schooling. Of course, some philosophers were critical of the Church's education, and this criticism flavoured the radical rhetoric of the French Revolution. Along with removing the Church from the schools, these critics proposed a grand plan for a new education coordinated by a central university with its satellites in each province. The university, in this scheme, was to be a central coordinating unit to design curricula and prepare examinations. But the revolutionary leaders were unable to translate these dreams into practice, and the actual consolidation was left to Napoleon. While Napoleon was able to launch the grand plan, owing to his military commitments he was unable to fund all of the components. He focused mainly on the *lycée*, and the technical component of higher education. Indeed, in the 1801 Concordat with the Papacy, Napoleon re-invited the Church to take responsibility at the primary level. So a double divide emerged in the French system between primary and secondary education and between private and public education (Judge, 1994, p. 41).

Following Napoleon's defeat, France for some time was a crippled nation with few educational policy initiatives. The new government formed in

164

1830 expressed its determination to reform education; Guizot assumed the pivotal role in this endeavour. A commission under Cousin was charged with the task of examining the educational systems of other European nations with a special focus on Prussia. The ensuing reforms included the establishment of a central *grande école normale* [3] to specialize in educational theory and normal schools in each province to train teachers for their schools (these were differentiated by gender). The reformed French system had a central curriculum for all grades that was secular and encyclopaedic. Students were expected to take examinations at every grade level as a condition for advancement. The teacher's job was to convey the curriculum precisely to students. The teachers were encouraged to help students as much as possible, but finally the students' fates were to be decided by external examinations. The challenging examinations resulted in a high rate of failure and drop-outs. Thus, only a small elite group of students survived to enter the top *lycée* where teaching was more spirited and free.

The main outlines of this system were followed until the Second World War. There were periodic reforms following, for example, the revolution of 1848 and France's defeat by Germany in 1870. One outcome of the subsequent reforms was a further narrowing of the job of the teacher.

England

England was not as impressed by the modern movement as its neighbouring European societies. While parliament periodically debated the merits of public education, the state was reluctant to intervene. Thus, independent private schools were left on their own to respond to the popular demand, and it was the most prestigious of these that provided the model for education. The ideal teacher of these schools has been described in various nineteenth-century novels. This teacher was a generalist who was born to teach. The teacher had moral convictions that he readily conveyed both in the classroom and in his other school roles as coach, master, and counsellor. The ideal teacher was a graduate of the school where he taught who had gone on to obtain a degree at a prominent English university. This system worked well for the upper tier of educational institutions that educated the elite.

While there was much indifference to popular education in England, some liberal politicians, as well as the emerging socialist movement, exerted pressure that was finally fulfilled in the Education Act of 1870. This Act enabled a slow spread of popular education. But, in contrast to the continent, the English approach was very much a bottom–up approach. Local education authorities were established and given the opportunity, but not the obligation, to provide popular education. The national government did not specify a detailed curriculum nor did it take adequate steps to prepare teachers for the prospective new schools. In the absence of teacher training institutions, the majority of primary-level teachers continued to learn on the job. As in the elite schools, teachers by default enjoyed considerable autonomy.

Beyond the elementary school, the educational structure in England varied by region and this characteristic persists. The most common offering in the nineteenth century was the academic grammar school, complemented in some areas by vocational schools. And of course, alongside these institutions were the long-standing public schools, which, while few in number, had considerable prestige. Later, in the publicly funded sector both secondary modern schools and comprehensive high schools were added in particular areas. Thus, there was considerable diversity in the structure of secondary education. In the public sector there was usually a divide in terms of qualifications and workload between those teaching in primary schools and those teaching in secondary schools (Judge, 1994, p. 160).

The first institutes specializing in training teachers emerged only in the late nineteenth century in England. These institutions placed as much stress on in-service training as on pre-service. Most schools recruited a substantial proportion of their staff directly from the pool of college and university graduates, set them to teaching first, and then sent them for training later. As in the case of the public schools, the belief persisted that a good teacher was born and not made.

USA

Americans initially followed the English model of the private provision of education, except in certain states, notably Massachusetts and New York, where there was a clear commitment to public education. From the 1830s these states began to take steps to establish 'common schools' in every community. The common school ideal involved the provision of classes for several grades, with separate teachers for each of the classes. This created a sharp acceleration in the demand for teachers, far exceeding the available supply. This shortage was further aggravated by rapid population growth as new immigrants arrived and looked to the local schools to prepare them and their children for the American way of life.

Owing to the shortage of suitable candidates, local communities searched for new solutions. Volunteers with a reasonable level of education were invited to fill the gaps. And from a comparatively early date, the American school came to recognize that young women could be as effective as young men in primary education. Given the unorthodox staffing of schools, high expectations were placed on the principals of each school to provide coordination and leadership in the instructional process. New manuals on school administration were published telling principals how to manage 'teacher-proof' schools through pre-selecting basic textbooks, requiring daily and weekly lesson plans, administering standardized tests, holding back the salaries of non-performing teachers, and other means (Lortie, 1975). Later, this same orientation led to the creation of a variety of specialist jobs such as counsellor, reading specialist, and mathematics specialist to supplement the work of the 'inadequate' teaching force.

In conjunction with the common school movement, the first normal schools were established in the USA in the mid-nineteenth century. Attendance at a normal school gradually came to be expected of new appointees in public schools. However, the continuing shortage of supply led to many compromises with this requirement. Also, in that most normal schools were established to serve local areas, they were small in scale and unable to provide much specialization in their curriculum. Thus, training for secondary education closely paralleled that in primary education and the local school systems came to offer essentially equal status and working conditions to teachers at both levels.

Japan

In the Tokugawa period, Japan had a strong tradition of caste-based traditional education, but the Meiji Revolution brought a radical shift. The caste hierarchy of the feudal system was formally abolished and along with it went the tradition of separate schools for samurai and commoners. In addition, the new universal modern education was to place a strong emphasis on the Westernizing subjects of mathematics and science as well as Western history and culture. At the same time, the new state was concerned to foster nationalism and saw education as a means to build loyalty to the new state. And so education needed to focus not only on cognitive skills but also on values and physical strength. These dramatic changes were embodied in the new curriculum drafted by the central government.

Japan's determination to provide compulsory education for both boys and girls created a tremendous demand for new teachers. The state drew on the French model to respond to this demand. Normal schools were rapidly built so that by 1887 there was at least one in each prefecture. These schools tended to be residential and to have a militaristic atmosphere. Students would get up early in the morning, express their loyalty to the Emperor, and engage in callisthenics and drill prior to breakfast and a well-organized day of study and practice. Schoolmasters, especially in rural areas, were urged to send their best students to the normal schools. Prospective students were exhorted as a patriotic duty to consider a teaching career. Free tuition and board proved a powerful incentive in motivating many able young people to accept this opportunity.

Russia

Soviet Russia also faced a great challenge in training sufficient numbers to provide mass education to a vast territory and a virtually illiterate population. At the same time as the Bolshevik government was considering its educational challenge, it was engaged in a civil war against the 'White'

Russians who opposed the new socialist direction. Partly for these reasons, women were more readily drafted to teaching and to other professional work in crash programmes to build the new nation. In contrast to the classical education of the past, the new Russia designed a simplified general school with a manageable curriculum covering a small set of core courses. This new curriculum was organized in such a way that a single teacher could continue with the same group of students for several grades at the beginning of their studies. This approach required fewer strata in the teacher training system and facilitated an efficient response to the pressing demand.

In the tsarist educational system, higher education was under the control of the various government ministries and university education enjoyed considerable autonomy. With the Bolshevik Revolution, most of these higher educational institutions were placed under the central Commissariat of Enlightenment (*Narkompros*). One of the early steps of the Commissariat was to expand access to higher education through treating secondary school graduation as sufficient proof of qualification for further study. The expansion of higher education along with the new programme of specifying the job designations of tertiary level graduates enabled the Commissariat to direct a rapidly increased number of qualified people to the expanding school system. While the demand was always behind supply, in this way the Soviet educational system was able to achieve rapid expansion in the teaching force.

Recruiting Teachers

These early experiences in establishing modern education had a lasting imprint on a variety of norms affecting the status of teachers and teaching. In England and the USA, the new education emerged in relatively tranquil times. Neither nation was facing a major external threat during the gestation period, especially one that highlighted the need for mass education. In both nations, the development of popular education was the responsibility of local governments, where the enthusiasm for rapid progress varied.

Still comparing these two decentralized settings, it would appear that the supply of qualified candidates was more abundant in England. While education was expanding in both settings, the population in the USA was more rapidly swelling owing mainly to the steady influx of immigrants. As many areas in the USA experienced a shortage of qualified candidates, gradually a culture developed of settling for whatever was available – and somehow compensating for weak teachers through introducing teacher-proof practices managed by strong school principals. Also, to fill the gap, the American schools from early on exhibited a greater willingness to recruit women to the position of schoolteacher.

In contrast to these tranquil settings, modern education in the other settings emerged in a period of national challenge where education was accorded an important role in the response. Thus, in these challenged

168

settings, a more coordinated national or centralized approach to recruiting and training emerged. Generally, recruitment preceded training, and public authorities took responsibility for both.

In most of the systems, at least in the early stages, teaching was viewed as a good job. It was a respected profession with reasonable hours and a more or less attractive workplace. And at least in the case of Germany and Japan, the compensation was competitive. This was especially so in Japan where recruiters directed their search to the second sons of rural families of modest income. These conditions made the job attractive to the intellectually inclined youth of lower middle-class homes. Over time, the social class of recruits declined somewhat and women came to make up a larger proportion of the teaching force.

Academic qualifications were an important recruitment criterion in all settings. In the initial decades of modern education, teachers were expected to have at least two to three more years of education than their most advanced pupils. Thus, in Japan middle-school graduates were recruited to teach in the primary schools. This standard was gradually raised. Moral character was another important criterion. In England, and especially in the USA, candidates were expected to have firm religious convictions; many of the early American teachers were graduates of religious seminaries or colleges who combined teaching with a part-time position as pastor in a nearby church. Japanese recruiters preferred children from rural families, believing that they were less likely to have been spoiled by the corrupting glitter of the new urban life.

Training the Modern Teacher[4]

In the USA and England, the recruiters generally were single schools or small school systems. Lacking extensive resources, they typically sought individuals who had the background appropriate for the available teaching job. These small systems did not have a special facility to provide pre-service training for their recruits. Thus, they viewed the responsibility for preparation to lie with the prospective teacher prior to their seeking a job. These circumstances gave rise to a tradition of teachers obtaining basic skills on their own, then going back for more training once they gained a foothold in an educational workplace. In these circumstances, a respect for practice was important at the recruitment stage and in-service training was encouraged as a means of enhancing competence.

In contrast, in the other settings recruitment often preceded training. Once recruited, a prospective teacher was assigned to a pre-service training experience that might last from a few weeks to several years. In the pre-service setting, which was often at a residential college, trainers were concerned to provide as extensive a training experience as affordable before sending their students out to the classroom. In France especially, the pre-service experience involved a strong knowledge component reflecting the need to prepare teachers to teach the encyclopaedic curriculum – thus the curriculum there tended to require several years for completion. In Japan and Russia, where there were more streamlined curriculums, the pre-service experience ranged from six months to two years.

As the systems to which the newly trained teachers were being assigned were undergoing rapid expansion, the responsible governments usually lacked sufficient resources to worry much about in-service teacher skill development. The supervisory system was looked to as one means of in-service training; however, supervisors were often overly burdened with routine paperwork and could not adequately respond to this need. Japan was perhaps the most creative in devising a supplementary approach. The Japanese pre-service experience was briefer than on the European continent and the in-service contribution of inspectors was also limited. To fill the gap, Japanese schools came to develop a rich routine of in-service training. One component was the mentoring system (building on the tradition of apprenticeship) where senior teachers were given formal responsibility for helping specific junior teachers adjust to their new life as teachers and colleagues. In addition, at least once a month the entire staff of each school gathered for a research meeting involving the common observation of a teacher demonstrating a pedagogical technique followed by critical discussion and reflection. In many districts, the local education authorities also organized periodic district-wide meetings where several teachers provided demonstrations to a critical audience (Shimahara, 1995).

In the early decades of the modern education experience teachers were only expected to have a few more years of education than their students. By the end of the nineteenth century, most systems came to believe that primary teachers needed at least a high school education before they began their teacher training. Other reform ideas included the unification of the training for primary and secondary education (more subject matter for primary teachers, and more pedagogy for secondary teachers), the location of all training in teacher colleges, and the affiliation of teacher colleges with universities in order to upgrade academic rigour. These various reform ideas had differential success in the respective settings.

Posting and Rewarding the Teacher

The administrative framework of the respective modern systems had an important influence on the patterns of deployment and pay of teachers. In the centralized systems, teachers were recruited to the civil service and once thus recruited could in principle be assigned anywhere. In contrast, in the decentralized systems teachers were locally hired and could only be assigned within the schools of a limited locality. In the highly localized USA, local systems often had only schools at each academic level. In between these extremes were the quasi-centralized systems that depended on a large share of local finance.

In the large and rapidly expanding centralized systems of Japan and Russia, teaching came to be viewed as a career. In Japan, the expected period of tenure at a particular school was six years, with the rationale that teachers who spent a long period at a particular school might become too comfortable in that setting and lose their professional edge and motivation for continuous improvement. Newly recruited teachers might initially be given an assignment in a supportive environment so that they could develop their skills. Once the teachers gained experience, they might then be asked to move to more challenging schools in rural and out of the way places. Incentives of promotions and special allowances were associated with these moves. At a yet later stage, the teacher, after having paid his/her dues, might transfer back to a more attractive setting. Towards the latter stages of the teacher's career there were possibilities for promotion to the position of principal or to a supervisory position in a local administrative office. The Japanese and Russian systems placed the greatest stress on assigning qualified teachers to newly established schools in challenging settings. On the continent, where local governments shared in the finance of education, teachers were more likely to continue at a single school or to rotate within a limited geographical area. This centralized pattern of organizing a sequence of transfers for teachers was complemented by a practice of remuneration that started with a modest initial basic salary with steady increments for years of service. On top of this basic salary were various increments to reward hardship and administrative responsibility.

In contrast, in the decentralized systems each school or local system had the challenge of recruiting from the pool of those interested in teaching, some with little experience and others already engaged in teaching elsewhere. Especially in the USA, where owing to rapid population growth there was often a shortage of candidates, these market conditions created pressure to offer a generous starting salary. But once teachers were on the payroll and settled in their new locale, the local system was under little pressure to raise salaries. If teachers wished to move, they would personally have to shoulder the costs associated with relocation. And so in the decentralized systems salaries tended to peak early. Also, career options for teachers were limited as school management came to be treated as a separate class. In order to enter the administrative class, teachers had to obtain special training that would qualify them to move out of their class.

Contrasting these two situations, the decentralized system was under pressure to provide relatively generous starting salaries with limited increments thereafter, and the centralized system was more likely to provide modest starting salaries but to offer job tenure and the prospect of career promotions and salary increments. Because of these differences in job assignment and remuneration, teachers in the centralized system enjoyed greater incentives for continuing as teachers throughout their working life. And as length of service was associated with steady salary increases (contrasted to the early peak in the USA), the average pay in centralized systems tended to be higher. Contrasting the centralized systems, Germany stood out in the early nineteenth century for the generosity of its remuneration. France was possibly most generous in the late nineteenth century. Japan also had a policy of paying competitive salaries in order to reinforce the status of teachers and to attract recruits of high quality.

These differences in posting and pay persist down to the present day. The Organization for Economic Cooperation and Development (OECD) conducts an annual survey of patterns of remuneration for teachers in OECD and related nations. Table 7.1 summarizes several features of the remuneration package for the six societies discussed here.[5] As can be seen from this table, the USA and Germany stand out in terms of the amount offered as starting salaries. While US salaries are comparatively high, they are exceptionally low relative to GDP per capita and they are average in terms of annual increments. Also, US salaries make no differentiation between teaching at the primary and the secondary level. Japan and Russia also make no salary differentiation for primary and secondary level teaching, presumably reflecting the high value these systems place on primary education; in contrast, the European systems pay somewhat more to teachers at the secondary level. Japan stands out for the size of the career increment, the long period before salaries peak, and the size of the average salary (adjusted to Purchasing Power Parity (PPP)) relative to per capita income.

	Starting salary for primary school teachers	Salary after 15 years' experience for primary school	Maximum salary for primary school	Ratio of salary after 15 years' experience to starting salary for primary school	Ratio of salary after 15 years' experience to GDP per capita	Salary after 15 years for upper secondary general school	Ratio of salary of secondary school after 15 years to primary school salary after 15 years
England	22,428	35,487	35,487	1.58	1.48	38,279	1.08
France	20,199	27,172	40,091	1.35	1.17	30,124	1.11
Germany	31,213	37,905	41,021	1.21	1.52	43,881	1.16
Japan	22,670	42,820	54,663	1.89	1.62	42,845	1.00
Russia	3,735	3,735	3,735	1.00	0.54	3,735	1.00
United States	27,631	40,072	48,782	1.45	1.12	40,181	1.00

Table 7.1. Teachers' salaries. Source: OECD, 2002.

The Context of Teaching

The different institutional histories of the teaching position have created distinctive contexts for the practice of teaching. Several of these differences will be outlined below, and illustrated with contemporary data. Chapter 8 will consider how these contextual differences influence the practice of teaching.

In the centralized systems, most of the administrative decisions relating to finance, curriculum, personnel, and even student placement and promotion are handled by the central administration. Thus, the staff at the district and school level are able to focus primarily on teaching. For example, in several of these systems the principal is classified as a headteacher rather than as an administrator. At any rate, there is less duplication of administration at the different levels of the system. Partly for these reasons, as previously illustrated in Table 4.2, the proportion of educational personnel responsible for administration and support is less than is the case in the decentralized systems.

In the centralized systems, as the centre devotes much care to the preparation of the curriculum, the selection of textbooks, and the selection of related instructional materials, the task awaiting the teacher is highly specified – getting the material across according to the weekly schedule of the national syllabus. Given the clarity of the job, several of the more centralized systems authorize comparatively large class sizes and hence relatively high student–teacher ratios.

	Student Teacher Ratios for Primary/Lower Secondary/Upper Secondary	Teaching Time (hours per year) in Primary/Lower Secondary/Upper Secondary	Intended Instructional Time (hours per year) for Students who are 14 years old	Teacher working time per week in primary schools (hours per week)
England	22.5/17.4/12.4	930/814/814	972	32.5
France	19.6/12.9/12.7	892/634/589	979	27.0
Germany	21.0/16.4/12.4	783/733/685	921	38.5
Japan	21.2/17.1/14.1	658/507/492	875	44.0
Russia	17.6/11.5/11.5	686/686/686	945	n.d.
United States	16.3/16.8/14.5	958/964/943	980	33.2

Table 7.2. Student–teacher ratios and other indicators of teacher workload.
Source: OECD, 2001; 2002. Some figures were not available for the current period and thus estimates were made based on the practices of 'similar' systems. English figures for teaching time are estimated as an average of the reported times for Ireland and Scotland. The Japanese figures for teaching time are estimated from data reported for Korea.

Figure 7.2 suggests several other differences in working environment. Official working hours per week differ somewhat across the systems, with the French, English and American systems having the shortest working hours. However, when it comes to teaching time at the primary level, the English and American expectations are the highest, suggesting that the teachers in these two systems spend most of their time in the classroom whereas the teachers in the other systems are allocated more time at their workplace to prepare for their classroom duties.

Also, as one moves from the primary level to lower secondary and upper secondary, a gradient associated with increasing complexity of the subject content, in the Japanese and French systems the number of hours of teaching time sharply decreases; it moderately decreases in the English and German systems; and in the Russian system the expected hours of teaching time are relatively low from the primary level and stay that way through the secondary level. In contrast, in the US system, the expected hours of teaching time are comparatively high for all three levels with no decrease from primary to upper secondary. In contrast with the other core systems, the American system does not appear to make allowances in the time budget for teacher preparation. Finally, the American system is the only system where the expected teaching time for individual teachers is equal to the intended instructional time of students. In all of the other systems, there is a considerable gap – another indication that most of the core educational systems recognize the value of teacher preparation.

Barnard, in his inspection of nineteenth century European classrooms, was impressed with the energy of the German teacher (1851, p. 46). Yet Barnard also described the German teacher as a drillmaster who was primarily focused on covering the required material according to the official schedule with little concern for student learning difficulties. Broadfoot & Osborn (1988, pp. 270, 273, 277), in their comparative research on French and English classrooms, observe that the French teachers, like their German counterparts, have a narrow understanding of their task, focusing primarily on content that they communicate during school hours; the French teacher minimizes contact with parents and community leaders. In contrast, the English teachers are equally concerned with the cognitive learning and the overall socio-emotional development of their pupils; and the English teacher is more inclined to work with parents and the community.

The organizational intensity of the centralized systems (reflected in a more systematic preparation of curriculum and a clearer plan for the recruitment and training of teachers) is accompanied by the more ambitious nature of their intended curriculums and the greater success they have in conveying the curriculum to their pupils. In chapter 8, we will draw on International Association for the Evaluation of Educational Achievement (IEA) data to argue that at least certain of the centralized systems excel in curriculum implementation whereas the decentralized systems encourage more experimental approaches that have many beneficial results but tend also to result in the coverage of less content.

Teacher Associations

Teachers have many matters for discontent, some pedagogical and others relating to low pay and poor job security. Educational managers, like managers in other sectors, have opposed the efforts of teachers to organize into unions that advance their concerns. In small systems, managers can easily threaten to dismiss those teachers who consider organizing. In large systems, the managers can invoke civil service laws that often declare that public servants have limited rights to organize and strike. In centralized systems, the states often attempt to create teacher associations effectively managed by the state as a tactic for undercutting independent organizational initiatives. Thus, many obstacles have been placed in the path of teachers seeking to organize for the purpose of improving their working conditions. Nevertheless, in several settings independent associations did form with a focus on both educational and employment conditions.

The first major independent teacher association emerged in Germany in the 1840s, and its members participated in the revolution of 1848 that gave imperial Germany a brief encounter with liberal democratic institutions. While the government had opposed any association of teachers, many of the teachers employed in primary schools lacked job security or even a fixed salary. A variety of local protests finally led in the 1840s to most states granting contracts with guaranteed salaries. Encouraged by these gains, several of the local groups formed a national front to press for Pestalozzian educational reforms that would liberalize the character of primary education and allow the teachers to be educators rather than drill masters and to teach universal values rather than the particular values of the Church and State. The teachers proposed that the requirements for training be upgraded to place more emphasis on independent psychological and cultural judgements by the teacher, and thus to shift teacher education from normal schools to the university. These bold proposals received a favourable hearing with the new but short-lived revolutionary government. With the government's overthrow, the union was crushed and over 100 of the leaders were imprisoned. New associations were allowed some thirty years later, but these associations tended to enjoy limited recognition in the German context until after the Second World War. Even then, a divide persisted between the unions representing lesser teachers and those representing teachers in the esteemed *Gymnasiums* and universities.

Ironically, while England was relatively late in developing a modern concept of teacher status and training, it was among the first places where teachers combined in an independent association to present their demands to employers and the state. The National Union of Elementary Teachers was formed in September 1870, only one month after the promulgation of the Elementary Education Act. This union issued a policy statement with four requests of the newly created local school boards: (1) a standard contract of service, (2) freedom from compulsory extraneous duties such as training a choir or playing the church organ, (3) freedom from 'teacher interference' by managers in internal school affairs, and (4) adequate salaries. From the central government, the union demanded (1) more stringent requirements for entry into the teaching profession, (2) the official registration of qualified teachers, (3) the right of teachers for promotion to the independent Inspectorate, (4) the right of appeal against an Inspector's recommendation to cancel a teacher's certificate, (5) the restoration of an adequate superannuation or pension plan, and (6) the abolition of the system of payment by results. The remarkable currency of these issues can be illustrated by a comparison of the 1870 and 1965 policy goals of the same union. The only significant addition in 1965 was the demand for the right to a closed shop.[6]

In the USA teachers were slow to organize. Both the highly decentralized nature of American education and the resistance of public authorities slowed their efforts. Eventually two major associations were formed that placed a heavy emphasis on educational ideals relative to working conditions. But from the mid-twentieth century they came to place more emphasis on wage issues and eventually resorted to the tactic of strikes and other agitation to advance their concerns.

Perhaps the largest non-government union is found in Japan, thanks to the encouragement of the post-war US occupation government. This government initially encouraged the formation of labour unions as a means for strengthening democracy. Several teacher unions were formed that eventually combined in the All Japan Teachers' Union or Nikkyoso. But almost as soon as the Union was formed, the US government experienced the 'fall of China' and came to fear the threat of communism in Asia. Thus, the occupation government cooperated with the conservative Japanese government in curtailing the activities of Nikkyoso. Ultimately, the union was deprived of its right to collective bargaining (Duke, 1973), and thus could only focus its energies on pedagogical issues where it provided effective educational leadership for several decades.

In Soviet Russia the state formed an association of teachers and had no tolerance for an independent union.

Conclusion

This chapter has reviewed the emergence of the teaching profession in six national settings, including practices relating to recruitment, pay, deployment and professional development. Each of these settings faced distinctive challenges and early on developed its respective response. Germany is usually credited with devoting the most resources to the development of its teaching corps, followed perhaps by France and Japan. The two decentralized settings of England and the USA were least attentive: in the English case, this was due to a belief that good teachers are born rather than made and in the US case it was due to a rapidly expanding population of young people which placed a continuing challenge on educational managers to keep up with demand. It is argued here that the early approaches to addressing the different circumstances led to the establishment of different traditions that have tended to persist. Some challenge the effectiveness of the respective traditions, but these challenges have not usually led to big changes. Table 7.3 summarizes several of the characteristics of the respective traditions.

Country	Germany	France	England	USA	Japan	Russia
Ideal Teacher	Energetic, Good education, religious	Intellectually promising	Teacher is born; is an alumni of the school	Earnest, patient, tolerant	Serious, patriotic, collegial	Committed, able to learn, compassionate
Job Scope	Teach all subjects	Subject specific from the primary level	Teach all subjects	Teach all subjects	Teach all subjects	May teach all subjects for several grades
Level in Charge	Centre with local involvement	Centre with local involvement	Local government	Local government and school	Centre	Centre with local involvement
Demand	Good balance of supply and demand	Good balance of supply and demand	Good balance of supply and demand	Rapid population growth means short supply	Goal of rapid expansions necessitates continuous recruitment	Goal of rapid expansions necessitates continuous recruitment
Recruitment Timing	Candidate recruited and assigned to normal school	Candidate recruited and assigned to normal school	Candidate begins job, and later pursues training	Usually after candidate pays for and completes training	Candidate recruited and assigned to normal school	Candidate graduates from state approved course and is assigned a teaching job
Recruitment Criteria	Good student, moral character and religious devotion	Good education	Good education, Moral character,	Whoever is available, very partial to female candidates, moral character	Conservative values, good personalities, able to learn	Socialist values, good student, energetic
First Salary	Very competitive	Somewhat competitive	Somewhat competitive	Competitive	Very competitive	"Competitive"
Salary Increments	Steady increases for first 15 years or so	Steady increases for first 15 years or so	Modest	Minimal	Slow increases, but can rise to 2.5 times initial pay	Modest increases
Deployment	State reassigns, but tendency to relocate to better schools in local area	State reassigns, but tendency to relocate to better schools in local area	Some reassignment within LEA	Market	State reassigns every 6 years	State reassigns, but tendency to relocate to better schools in local area
Training	Pre-service by state	Lengthy pre-service by state	In-service by state	Usually pre-service on your own	Pre-service by state	Pre-service by state
Professional Development	Well developed in-service	Some in-service	Some in-service	Minimal	On-service by teachers themselves	Periodic in-service as well as on-service
Teacher Association	A state-run association	A state-run association	Strong national association with collective bargaining rights	A voluntary "professional" association	In pre-war, a state-run association	A state-run association

Table 7.3. A comparison of teacher characteristics in the early modern period.

Notes

[1] The government's additional measure of establishing advanced in-service teacher training colleges has not, however, been roundly applauded by the majority of teachers, who question the purpose and effectiveness of these institutions.

[2] Lynch & Plunket (1973, p. 19) remind us that these foundation patterns have remarkable resilience to resist cultural change.

[3] Many notable French intellectuals have held positions at the Grande Ecole Normale including Emile Durkheim.

[4] Barnard (1851) states that the first normal schools were established in 1775 in Prussia, 1808 in France and 1840 in England.

[5] The Russian data are presented as reported. Currently, as suggested by Table 7.1, the salaries of Russian teachers are low relative to others with similar educational qualifications. Interestingly, the Russian salary scale provides no increments for years of service but, rather, provides increments related to certification and the assumption of additional responsibilities. Teachers with greater lengths of service do tend to seek higher academic qualifications and to assume greater responsibility and so their actual salaried income may rise – but this is not automatically computed by years of service but, rather, by accomplishments.

[6] The National Union had 270,000 members in the 1970s and through its alliance with Labour was, at least for a while, an important political force.

CHAPTER 8

Teaching and Learning

It is time to reestablish the grand principle, which seems too much misunderstood, that children belong to the Republic, more than they do to their parents ... We must say to parents: We are not snatching them away from you, your children, but you may not withhold them from the influence of the nation. And what can the interests of an individual matter to us besides national interests? ... It is in national schools that children must suck republican milk. The Republic is one and indivisible; public instruction must also be related to this centre of unity.
(Danton, 1794)

In their curriculums, the modern nation states outlined the values and knowledge they expected future generations to learn. And they looked to the new cadre of teachers, recruited by the state and trained according to state-specified guidelines, to guide the development of young people so that they acquired the specified values and knowledge.

States, however, varied in their degree of determination. Revolutionary France was most explicit in its declaration of intent, but it failed to accompany this declaration with the necessary resources, especially for the early grades. Japan and Soviet Russia were the most committed to transforming young people from the first years of their primary education – their schools welcomed all young people regardless of gender, race, or class; their curriculums were the broadest in scope and possibly the most ambitious in content; and their teachers were the most thoroughly subjected to an ideologically 'correct' training experience. In England and imperial Germany the central state organized the formative educational experience in cooperation with local governments and communities, and this led to various compromises that diluted the control of the state and favoured a more diverse and less ambitious effort. In the USA the several states were responsible for this endeavour.

Some of those nations that allowed compromises in the early grades intensified their influence over education in the later grades. France and Germany were notable for the quality and intensity of their secondary schools, and the USA became renowned for the responsiveness of its collegiate and university education.

These differential starts, already reviewed in the earlier chapters, have had an enduring impact on the practice of education over the long history of modern education. In this chapter, we leap forward from the nature of education in the formative years to present some evidence on what, it is believed, is the lingering impact of the formative period. The main focus will be on primary education, though there will also be a brief look at some other issues.

The Learning Challenge

Much thought went into the early designs of the modern school experience, drawing on both practical experience and the emerging theories of human development of such notables as Comenius, Rousseau, Herbart, Pestalozzi, Fukuzawa, Piaget, Vygotsky, and others. While many issues were considered, four broad sets of questions stand out as differentiating this early thinking.

Ability versus effort. In pre-modern societies, most work was ascribed and young people were generally expected to assume the same work as their parents. Work differed in the nature of its intellectual demands, and to legitimate the differential assignment of workers, it came to be assumed that individuals differed in their inherent ability to think and learn. Those who inherited high positions were said to have greater ability, those in low positions were said to have limited ability. In other words, ability was passed on from generation to generation. The modern revolution tended to break down feudal hierarchies, and with this shift emerged a new way of considering potential: while an individual's social station might influence their potential, there was also the possibility through hard work to achieve new heights. Towards the end of the eighteenth century, Samuel Smiles composed a popular book titled *Self-Help* (1866) that featured biographies of a wide range of ordinary people who through extraordinary effort had been able to make successes of themselves in the new industrial society. Among those included was Benjamin Franklin, the son of a poor New England craftsman, who took up the occupation of printing and eventually was able to launch his own printing firm, realize affluence, and then turn to the worlds of science and diplomacy where he achieved remarkable results. Smiles's book, which achieved considerable popularity in his home country of England, became a best seller in Meiji Japan. Meiji leaders were known to encourage young people to 'be ambitious', and it was no accident that Japanese pedagogy came to place near total reliance on effort as opposed to ability as the key to learning. Similarly, Soviet pedagogues argued that individual achievements were socially determined; with the Revolution, the class obstacles to achievement had been removed, leaving accomplishment in school and work up to each individual's effort. Hess et al (1986) and Stephen & Stigler (1994, pp. 94-112) report that this distinction is still helpful for cross-cultural comparisons of pupil motivation to learn.

Cognitive intelligence versus holistic learning. Educational ideals in the medieval period focused on the development of the whole person as the faculties of that person were variously described – head and heart, mind and body, reason and will. Enlightenment thinking which was prevalent at the birth of modern education tended to focus more narrowly on reason or what currently is termed cognitive intelligence. And it might be said that the main thrust of French education has followed that lead. While the revolutionary leaders placed much stress on loyalty to the new republic, these ideological themes were gradually attenuated in the very demanding encyclopaedic curriculum of the modern French school. Both English and American schools initially stressed holistic education, but at least in the USA a series of 'Church versus State' legal decisions led to a narrowing of pedagogical objectives. In contrast, Japan's Meiji leaders were convinced of the importance of fusing a modern scientific curriculum with a firm foundation of 'Eastern values'. Moreover, they believed in the importance of physical strength and aesthetic sensibility and included all of these themes in the new curriculum. The Soviet Russian educators also favoured the development of the whole person in their schools (Bronfenbrenner, 1970).

Documentary versus rhetorical exposition. Nakayama Shigeru (1984) argues that the West from the time of Plato favoured a rhetorical approach to learning in contrast with the East Asian disposition towards documentation. To develop his argument, Nakayama points to the example of Socrates spending his days engaged in sophisticated arguments with his contemporaries, with his students recording these arguments for posterity. In contrast, in Imperial China the great minds were recognized for their written expositions on politics, art, religion and other matters. Nakayama notes that Western universities well into the twentieth century subjected candidates to oral examinations as a condition for graduation, whereas in China the famous test for the Imperial Civil Service was a three-day written examination. Nakayama goes on to suggest that the early education in the respective areas has developed in such a manner as to prepare young people for these culminating experiences. Thus, he posits that the East Asian school places greater stress on written exposition, and the Western school places greater stress on oral exposition. This differential stress is presumably deeply ingrained in the respective cultures and shapes the expectations of young people as they participate in schooling, the Asian child being more comfortable with writing and the Western child more comfortable with speaking. Within the West, the commitment to the oral tradition varies, being most firm in Soviet Russia, where oral examinations are still common in the schools and universities, and England, where universities place a high value on oral tutorials, and perhaps least firm in the USA.

Language versus logic. The Western educational tradition through the Middle Ages continued to favour the classical texts, with their extended logical arguments on such matters as the conditions for ideal government, the proof that God exists, or the possibility that a thousand angels could stand on the tip of a pin. The task of education was to provide young people with the necessary tools so that they could eventually understand and contribute to these arguments. Early learning then featured a progressive exposure to argumentation and proof in such subjects as logic, grammar, rhetoric, geometry, and so on. The good mind was the mind well honed in reason. Yet there were those in the West who questioned the singular focus on logic, arguing that the young mind needed to acquire a foundation in essential language skills so as to understand the broader concepts that might be featured in arguments or other forms of discourse. The stress on the acquisition of language skills emerged relatively late in the modern period and is attributed to such thinkers as Piaget and Vygotsky. In theory, the stress on language skills need not be seen as an alternative to the stress on essentialism. But many educators have tended to frame arguments along those lines. And similarly, educational systems tend to lean in one direction or the other: the Russian system places a strong emphasis on language skills, and most systems are moving in that direction, except especially the French system.

Country	Ability/effort	Cognitive/whole	Rhetoric/document	Logic/language
Germany	Ability	Middle	Middle	Logic
France	Ability	Cognitive	Rhetoric	Logic
England	Ability+	Whole	Rhetoric	Middle
USA	Ability	Middle	Middle	Middle
Japan	Effort	Whole	Document	Language
Russia	Effort	Whole	Rhetoric	Language

Table 8.1. A comparison of the learning and pedagogical assumptions of the core systems.

Table 8.1 seeks to summarize these generalizations concerning learning potential and the best strategies for promoting learning of the core societies. In so far as these placements fit the respective settings, it can be said that there are distinct differences in the learning assumptions and strategies. These differences could easily lead to different learning outcomes. Before examining the outcomes, it will be helpful to consider some of the resources and processes the core nation states mobilized for their educational projects.

The School as the Central Life Experience?

In pre-modern society, the home was always an important teacher. Most social positions were hereditary – children succeeded their parents and thus learned the necessary skills for life in the home. Rousseau in *Emile* romanticized home education, arguing that this setting could provide the most natural environment for healthy child education. For more advantaged families, the home continued to be the key place for education well into the nineteenth century. Privileged children were educated by tutors or in local dame schools. Parallel to the home was the real world and the lessons learned from peers, relatives, and members of the broader community. Many pre-modern communities also organized formal youth groups to provide opportunities for entertainment and education during the adolescent years.

The founders of the early modern schools were aware of these competing influences and introduced various measures to limit their influence, or alternatively, to make the school a 'total society' (Goffman, 1962) monopolizing the energies of young people. All children were expected to come to school on a regular basis, and parents might be charged with criminal negligence if their children did not comply.

- Parents and outsiders were not allowed on the school grounds in the modern school, except at specified times.
- Children were expected to wear uniforms to symbolize the distinct setting of the school.
- Schools had long hours, and also assigned homework to occupy children after school.
- Schools provided a co-curriculum of clubs featuring sports, music, and other activities to keep children attached to school life.
- In some cases, schools were residential institutions and visits from outsiders were banned or curtailed.

Societies varied in their emphasis on these various practices. Possibly, the stress on school participation was most extreme in nationalistic and late-developing societies – revolutionary France, late nineteenth-century Germany, and the late Meiji era of Japan when the nation became involved in empire-building wars with Russia and China.

Within a society the practices varied over time. For example, in Japan these practices intensified over the 1930s as Japan began to extend its imperial ambitions to China and South-east Asia. Ironically, in the USA, these practices appear to be more intense today than at any previous time: the number of school days is being increased, with some school systems discussing year-round schooling, children are beginning to wear uniforms, co-curricular activities are expanding, homework is increasing. US practice is only now beginning to equal the level of intensity of other advanced societies

Within any society the prevalence of these practices is likely to vary by school. For example, the pace of school learning, the number of required hours in school, the variety of co-curricular activities, and the amount of homework picks up as the grade levels advance. And the intensity is likely to be greater at vocational schools, normal schools, and military schools relative to schools in the academic stream.

The Impact of the School

It is sometimes argued that the relative impact of the school is at least in part related to its totalism – this simple idea has been the inspiration for collecting data on the number of hours per year children are in class in a school. Table

6.3 presents some comparative information from a recent Organisation for Economic Cooperation and Development (OECD) survey. According to this survey, children in the six core societies spend about the same amount of time in actual classroom instruction.[1] On the other hand, there are significant differences in the amount of time children spend on instruction at supplementary schools and on homework.[2]

Practice	France	England	USA	Japan	Russia
Lesson Length	Varies	Varies	Varies	45 minutes	40 minutes
Getting Settled	1 minute	10 minutes	10 minutes	1 minute	1 minute
Sequencing Instruction	Long lesson introduction, sequence of episodes involving both seatwork and exposition, single task, abrupt conclusion	Often a long session introduction on procedure, short lesson intro, unitary task or series of episodes, conclusion	Long session introduction with loose connection to short lesson intro, often a long unitary task, short conclusion	Strong introduction, student work on problem (often in groups), presentations, conclusion	Strong introduction, sequence of episodes, conclusion
Task demand	Emphasis on acquiring new knowledge and applying existing knowledge	Emphasis on practice, applying existing knowledge	Emphasis on practice, applying existing knowledge	Emphasis on acquiring new knowledge and applying and existing knowledge	Emphasis on acquiring new knowledge and applying and restructuring existing knowledge
Learning Activities	Talk to class, work from blackboard, write at desk, answer questions, read silently	Read silently, read to teacher, work from worksheet, write at desk	Work from worksheets, write at desk, collaborate in groups	Answer questions, Write at blackboard, talk to class, collaborate in group, work from worksheet	Answer questions, assess peers, talk to class, work from blackboard and text
Time on task	High	Moderate	Low	Very high	Very high
Instructional Pace	Fast	Slow	Slow	Fast	Very fast
Classroom Assessment	Leans to oral	Mixed	Mixed	Written	Oral

Table 8.2. Pedagogical practice in five societies. Source: Alexander (2001), pp. 297, 298, 349, 354, 416, 400, 373; inferences for Japan were made from Stigler & Hiebert (1999).

The OECD survey focuses on children in particular school grades. Depending on the logic of a system, certain grades are more important than others. For example, in the Japanese system, the twelfth grade is the critical year, as towards the end of that year young people write their entrance examinations; another critical year is the ninth grade, as preparation is made for the high school entrance examinations. In the American high school the eleventh grade is perhaps the most critical year, as that is the time young people prepare for college. In England, the tenth grade may be most important, as young people prepare for their General Certificate of Secondary Education examinations. And in France, the critical year may be the ninth year of schooling, as young people compete for places in the top *lycées*. It can be expected that young people tend to buckle down to more intensive study at these critical points, and a survey directed at a particular grade may not catch the point of greatest intensity across the several systems.

Also, the hours young people are involved in instruction (or homework) is not necessarily equated with the quality of those hours. Is the instruction perceived as interesting and challenging? Are the teachers successful in communicating the curriculum to their students? Robin Alexander (2001) has recently reported his findings from a five-country study of culture and pedagogy that provides valuable insight on the quality of instruction in primary schools.[3] Table 8.2 provides a highly condensed summary of several of Alexander's findings.

At the risk of oversimplification, it can be said that the Japanese, Russian, and to a lesser degree the French teachers have the most predictable routines: the length of their class shows little variation, they get started promptly, and their sequencing of instruction is consistent. The Japanese and Russian teachers are most notable for providing equal attention to all of their students and for having more time on task. The Japanese and the American teachers are more likely to encourage group work. Reflecting the common continental influence, the French and Russian teachers are most similar in terms of the tasks they demand; also, the teachers from these two settings are most likely to rely on oral assessments whereas the Japanese teachers are most likely to rely on written assessments. The English and American teachers stand out for providing a less predictable classroom routine, for giving more attention to individual students, and for recognizing creativity in their assessment of pupils.

Alexander argues that these pedagogical differences are anchored in the distinctive cultural traditions of the respective educational settings. He is particularly taken by the Russian (and to a lesser degree the French) pedagogy that he compares to a musical symphony, with such features as form, tempo, melody, harmony, polyphony, and counterpoint. Alexander speculates:

> *It is hardly a coincidence that Central Europe has been a centre of gravity for both musical and pedagogical form. It is not implausible to suggest that cultures which responded to the imperatives of form in realms as diverse as music, art, literature, drama, architecture, philosophy, mathematics and science, might have applied that consciousness to education, a contingent field in which many of the great figures have had a more than passing interest. (2001, p. 318)*

185

Additionally, we suggest that the more focused and deliberate approach in the Russian and Japanese classrooms follows from the belief of teachers that all children can learn if approached with an effective instructional format and allowed to do their best. This belief contrasts with the belief of the English and American teachers that learning is shaped by inherent ability, and that much time has to be devoted to reaching out to each individual student. Also, the strong reliance of Russia on oral assessment and of Japan on written assessment reflects the lingering presence of the respective rhetorical and documentary traditions.

The above comparisons are for instruction at the primary level, where the Japanese and Russian traditions launched their representative schools. As children move to higher grades, it is likely that the comparisons will yield a different picture. Especially on the continent, it can be predicted that the pace of instruction will accelerate along with an increase in time on task and a more careful sequencing of instruction.

| | Mathematics/Science Achievement Means | | |
	4th grade	8th grade	12th grade
Germany		509/531	465/497
France		538/498	557/487
UK	513/551	506/552	
USA	545/565	500/534	442/480
Japan	597/574	605/571	
Russia		535/538	542/481
Average	529/524	513/516	501/500

Table 8.3. Comparison of TIMMS achievement means for different grade levels by country.

The International Association for the Evaluation of Educational Achievement (IEA) studies provide some evidence of these shifts in quality with the progression of grade levels. As illustrated in Table 8.3, Japanese young people are exceptionally strong in academic achievement at the sixth grade level. They continue at a high level through the high school years. However, the children on the European continent narrow the gap by the twelfth grade level. American children get off to a good start in the primary grades but their comparative performance drops by the eighth grade and takes a further decline by the twelfth grade, though the expectation would be for them to make significant gains over the collegiate years.

The Rise of Other Teachers

While the modern school sought to capture the hearts and minds of young people, these young people had at least one foot in the other worlds of family, church and community. With the shift of the population to urban settings, other educational influences emerged, including the daily newspaper and popular books. From the 1930s, radios were widely prevalent in the core societies, and, as Daniel Lerner (1958) reminds us, by the 1950s they were also widely available in developing societies and with their hot messages serving as one of the most important educators. Currently, the press and radio are being surpassed by television and the Internet. Thus, with the passage of time the diversity of alternative teachers has increased, and so probably has their influence on the education of young people relative to the modern school.

The impact of these other teachers is likely to vary within a given society. Generally, the affluent have greater access to the other teachers. Also, the older a child the more access they have to a diverse range of outside influences. Figure 8.1 presents the average salience (self-reported) of key outside influences by age, for a sample of Japanese young people (Cummings, 1987, p. 25). According to these youth, home influences are salient in the early years, school in the first years of primary education, and friends, television and the press after that.

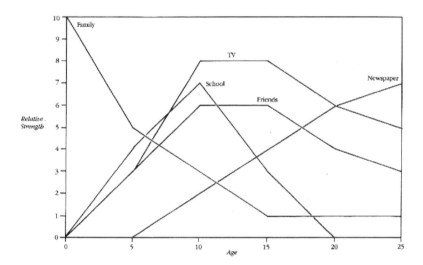

Figure 8.1. The influence of different teachers.

In the modern society, outside of the school there are many teachers available to influence the education of young people. These other teachers are often perceived as competitors with the school, but that need not be the case. Parents often serve as resources to help young people master their schoolwork. Additionally, particularly in East Asia, a large variety of supplementary schools have been established to help young people with their schoolwork as well as with the development of other important skills. In Japan, these supplementary schools initially focused on such areas as

187

calligraphy, music and art. But, as growing numbers of children encountered difficulty in keeping up with the fast-paced school lessons, these supplementary schools also came to focus on remedial and enrichment instruction (Russell, 1994). Today, four out of every five Japanese school-aged children attend these schools at some point over the course of their formal education. The public school system recognizes the essential contribution of the supplementary schools in helping young people learn. Such supplementary schools are also common in Korea, Taiwan and Hong Kong. Just as parents and supplementary schools reinforce the lessons of the schools, so may friends, the press and the media.

Evidence of the Influence of Other Teachers on Learning

Over the last four decades, an important comparative effort has been undertaken by such entities as IEA and OECD to determine how much young people learn as well as to identify the influences on their learning. Much attention has been given to the relative standing of nations in terms of the average academic achievement of their young people. Several other patterns in the findings should be highlighted:

Schooling is most important in the early years of the modern state. The modern state, especially in its foundation period, devotes much effort to ensuring that schools capture the attention of young people. In the first rounds of these studies, conducted from the 1960s to the 1980s, it was found that 'school effects' were relatively greater in newly independent developing nation states when compared to the mature industrial nations (Heyneman & Loxley, 1982).

The effects of the home and other teachers tend to increase as a society matures and develops. In a given society, the relative influence of home and other effects becomes greater over time. In mature industrial societies, the influence of home and other effects generally tends to be at least as great as that of school effects (OECD, 2002). In the few studies that have looked at mature industrial societies over time, there is some indication that the influence of home and other effects increases (Cummings, 1980). A recent comparison of the findings for developing countries in the early 1980s and the mid-1990s reports a dramatic increase in the magnitude of home and other effects over this twenty-year period (Baker et al, 2002).

Evidence of the Influence of Institutional Patterns on Learning

The aforementioned studies have also been used to draw a variety of inferences about the impact of schools on learning. The following are a few examples of the likely links between the institutional framework of modern educational systems and the patterns of learning outcomes revealed in these studies.

Gap between the intended and the achieved curriculum. There are substantial differences in the gap between the intended and the achieved curriculum. In the initial studies of this issue, careful measures were made of the proportion of international test items that were included in each nation's curricula, the proportion of those items that teachers said they actually taught in their schools (sometimes referred to as the 'opportunity to learn'), and the proportion of the items teachers taught that students actually learned (Livingstone, 1986). The gaps were relatively small in the Japanese system, intermediate in the French and English systems, and relatively large in the American system – differences that might be due to the relative complexity of implementing a curriculum over several levels of a highly decentralized society. More recently, this same issue has been examined with new methods and has yielded essentially the same conclusion. Singapore and Japan stand out as highly systematized with modest gaps (Schmidt, 2001). The USA is very weak in systematization and has substantial gaps between the intended and achieved curriculum. And so centralism and systematization seem related to opportunity to learn and in turn to actual learning.

Gender difference in curriculum achievement. In most subject areas, boys tend to achieve slightly higher scores than girls. These differences are especially evident in the sciences at the secondary level. The gender gap is largest in physics, least in biology (Figure 8.2). Similarly, of the various sciences courses, girls are most likely to study biology and least likely to study physics. Indeed, in several societies girls are more likely than boys to study biology.[4] The overall pattern of results suggests that the gender gap is least in socialist societies where gender segmentation is less common and greatest in England and Western Europe were there remain many vestiges of gender discrimination.

'Within-school' variation in achievement. Nations that assume effort is the key to learning and that do not stream children by ability tend to have lower within-school variation in achievement. For example, in the recent OECD (2002, p. 83) study of reading literacy, within-school variation was lowest in the East Asian nations of Japan and Korea and the East European nations of Poland and Hungary.

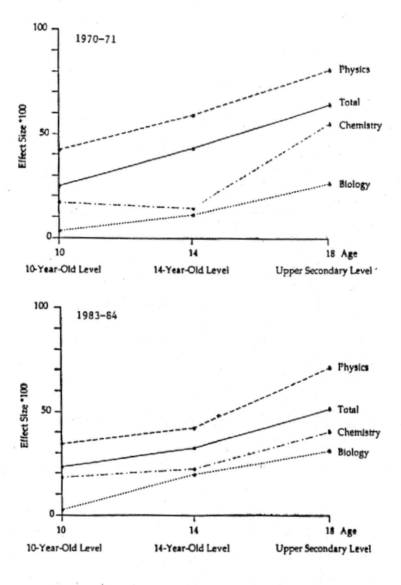

Note: The difference recorded is called an *effect size* and is obtained from:

$$\text{Effect size} = \frac{(\text{boys score} - \text{girls score}) \times 100}{\text{pooled standard deviation across countries}}$$

Figure 8.2. Sex differences in science scores and subscores at different ages, 1983-84.

'*Between-school*' *variation in achievement*. Nations with more centralized systems tend to allocate resources more equally across school districts and across schools within those districts. Thus, it is not surprising that the between-school variation in these systems is relatively small. On the other hand, to the extent that these systems establish numerous tracks and/or segments, the variation between schools increases (OECD, 2002, p. 83). Scandinavian countries tend to combine centralization and minimal tracking and thus their between-school variation is relatively modest. Continental and Eastern European systems influenced by the polytechnic tradition for the secondary level tend to have relatively large between-school variation, at least at the secondary level.

Average national scores. The finding that has received the greatest attention is the relative standing of different societies. Generally, East Asian societies achieve the highest average scores, especially in the subject areas of mathematics and science. East European societies such as Finland and Poland also often achieve impressive results. Continental European countries tend to fall in the next tier, with their scores somewhat less impressive in the lower grades and more impressive in the upper grades (as noted earlier in this chapter). Among mature industrial societies, average scores for the USA and England tend to be comparatively low. This overall pattern of differences in average scores is consistent with the argument of this book that the East Asian and East European educational approaches stress learning in the early grades, the continental European approaches stress learning at the secondary level, and the US approach stresses tertiary education.

Conclusion

This chapter has explored various dimensions of the learning environment. There is much important research under way exploring differences in the classroom experience across societies, and this research has provoked an interesting argument about the relative salience of cultural/institutional factors (LeTendre et al, 2001 vs Anderson-Levitt, 2002). Given the preponderance and persistence of national differences in learning environments over the entire modern era, this discourse is most puzzling. How else can such differences be accounted for than by reference to the link of culture and pedagogy? Perhaps the greatest weakness of these debates has been their overly narrow focus on schooling. Learning is a function both of the school and other settings. The presence of multiple teachers was recognized from the earliest days of the modern school. And so in future studies of learning there needs to be a broader perspective that considers the role of all of the teachers.

Notes

[1] It should be noted that the survey makes some questionable assumptions. It observes that the class period in Japanese schools is much shorter than in American schools. It also discounts the time in school devoted to club and other co-curricular activities.

[2] Again, the OECD figures on homework are quite different from those reported in other surveys such as Lapointe (1989).

[3] Of the six core societies that are the focus of this book, Alexander's study included France, England, Russia, and the USA. Stevenson & Stigler (1992) as well as Stigler & Hiebert (1999) provide parallel information that enables comparable estimations of several features of Japanese education. Germany was also discussed in the latter volume, but as the information was less complete, I decided against making comparative inferences about German pedagogical practice.

[4] In Hungary, girls are also more likely to study chemistry.

CHAPTER 9

Evaluation and Examinations[1]

It is essential to accurately classify students according to their learning stage. Inaccurate classification will create an obstacle to learning progress. In order to advance from a lower grade to a higher grade, students should be required to pass examinations for the subjects they have finished. Unless they pass these examinations, they should not be upgraded. Those who fail should stay in their present grade and thoroughly review the subject matter. Monthly tests should be given for each subject, and the seating order in the class should be determined based on the results. In this way, the students will study harder and look forward to progress in each subject and better placement. (Morokuzu Nobuzumi, First Principal of the Tokyo Normal School, Indispensable Book for Elementary Teachers, 1873)

Evaluation in education assumes diverse forms and serves many purposes. The procedures for evaluating pupils and other participants in education systems have become progressively elaborated since at least the middle of the nineteenth century to the point where they now command substantial resources. Upwards of 10 per cent of instructional time is devoted to such procedures in many systems, and as much as 10 per cent of educational expenditure may go – either directly or indirectly – for evaluation.

Educators' evaluation activities are of many kinds. Policy-makers appraise the school's learning goals to determine whether such goals are the ones most suitable for the society and for the learners' aptitudes. Administrators assess the school's management system to decide how effectively it promotes educational outcomes. Governing boards appraise the sources of school funds to judge if those are the most appropriate sources. The personnel who operate the education system – teachers, headmasters, school psychologists, support staff – are also evaluated to determine how well they perform their functions.

However, among all the types of assessment, the most frequent and pervasive is that which focuses on the learners. Students are evaluated to determine how much they know (knowledge), how efficiently they perform (skills), what convictions they hold (values, attitudes), and how much potential they have for further learning (aptitudes). Assessments of student performance are often categorized as either formative or summative evaluations. Formative evaluation is the kind continuously conducted during the students' learning activities. It consists of day-by-day teacher judgements of how well pupils are mastering each step of the learning process. The resulting information is typically used to guide teachers' decisions as they help students overcome learning difficulties and as they determine when students are ready for new learning tasks. Among the techniques used for deriving formative information are: written tests that accompany a textbook, teacher-made quizzes, standardized tests, workbook exercises, oral questions that students answer during group discussion, pupils' essays, the teacher's judgements of products students create (charts, graphs, maps, models, exhibits, experiments), observations of pupils' performance (their use of a computer, their skill in games, their participation in group work), and more.

Summative evaluation, on the other hand, refers to assessment conducted at the end of a lengthy period of study, such as at the end of a semester, of a year, or of a major segment of the schooling hierarchy (the end of elementary school, or of junior secondary school, or of senior secondary school). Information derived from summative evaluation is typically used for deciding what final mark or grade a student deserves, whether the student should receive a diploma or certificate, and where the student will go for the next stage of his or her schooling.

Reviewing all of the foregoing facets of educational evaluation is far beyond the scope of this chapter. Thus, one aspect that is currently of key international interest has been selected for analysis. That aspect is the use of summative evaluation – in the form of written or oral examinations – for guiding decisions about the next step in students' school careers. Although the focus will be primarily on examinations, some passing attention will also be directed to the assessment of the value of educational innovations, the assessment of teacher and school performance, and the generation of information to help decision-makers plan ahead (Bloom et al, 1971, p. 7; Lewy, 1981, p. 4).

While evaluation pervades the educational system, many of its characteristics become most evident through the role it plays in shaping the linkage of schools and universities (Clark, 1984), and so the major focus of this chapter will be on that transition. Some recent studies tend to look for commonalities in national evaluative styles (Eckstein & Noah, 1989), but there are also marked differences. And these differences in evaluative styles provide some striking revelations of how education systems vary. Some national systems evaluate selected subject matter areas or skills, while others focus on a broad range. Evaluative procedures take many forms, ranging from oral to written assessments, from predetermined to open formats, from pre-test to post-test, from aptitude to achievement. Similarly, the institutional locus of evaluations varies widely: in some systems national governments supervise evaluation, in others special independent examining bodies perform this function, while in yet others teachers have extensive responsibilities.

In this chapter we seek to understand (1) why evaluation has become progressively more prominent in educational systems; (2) what the major variations in evaluation are; (3) how this variation can be explained; and (4) what the educational implications are. The discussion begins with a brief review of the history of examinations, then describes how this history helps explain the present-day role of examinations in Germany, France, England, the USA, Japan, and Russia. The chapter closes with comparative reflections on systems of evaluation, and speculation about what might be expected in this field over the years ahead.

The Origins of Examinations

Rigorous forms of evaluation of formal educational achievement are generally believed to have first been developed in China by the Sui (AD 589-618) emperors (Miyazaki, 1981). Prior to that, during the Han period, informal means of evaluating the qualifications of members of aristocratic families had been employed to select those who would assume key posts in the imperial household. But in the earlier evaluations, which tended to focus on attributes of character and style, relatively little attention was focused on specific content taught in schools.

Two major factors account for the introduction of formal examinations by the Sui emperors. Perhaps most important was a tactical need, in that the Sui were outsiders attempting to establish control over an entrenched aristocratic system, and so they developed a means of selecting officials that would provide legitimacy for the new ruling group. Recognizing the high prestige of the Confucian intellectual heritage, the Sui leaders hit upon the idea of testing aspirants in terms of their knowledge of this prestigious heritage. They reasoned that the aristocrats would have no special advantage in these tests over other candidates from, for example, their own society. The crucial determinants of success would be natural ability and effort in mastering the prescribed subject matter.

Secondly, as Shigeru Nakayama (1984) observes, China, by virtue of the special characteristic of its intellectual heritage, was uniquely in a position to devise a formal examination. Nakayama suggests that two major approaches have emerged for the development of knowledge, the documentary and the rhetorical. In the rhetorical tradition, which was characteristic of the Judaeo-Hebraic tradition and received its highest development in classical Greece, knowledge was developed through verbal assertions and argumentation. The standard of proof was success in convincing a group of peers of the soundness of a particular viewpoint. Plato's *Dialogues* are an example of this form of knowledge creation; significantly, the *Dialogues* were written down by Plato's students long after their original presentation. The rhetorical tradition did not depend on a written record. In contrast was China's documentary tradition where knowledge was developed and recorded on paper rather than expressed in

195

debate. Additions to knowledge made reference to antecedents either directly or through symbolism. The core documents in the Confucian tradition were the five classics and the four books. The later books in this corpus made consistent reference to their precedents as they explored new themes. Professional scholars working in such areas as medicine, astronomy, or even poetry observed the same discipline.

There are extensive debates on the relative merits of these two forms of knowledge development (Needham, 1956; Lach, 1977; Boorstin, 1983). Regardless of the conclusions, undisputed is the much earlier development in China of a flexible writing system and an extensive body of recorded knowledge. Thus, China was in a position, at a much earlier time than the West, to develop written knowledge-based examinations.

The Chinese examination system was designed to test the pupil's comprehensive mastery of all this written material. Aspirants were expected to prepare for the examinations on their own in private schools run by able scholars or through private tutorials. It has been estimated that an exceptional youth who could memorize 200 new characters a day (the equivalent of a page in this book) might be prepared for the first round of examinations by the age of fifteen; most aspirants took much longer, continuing their studies even into their thirties. A system of regional testing was devised to screen out poorly prepared students. Those who survived these hurdles were invited to travel to the capital city to take the highest examination over a continuous period of three days. The candidates' answers were evaluated by a special examining board appointed by the emperor, focusing their appraisal on correct referencing, literary quality, and penmanship. Each time the examination was offered, a fixed number of aspirants were accepted into the imperial bureaucracy.

Examinations in the West

There are various accounts concerning the origins of examinations in the West (Montgomery, 1965; Durkheim, 1969; Amano, 1990). An enduring theme in Western societies, drawing from the rhetorical tradition, has been the reliance on oral and other less-structured forms of evaluation, such as recommendations and practical achievements. For example, in continental Europe, most secondary school-leaving examinations have an oral component; and the interview is a major component of evaluation for entry to top English universities. Through the seventeenth century, evaluation in the West relied almost exclusively on such criteria. But from about that time, written examinations became progressively more prominent, and it is generally assumed that this was due to admiration for the Chinese example.

It is not altogether clear how the West became aware of the Chinese system. For example, Matteo Ricci, a Jesuit missionary, was said to have provided glowing descriptions of this system in the letters he sent from his China post. His letters and subsequently the prominence of Matteo Ricci in the Jesuit order are pointed to as factors behind the introduction of rigorous examinations into the Jesuit schooling system from the early eighteenth century (Durkheim, 1969). The quality of Jesuit schooling, it has been suggested, eventually led to imitation by other educational institutions.

Ikuo Amano (1990), who has written the most comprehensive study of the role of examinations in modern education, suggests that Prussia was the first European society to rely on such assessments for the selection of public officials. From as early as 1748 Prussia depended on examinations for filling all government administrative posts. University education became a prerequisite for seeking a government office, thus leading to competition for university entrance (Ringer, 1974). In 1788 the *Abitur* examination was introduced as a means for determining who was qualified to graduate from the middle schools (and thus have claim to a place at the university). Over the succeeding years, examinations were introduced at lower levels The German example was the inspiration for selective reforms in other nations of continental Europe during the late eighteenth and early nineteenth centuries.

Another account (Montgomery, 1965) suggests that the British East India Company admired the Chinese examination system, and decided from the early nineteenth century to introduce a similar method for the selection of its local-hire personnel. Eventually the system was elaborated to become the basis for all new appointments to the East India Company. And following this example, in 1872 the British government introduced competitive examinations for all civil service appointments.

Amano observes that, while there are various accounts of the origins of examinations, what stands out is the pervasive interest from about the middle of the nineteenth century in examinations as a means of social selection. Thus, he calls this period the Age of Examinations. The key background factor in this era is the emergence of large public bureaucracies to collect revenues and administer various services. These bureaucracies sought effective means of selecting staff. One after another, they turned to some form of examination for this purpose. Examinations were also used for entry to other important positions, including those in medicine, the judiciary, and even the clergy. In some areas, the professions introduced examinations ahead of the civil service. But especially from this period, the examinations for entry to the professions became more rigorous, and often the state played some role in the administration of the examinations.

Because schools had been the traditional source for supplying staff to the bureaucracies, the schools themselves began to introduce examinations, in part, at least, as a means of preparing students for the official examinations. There are interesting national peculiarities in the structure of school examinations of that time which persist in considerable degree down to the present, as demonstrated in the following examples.

The German Pattern

In Germany, which pioneered in the introduction of civil service and professional examinations, students move at a relatively early age into one of several tracks. Currently, these are the *Hauptschule* (main school), leading to terminal vocational training at about age eighteen, the *Gymnasium*, which provides preparation for universities, and the *Realschule*, which directs youth to intermediate positions in the occupational hierarchy (Teichler, 1985, p. 46). Once students are in these tracks, there are relatively few examinations until their conclusion; and, even at that point, the pressure of the examinations is not insufferable, for there is reasonable balance in the number of openings in the next respective stages (Teichler & Sanyal, 1982). The *Abitur*, which covers only certain subjects, is the examination administered at the conclusion of the *Gymnasium*. Students who pass this test are entitled to continue studies at their local university, and in principle are qualified to attend any university throughout Germany.

The French Pattern

In France there are frequent examinations at every stage over many subject matter areas, and many pupils fail, with the result that they have to repeat grades and even drop out.[2] For those experiencing difficulty, various terminal vocational educational opportunities are provided. Those who endure the gauntlet of academic tests enter a *lycée* where they can pursue either a science or arts course (Neave, 1985a, p. 24). At the conclusion of each year, students are required to take year-end tests, and the failure of a test in any subject area necessitates the repetition of the entire school year. At the completion of the *lycée*, students are tested with both a written and an oral examination as a condition for further study. In contrast with Germany, where the universities are paramount, the most prestigious concluding step to educational careers in France is one of the *grandes écoles*, which specialize in fields of practice, such as engineering, finance, or education. Only a small proportion of *lycée* graduates are able to gain entry to these institutions. Relative to other European systems, the French system is viewed as highly competitive and singularly shaped by the series of selective examinations devised by the Central Ministry of Education.

The English Pattern

England was a late entrant to the Age of Examinations. England's great universities and her well-known public schools were for the benefit primarily of the upper classes, and many of the places in these institutions were reserved for the descendants of these special groups. Under such circumstances, there was natural resistance to testing the qualifications of students. However, in the mid-eighteenth century, the University of

Cambridge introduced an honours examination to confer recognition on those students who applied themselves with special vigour. Oxford followed suit in 1800, and this practice was also emulated in several of the public schools.

In contrast to Prussia and France, schooling in England was much more decentralized, and the state had a minimal role in the popular educational system, which was quite diverse. To bring some unity to this system, in 1861 the state proposed a special national test, with provision that local governments whose students did well would receive certain subsidies. Thus, a pattern was introduced linking state involvement in local educational systems with the examination performance of the students of these systems. And so in England examinations were introduced from above as a means of promoting quality in certain subject areas offered by the schools of a highly decentralized system and not as part of a monolithic programme for realizing a fully integrated system under the control of the centre. This same principle was manifest in later examination reforms. Especially noteworthy after the Second World War was the 11 plus examination, which schools were encouraged to use as a means for selecting young adolescents for entrance to the secondary schools which provided university preparatory courses (Young, 1958). As the secondary school system expanded, it became necessary to devise a means for selecting individuals for those university places not allocated on the basis of heredity. In response, the major universities formed examining boards, which devised a series of subject-specific examinations. These became known as the ordinary examinations (O levels) and advanced examinations (A levels). Students could take as many of these as they wished, but a high performance in at least three A levels came to be essential for advancement to university studies.

The reforms associated with the Education Reform Act of 1988 are, at least in the views of some, a further extension of the traditional principle of limited state intervention, with reward tied to evaluation (Johnson, 1989). The main difference in the current round is that the state has prescribed a fixed national curriculum, and the state's evaluation will focus on the success of schools in implementing that curriculum as measured by student performance in national examinations tied to this curriculum.

Evaluation in the USA

Until the middle of the nineteenth century, American education was largely modelled on the English pattern, with a minimum of formal evaluation of student performance. However, as a new nation that was conscious of its backwardness, America was highly alert to the latest trends on the continent of Europe, including the use of written examinations. Thus, as early as 1850 systematic testing began to appear in the school systems of large urban areas, and in 1865 in the state of New York the Regents Examinations were introduced along the lines of the German *Abitur*. But these examinations were peculiar to New York.

Two other traditions that emerged during this period had a more enduring influence on the selection of college students. According to Wechsler (1977), the University of Michigan pioneered in the identification of reputable high schools and in reliance on their recommendations as a basis for admitting students. Eventually this approach was modified to take account of the averaged grades received by their students (GPA or grade-point average). But the elite colleges of the East Coast, while also maintaining special relations with selected high schools and preparatory schools, did not want to be solely tied to such a principle. Nicholas Murray Butler of Columbia University was particularly firm in pressing for some form of entrance examination. Eventually this led him in 1901 to take the lead in forming a small consortium known as the College Entrance Examination Board. This Board devised an essay-style entrance test to be used jointly by participating schools as one means for evaluating prospective entrants. While the first examinations followed the English pattern of essays, over the early decades of the twentieth century the philosophy changed under the influence of the emerging discipline of psychology. To understand this shift, it will be helpful to consider important developments of that time in American society.

At the turn of the century, America was just moving into a stage of rapid growth of industrial and governmental organizations, with their needs to recruit employees and make good use of them. For example, the new factories for the mass production of cars needed to evaluate the applications of several thousand employees in a short period of time and make appropriate assignments of their workforce to a great diversity of jobs. The new discipline of psychology was turned to for assistance in making these decisions, and it responded with various tests of ability, personality types and intelligence. Noting that new Southern European immigrants and Blacks generally faired poorly on these tests, some critics suggested that the tests served as a means of providing 'scientific' legitimacy for discriminatory personnel practices. Subsequently, psychological testing achieved a new level of legitimacy in the First World War when it was used as a means of screening recruits for military service (Young, 1958).

With this background, it was only a matter of time before educational institutions would turn to psychological testing to assist them in making various decisions. Indeed, as we will indicate in the next section, some American school systems have institutionalized psychological testing as a key element in virtually all decision-making areas. But prior to outlining that comprehensive approach, it will be helpful to point out some of the distinctive features of American testing.

In contrast to continental Europe, where schools were oriented to conveying a commonly accepted curriculum, American educators were less certain about what should be taught at the various levels. In the absence of agreement on content, they tended to look at schools as settings for the stimulation of thought processes and overall human development. Thus, in thinking of ways to evaluate students, they were as much concerned with measuring the students' ability or aptitude as their achievement. Indeed, many of the educational tests developed over the twentieth century had this character.

Perhaps most notable among these is the Scholastic Aptitude Test (SAT), which was developed after the Second World War under the sponsorship of the College Entrance Examination Board. Following the War, a large number of Americans returned from their military duties with the intent of seeking further education. As the soldiers had been away from their studies for a long time, it seemed unfair to examine them on the basis of what they knew. Thus, a new test was sought which would measure their aptitude for collegiate study. This test was to be divided into two sections, one for verbal aptitude and one for mathematics aptitude. To develop the SAT, the independent, non-profit Educational Testing Service was established, and over time this organization has developed impressive sophistication in the design of various other tests. Most such tests take a multiple-choice format, which, while costly to produce, as they require considerable expertise for the framing and selection of questions, can be efficiently graded. Thus, they are suitable for the common evaluation of large numbers of students.

The SAT was first administered in 1947 and rapidly became institutionalized as one of the principal criteria that American colleges use for deciding on the admissibility of applicants. The test supposedly taps basic aptitudes and thus ostensibly is not one that individuals can study for or that teachers can teach to. It is not tied to the study of specific subjects, and so the particular curriculum a student has covered should not have great bearing on their results. The test also is supposed to be culturally unbiased so that students of different ethnic and racial backgrounds have an equal chance to do well. These 'supposed' characteristics are highly attractive, and thus have caught the attention of educators around the world who are concerned with such issues as cultural bias, teaching to the test, diverse academic backgrounds of students, and inefficient testing procedures. Therefore, a number of countries, ranging from Japan to Indonesia, have attempted to introduce elements of the US model into their procedures for university admissions.

Not all American educators have been as enamoured of the aptitude tests as are personnel of the Educational Testing Service. Many observers question the appropriateness or accuracy of numerical measures of an individual's worth, especially when these measures are based on multiple-choice questions. Critics can point to other possibilities for evaluation that are equally sensible (Owen, 1985). And they ask whether some areas of knowledge can be meaningfully measured with multiple-choice questions. They also ask if the tests measure the full range of aptitudes or intelligences that American education seeks to cultivate (Gardner & Hatch, 1989).

201

Over recent years, the 'supposed' characteristics of the SAT have further been called into question by a number of researchers who show that, despite the efforts of the Educational Testing Service to construct culture-fair measures, many of the test questions retain a strong cultural bias. A number of private tutoring or 'cram' schools have achieved excellent results in raising the test scores of students (Slack & Porter, 1980), and the academic preparation of students has been shown to have a strong relationship to aptitude as measured by the SAT. Thus the SAT's reputation has been in decline as a panacea for educational evaluation. Many American educators are urging a shift back to more curriculum-specific achievement-based tests as a fairer way of evaluating student progress, and many leading colleges are de-emphasizing their reliance on the SAT as a criterion for admissions.

Another important American contribution has been the vision of a comprehensive educational evaluation system. In no other country have schools shown such an interest in testing as in the USA. For example, the Ninth Mental Measurements Yearbook (Mitchell, 1985) describes 1409 published tests in current use. Furthermore, in no other country have computers been so extensively mobilized to store and analyze test results. Tests have been used by American schools not only for measuring student aptitudes and achievement but also for assessing student personality profiles, teacher aptitudes, school climate and management styles, and a host of other characteristics. In recent years, some educational evaluators have begun to see how these various pieces of information can be linked so as to produce a comprehensive system for the evaluation of education. Perhaps the best way to illustrate this vision is to cite the example of the state of North Carolina, where considerable progress has been made towards the realization of the formal testing portion of this goal.

In North Carolina, all children in all grades are administered an achievement test in selected subjects each year. The test results are coded in such a manner that the scores of a student during one year can be compared to that student's results for the previous year, thus providing an indicator of how much he or she has gained during the year. The results can also be analyzed to determine how much the students of particular schools or particular classes in schools have gained in a year. Such results also enable comparison of the relative level of achievement of individual children, classes and schools. Information of this kind can be put to a variety of uses, including the mobilization of remedial work for individual students, classes or schools where insufficient progress is shown. Other uses could include linking teacher salary increases to the tested performance of the students they teach, or keying principals' salaries to the test scores of their schools.

In North Carolina, the system thus far has been used only for student-related decisions. However, the possibilities for applying test results appear great indeed, and that is one of the concerns of watchful educators. For instance, is the information in this system appropriate for making all sorts of decisions about students, teachers and administrators? Might the privacy rights of students and teachers be violated by certain uses of such a system? These are some of the disturbing questions raised by that type of comprehensive testing programme.

The Japanese Pattern

Japan, which wakened from a deep feudal slumber in the mid-nineteenth century, was much impressed by the technological advances of the West and concluded that the key to catching up would be the rapid development of Western-style education (Spaulding, 1967, p. 23). Thus, in 1872 the new government proposed compulsory primary education and took rapid steps to develop a university system of high quality.

The Japanese began the development of their education system just at the time the West was at the peak of its Age of Examinations. Hence, a major theme in the early Japanese thinking about education was the use of examinations to stimulate learning. In local areas, a series of learning competitions was set up between primary schools. Top government officials would attend day-long sessions in which young students competed in jousts of mathematics or literary prowess. Through such competition, the young government sought to fan enthusiasm for modern learning (Amano, 1990).

Distinct from these popular competitions were the principles for evaluation built into the formal educational system. The early Japanese model was founded on European precedents, especially the French example with a centrally prescribed curriculum and textbooks, frequent tests throughout each school year, and a final test at the completion of the year. Passing the year-end test was, in principle, a precondition for moving on to the next level. But in the Japanese case, schools were often small, and able students found ways to complete the year-end tests ahead of schedule, thus accelerating their progress. At least in the early stages, most of the tests were devised by the teachers of the particular schools.

The critical tests that emerged in Japan were those determining who could move from one school level to the next. And concerning this transition, the Japanese eventually resolved on a different principle from that practised in Europe – the use of entrance examinations to the higher level rather than school-leaving examinations from the lower level. As the system now operates, in the transition from middle school to high school, middle school marks receive equal weight with the high school entrance test. But in transition to higher education, the examinations administered by the universities are the sole criterion. The final decision on a student's admission to a university is based on his or her performance in an examination prepared and marked by the faculty of that particular institution.

The formal reasoning behind this practice is that the content for the two levels is not always adequately articulated, and so it is important for the receiving institution to ensure that entrants have adequate preparation for the institution's programme. Indeed, to ensure adequate preparation, some of the middle and higher-level schools have created special preparatory courses. However, it has been argued that this modification reflects a strong theme in Japanese culture of setting strict conditions for the initiation of new social relations on the assumption that once a commitment is made it should be a lasting one. That is, the system is designed to preclude the failure of a student by a teacher or a school (Cummings, 1985).

Another interesting feature of Japanese evaluation is the comprehensiveness of the subject matter covered. For example, to enter upper secondary schools, students are required to take an examination in every subject, including physical education. Entrance examinations to universities typically cover five subjects. Even schools of music include the standard subjects of English language and mathematics in their entrance tests. Especially at the university level, Japan's entrance examinations are difficult, and quite a few students fail. Those who fail are not considered unworthy for the next level, but the cause is assumed to be insufficient effort in their preparation. Therefore, a student who has failed once can try again the following year and again and again. In other words, the system recognizes and even applauds the value of hard effort.

Soviet Russia

Soviet Russia inherited a classical European educational system that the new Soviet leaders sought to humanize and democratize. Their early goal was to establish a unified school that all young people could attend from grade 1 to 10 with no artificial barriers such as local or national tests, but, rather, with promotion based on their individual teacher's evaluation. This bold goal proved impractical, and so in Stalin's times a preliminary screening was introduced between grades 4 and 5 to obtain an early estimate of academic ability (with some children being ushered out of the school system) and a more serious evaluation at grade 8 leading to the tracking of children into academic and vocational preparatory courses. The examinations introduced at these lower levels were typically prepared by local governments in the appropriate local languages. Finally, at the conclusion of general academic studies, those young people seeking to advance to further studies were expected to take examinations offered by the respective vocational-technical institutions and universities. Particularly at the top universities, the competition for entrance was quite stiff and as many as nine out of ten did not succeed. Success rates were greater at the lesser universities and especially in the vocational and technical institutes that were rapidly expanded (Jacoby, 1975). Thus, while the Soviet system originally hoped to minimize the impact of examinations, the practical necessity of linking human resources with available opportunities led to the reintroduction of an examination system not unlike that practised in nations such as Germany. The examinations offered by the various post-secondary institutions tended to focus on the subject areas emphasized by that institution; thus, students

204

aspiring for a university place in foreign languages could focus their secondary-level effort on foreign language mastery while neglecting careful study of the sciences (though the student was expected to attend classes across the full spectrum of subjects).

Diploma Disease

The various measures of the Japanese government to promote education have resulted in extraordinary popular enthusiasm for schooling, such that universal primary education was achieved by 1900 and the numbers seeking entrance to the middle schools soon exceeded the number of available places. Over subsequent decades, additional middle schools were established so that the competition shifted upwards to focus on entrance to the higher schools and the universities (Kinmouth, 1981). The intensity of this competition came to be described as examination hell by some social observers. Students studied long hours, often with the aid of tutors or teachers at special 'cram' schools. Many of the aspirants, known as *ronin*, dropped out of school a full year or more specifically to prepare for the examinations, and a few who failed committed suicide. Yet, even those who succeeded were not always destined for a job fitting a university graduate.

Ronald Dore (1976), a leading Japanologist, found even more extreme examples of the same pattern in a number of developing societies he had occasion to observe, notably Sri Lanka and Kenya. He expressed his concern that the chase for diplomas was turning the schools of these nations into factories for examination cramming. Schooling in such late-developing nations was 'ritualistic, tedious, suffused with anxiety and boredom, destructive of curiosity and imagination; in short, anti-educational' (Dore, 1976, p. ix). Dore observed that the problem derived from the use of the evaluative activities in schools to double as society's mechanism for social selection. To relieve schools of their 'diploma disease', he urged such approaches as the use of aptitude tests (or forms of lottery) for social selection and a reliance on apprenticeship and mid-career education and training in place of the pre-career pattern.

Dore's views on the impact of testing on 'late developers' has since been questioned by other educators. For example, a careful analysis of Kenya's revised Certificate of Primary Education, with its related feedback system, suggests that is has provided important 'insight into the reasons for pupils' cognitive difficulties' and has had 'a major impact in improving the overall quality of education and in reducing quality differences among schools' (Somerset, 1987, p. 194). A number of educators believe that their educational systems can benefit from a strong dose of the diploma disease.

Regardless of whether one accepts Dore's analysis, it is certainly true that the evaluation practices of particular developing countries have tended to be modelled on those of their colonial mentors. Thus, in Sri Lanka and Malaysia, even though the languages of instruction are no longer English, the content of instruction is much as it was during the colonial period, and the same O level and A level examinations continue to be administered. Similarly, most francophone African countries employ an evaluation system identical to that found in France. It is reasonable to ask if these classical European approaches fit the new circumstances of these new nations.

Comparative Reflections on Systems of Evaluation

While each of the evaluative systems reviewed here has its strengths, we have also seen that these systems are the focus of much criticism. Indeed, it seems that, just as in the developing world, several of the advanced educational systems are searching for more suitable modes of assessment. As part of this effort, in recent years there has been a new wave of policy-oriented research on evaluation systems (Somerset, 1987; Heyneman, 1987; Heyneman & Fägerlind, 1988; Madaus, 1988). The following appear to be some of the major findings that have emerged from these studies.

1. Systems of evaluation have to be judged not only on technical criteria but also in terms of their political and cultural compatibility. We have outlined some of the characteristics of the examination approaches found in several of the more prominent advanced societies. The approaches have evolved over the course of development of these societies to the point where they have highly distinctive styles. Each reflects special concerns of the society – for local autonomy in England, for ensuring intellectual breadth in the case of France, for encouraging diligent effort in the case of Japan, and for ensuring the fair treatment of a diverse citizenry in the case of the USA.

2. Conceptions of the knowledge that schools should impart become important determinants of the style of evaluation systems. Berlak & Berlak (1981) have characterized differences in the way knowledge is perceived. In the classical view, knowledge is content, given, and holistic. In the modern view, knowledge is process, problematic, and molecular. Evaluation following the classical view is best carried out with essays, while the modern view is more amenable to short open-ended or multiple-choice questions. These differences are reflected in the evaluation procedures used by different fields as well as by different countries. Newer fields of knowledge and newer countries seem more comfortable with the short-answer approach.

3. Uniform evaluation systems are more easily developed in programmes with a clearly specified curriculum. Most educational systems with national curricula have developed some form of acceptable national examination for key transition points, while in more decentralized systems, such as England and the USA, much of the evaluation work is school based.

4. Evaluative formats involving multiple-choice questions may or may not be more efficient than essay examinations. Multiple-choice tests can usually be graded more quickly than essays, but they tend to take more time to prepare. Moreover, special skills are required for the preparation of questions and for their effective presentation in test papers. The additional

time required for preparation may equal the time saved in grading. Sometimes the issue is not whether gross efficiency results, but whose energy is saved. It makes a difference to teachers whether it is their time or someone else's time that is required to prepare tests and mark them.

5. Careful analysis and preparation are required for the development of a fair and effective evaluation system. Concerning the development of evaluation material, an extensive technical literature has emerged to guide the preparation of evaluative procedures that use multiple-choice formats, with the literature stressing such issues as bias, scope and balance, difficulty level, coverage of the full range of skill hierarchies (from recall to synthesis or higher reasoning), validity, and reliability. All of these issues have equal relevance for formats using other procedures. Whatever the format for particular questions, extensive planning is required to ensure an appropriate procedure for the presentation and the assessment of the evaluation materials.

6. It may be impossible and even unwise to devise an evaluation system that provides no encouragement for students to prepare their answers outside of school hours. In evaluation systems where the criteria are well known and are perceived to have consequences for the child's future, children do spend more time on homework and at special cram schools. Some critics, expressing concern that such children are robbed of their youth, urge the development of an evaluation system that cannot be studied for. While it was once assumed that carefully prepared aptitude tests could meet this need, recent experience indicates that it is even possible to provide cram school courses that will help children significantly improve their aptitude-test scores. Thus, it seems difficult to develop a study-free test. But it is just as difficult to develop a study-free learning process. No pill has yet been developed that enables a child to become brilliant and mature overnight. The acquisition of societally approved personal habits and critical knowledge still requires study, the more the better. Under the circumstances, it makes sense to publicize the goals and general structure of tests and to encourage children to study for them.

7. It is not clear that children in societies afflicted by the diploma disease receive a 'poor' education. Critics charge that the children who attend examination-oriented educational systems focus so narrowly on the task of passing the examinations that they experience boredom and their minds fail to be stimulated. But comparative studies suggest that children who study in such systems learn more than children in schools with more diffuse educational objectives. Moreover, the former children are more adept in answering questions that require higher reasoning skills. While children in examination-oriented systems take up their studies with the extrinsic motivation of passing examinations, they seem more likely to eventually develop a genuine love of learning than do children in less demanding systems.

8. The locus of critical evaluative assessments has a profound influence on the climate of relations in educational institutions. In most European educational systems, evaluation comes at the end of an extended period of schooling. The same teachers that are trying to motivate students in the classroom during the school year are the ones who determine the learners' fate at the end. The overlapping of the pedagogic and selection roles tends to encourage formal interpersonal relations. In contrast, in Japan and China, the critical examinations are administered at the stage of entrance to schools by the very teachers who will be receiving the students. Once the students are admitted, the teachers appear to feel a special responsibility to help the entrants complete the educational programme. The separation of the pedagogic and selection roles seems to lead to more intimate interpersonal relations.

9. There are rich possibilities for the expansion of the functions served by evaluative systems, but there are also important constraints. As illustrated in the North Carolina example, many local school systems in the USA have taken bold strides toward linking different evaluative functions in a comprehensive system. When similar procedures were proposed in Japan in the 1960s, the Japan Teachers' Union voiced its firm resistance, arguing that such information, in the hands of administrators, could be manipulated to discriminate against particular teachers or students. Thus, the proposal for a comprehensive approach was abandoned.

10. Evaluation methods have an important and visible impact on the way teachers and students use their time in class. In countries with explicit testing systems, government agencies or commercial firms are likely to develop and publish special exercises and tests. Teachers can rely on these externally created materials for many of their routine assessments. If the materials are well prepared, the amount of time that teachers and students need to devote to such assessments may be modest. In systems with less explicit evaluation methods, teachers may have to devote considerable time to the preparation and marking of tests and quizzes. Moreover, such teacher-made tests tend to absorb a considerable amount of class time while teachers write them out (perhaps on the blackboard) and while students participate in correcting the tests. With these ten comparative observations as a background, we turn now to what might be expected in the field of educational evaluation in the coming years.

Conclusion

Recent experience would seem to raise major questions about the value of systematic and comprehensive evaluation, whether of student learning or of other aspects of the educational process. Each new method of evaluation adds costs to the educational system while at the same time inviting compensatory adjustments for what may be undesired side effects – such side effects as pupils studying just for the tests or educators manipulating the material entered into data files so as to produce the results the evaluators seek. These adjustments then invite further refinement of assessment procedures by the evaluators, leading to yet another spiral of innovative manipulation and response. One might assume that after so many cycles of this kind, educators would be tempted to discard the process of evaluation altogether. But far from it – the current trend is towards a progressively more solid institutionalization of evaluation in education systems.

One prospective trend today is towards more centralized standards for evaluation. The UK Education Reform Act of 1988 for the first time placed on the shoulders of the central Ministry of Education the responsibility for formulating a national curriculum and for developing procedures for evaluating how well schools achieve curriculum goals. Considerable sentiment has also become evident in the USA for the creation of national achievement standards, or at least for more uniform standards across the nation, along with uniform ways of measuring progress towards the standards. And in most other societies, a system of national standards and assessment procedures is already in place, with the desirability of their continued use generally unquestioned. Thus, agreement seems to be emerging across the world on the value of establishing national criteria for educational achievement. At some distant date in the future, the next stage may well be the widespread recognition of international standards. A very early step in that direction is the International Baccalaureate programme adopted by schools in various countries.

A second prospective trend is towards linking educational evaluation with levels of support or reward for individual actors in the education system – a process sometimes referred to as accountability. A variety of formulas have been tried over time to attach rewards to the quality of individual educators' and individual schools' performance. Among these formulas are merit pay for superior teachers, opportunities for parents to choose which schools their children will attend, and promotion in the schooling hierarchy for effective administrators. However, the outcome of such schemes has often proved disappointing, partially because of the difficulty of assessing personnel and schools in a just and convenient manner. In recent years, there has seemed to be a hunger for new and more acceptable accountability procedures, ones that will produce accurate and fair assessment results with an economical expenditure of staff time and money.

As part of the trend towards greater accountability, more school systems may shift toward publicizing evaluation results so as to mobilize public participation in schools and to stimulate public action toward promoting educational improvements. As suggested by those who advocate publishing test results, teachers who repeatedly failed to educate their students effectively could be exposed through public records, and schools that continually displayed poor results in standardized examinations might find able students departing for schools with better test outcomes. Such an approach opens the road to a type of accountability that lies outside the normal bureaucratic processes which heretofore have dominated the use of summative assessments in nearly all education systems. However, the difficulties and potential dangers in implementing such plans are formidable. For example, all children do not have the same aptitude for academic success, and so a teacher who receives a large number of less adept learners will be blamed for the low test scores that such pupils earn. Furthermore, schools can differ markedly in the level of support for academic effort that is provided by the families from which the schools draw their clientele. Nor can all schools furnish the same learning facilities or have the same numbers of pupils per class. In addition, pencil and paper examinations do not provide suitable evidence about students' progress towards many of the school's goals, particularly in the arts and in character traits and moral values. These barriers to the fair implementation of accountability schemes are not easily dismissed. As a consequence, the proper role for evaluation in promoting educational accountability will continue to be a highly controversial issue.

A further future prospect is for the increasing involvement of workplaces in the evaluation of educational processes. Employers have traditionally relied on schools as a means of selecting highly educated personnel, with this reliance reflected in companies making an effort to encourage and recruit the best of the college graduates. At the same time, employers have tended to neglect the educational fate of those students who have not fared well in school. However, as the number of positions in the job market for unskilled and semi-skilled workers diminishes, employers face the need to become more active in their search for lower-level employees who can perform well in job assignments requiring literate, well-trained personnel. Thus, increasingly, employers find it in their best interest to focus attention on all levels of the education system, rather than solely on tertiary education. It seems likely that employers will increasingly tie incentives to the indicators of success provided by educational evaluation. An example of such incentives in the USA is the offer by certain industrial benefactors to pay the full costs of education to all workers who complete their high school studies. Another incentive is the provision of monetary rewards for good school reports. What is clear, in these efforts, is that the results of education are more and more seen to be closely linked with the success of national economies. As economic leaders become increasingly convinced that better schooled employees in all jobs foster productivity, they are seeking new ways to establish compacts or partnerships with education systems, while not excessively intervening with the actual educational process. One means of accomplishing this is to provide attractive incentives to learners who receive positive evaluations.

Finally, at no time in the world's history has the field of educational evaluation been so active as in recent years. This activity has involved an unprecedented number of researchers and practitioners proposing innovative means of assessment, devising improved methods of analysis and interpretation, and critically appraising the use of evaluation techniques. Never before has there been so much international transfer of assessment methods and of student achievement results. Therefore, despite the many problems associated with assessment procedures, it is likely that evaluation will become an ever more prominent feature of education systems in the decades to come.

Notes

[1] An earlier version of this chapter written by the author was published as chapter 5, Examinations and Evaluation, in M. Thomas (Ed.). *International Comparative Education: practices, issues and prospects*, pp. 87-106. Oxford: Pergamon Press, 1990.

[2] Since the Second World War, and especially since the reforms of the 1970s, French education has reduced the burden of examinations in the lower grades.

PART FOUR

The Replacement of Modern Education

CHAPTER 10

The Changing Context

In the coming age, people will no longer be driven to consume more resources, energy, and farm products. They will instead turn toward values created through access to time and wisdom, which is to say, 'knowledge-value'. (Taichi Sakaiya, 1991)

One of the greatest accomplishments of the modern nation state was to shift the major burden of education from primordial, religious and work organizations to a new institution, the public school. This reallocation of educational responsibility was possible so long as the state maintained its ascendancy as the controller and director of modern life. But in recent decades, there is increasing evidence that the state's position as the defining force in everyday life is crumbling. And as the state unravels, so does public education, at least as we know it.

What should be done? The earlier chapters highlighted various reforms that were carried out on modern education, fixing what has been built, engaging in the 'steady work' of improvement preferred by the many practitioners who have a vested interest in the present system. But disappointment with the fruits of reform encourages apocalyptic thinking, as do the seemingly multiple signs of natural, social and cultural decay. Thus, there are other voices, quieter and less certain, who say fixing is not enough, that the old, that is, the modern system, has to be thrown out and replaced by something new.

In this chapter, we review several so-called mega-trends that are influencing and eroding the foundations of modern education. Global theorists focus on the economic and technological trends that tend to be somewhat more universal in their impact. In contrast, there are equally powerful social and political changes that are not uniform across the core societies, not to speak of the many other settings that are certain to become more prominent in the twenty-first century. Thus, just as there were multiple paths through the modern era, it is reasonable to anticipate distinctive trajectories in the years to come. In the concluding chapter, we will speculate on future educational scenarios.

Economic and Technological Change

Towards a Global Marketplace

One of the important roles of the modern state was to establish boundaries around national territories so as to demarcate who belonged to whom and, just as importantly, who produced for whom. While trade in the Middle Ages proceeded independently of these boundaries, with the rise of the nation state trade became regulated by various tariffs and other restrictions. Governments, in order to encourage local producers to gain strength in specific areas, would seek to favour these producers with such protective benefits. In the early industrial era, farmers were often favoured with protective tariffs to ensure that they produced in sufficient quantity to feed the growing national population; in particular, staples such as wheat, corn and rice were protected against foreign imports that might come in sporadically when a neighbouring nation enjoyed a surplus. Over time in selected nations, notably France, Japan and the USA, these protective policies for agricultural products became an important feature of national politics, in that ruling parties came to depend significantly on the farm vote for their continuance in office.

As nations improved their industrial production, protectionism was extended to industrial products, both at the urging of manufacturers who sought to avoid foreign competition and of labour unions who did not wish their members to lose jobs. But the consequence of this protection was to leave prices in the protected country at a higher level than prices outside, thus depriving consumers of the advantage of more reasonably priced products.

One of the major movements of the post-Second World War era has been to induce governments to discuss the advantages and disadvantages of these trade barriers. A General Agreement on Trade (GAT) was reached among several of the more advanced economies in the 1950s to seek selectively to reduce these barriers, taking into account the particular circumstances of each nation. Over time there has been a steady reduction in official tariffs. Even so, nations are able to impose invisible barriers (such as arcane rules for inspecting imported products, the most notorious example being Japan's ruling that American baseball bats did not pass Japan's standards). An important recent continuation of this trend has been the establishment and/or consideration of various regional agreements, as among the nations of the European Economic Community and the North American Free Trade Agreement; discussions are now under way in both Asia and South America about similar agreements.

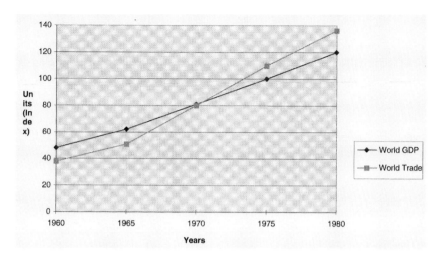

Figure 10.1. Increase of world trade. Source: United Nations, various years, *Statistical Yearbook*.

With the reduction of trade barriers, some national economies have significantly reoriented major sections of their industrial effort towards the promotion of exports. Over the past three decades, East Asian nations have been most remarkable in this regard. For example, Hong Kong and Singapore have raised the value of their exports to the point where they exceed the total value of their gross national product. Japan for many years exported much in excess of what it imported.

While certain nations have, at least in the short run, excelled in the promotion of exports, virtually every nation in the world has significantly increased the proportion of its agricultural and industrial goods that it either exports or imports. Similarly, many nations have become skilled in the export of services such as transportation, tourism and finance.

The reduction of trade barriers and the expansion of international trade is another factor behind the weakening of the influence of the nation states relative to other actors such as the transnational corporations and local governments. The increase in global competition places pressures on localities and individuals to keep abreast of new developments and to prepare for them through study and training. Of particular importance in the new competitive environment is the ability of localities to gain an edge in some area of high technology production. Those who can look ahead are likely to stay ahead, while those who ignore the new competition are destined for hard times.

217

The Rise and Decline of Transnational Corporations?

An important recent tendency in economic activity is for large corporations to sever their ties or commitments to particular national interests. Many of today's corporations locate their operations in various nations and operate in such a manner as to maximize the benefits from each location while minimizing the obstacles; such corporations are sometimes referred to as transnational corporations (TNCs).

Corporations by law have a special legal person status wherein the owners of shares in the corporation have limited liability. In the early stages of modern capitalism, most corporations were owned by investors who shared a common nationality and adhered to the tax laws of a single nation. But the sources of large capital are spread around the globe in the major financial centres such as New York, London, Düsseldorf, Amsterdam, Hong Kong and Tokyo. To accommodate the needs of corporations to gain access to these funds, laws were liberalized to allow the free flow of investments in corporations. The TNC inverted this condition by using the capital from various sources to invest freely around the globe.

In the early to intermediate stages of a corporation's life, there is a tendency for the corporation to expand its market share. Growth may benefit investors by increasing the value of their stocks. But at a certain stage, investors tend to press the corporate managers to emphasise the short-term gain of profits over the long-term gain of growth. The stress on profits leads managers to seek new sites for business that minimize costs, and these sites tend to lead a corporation to shift to new offshore production sites. Baran & Sweezy (1968), writing in the 1960s about US-based corporations, stressed this pattern and argued that it worked to the detriment of both the American worker and the workers in those countries gaining the new plant. From the 1980s the practice has been revived, not only by US-based firms but by the great majority of large firms irrespective of their origins. Particularly striking has been the tendency of leading Japanese firms such as Toshiba, Mitsubishi and Toyota to move offshore.

Baran & Sweezy argued that corporations moved offshore to take advantage of lower wages. Another reason is to move to locales where other costs such as the tax burden imposed by the state is more favourable. A view currently stressed by global theorists is that the major factor of production is knowledge, and that the TNCs are not just after low wages but also high skills. Thus, there is an incentive for local areas and individuals to build up their human capital (Reich, 1991).

Whatever motivates the offshore movement of TNCs, it is clear that the loss of a firm's activity erodes the tax base of a state, and hence the state's ability to provide services; and as the state's ability to provide services declines, so does its authority in the eyes of citizens who had come to expect more (Korten, 1995).

Ultimately, the TNCs also seem to be suffering. Despite the clever attempts of large TNCs to mover offshore and increase productivity, it would appear that firm after firm becomes the victim of new, leaner firms that challenge special areas of their product lines. This competition has forced extraordinary downsizing in such corporate giants as Worldcom, General Motors, IBM, AT & T, and Kodak, and it has led others, notably in metals, machinery and electronics, to declare bankruptcy. Of course, recent trends are not all one way; in contrast to the general trend of downsizing is the pattern of mergers in the communications, pharmaceutical and financial industries. But even with these mergers, there is typically an announcement of massive layoffs or worse. America Online and Time Warner merged in January 2001; for the 2002 fiscal year, they reported a loss of $98.2 billion – the largest ever for a US corporation. Thus, on balance it would appear that large TNCs may have peaked, and that a new balance is being pursued in the corporate world.

From the Industrial to the Cybernetic Revolution

Social theorists as distant as Karl Marx and Daniel Bell agree that technical innovation is the engine of change. The modern era emerged on the shoulders of a revolution in natural science that, among other outcomes, enabled the harnessing of energy. One outcome was the military revolution. Other early innovations included the smelting of iron ore to produce machine tools. The Industrial Revolution followed, with manufacturers building large mass production plants to spin yarn, weave textiles and produce fabrics; a host of other products such as shoes, dishes, pots and pans, furniture and tools came to be produced by these same high-energy production processes. With the success of industrialism, workers moved to the industrial areas, and urban industrial life came to replace rural agricultural life.

The rise of industrialism led to a profound re-ordering of productive life and, in turn, of rules for distributing its fruits. Whereas the pre-industrial society had been divided between those who owned land and those who did not, with a relatively small group involved in crafts and commerce, the industrial society offered its greatest rewards to those who owned and/or controlled the capital used to build the factories and procure the raw materials. The scale of industrial production was often so great that the owner-capitalists enjoyed boundless power over those they employed, and in many instances they used this power to extract extraordinary effort for a trivial compensation.

In opposition to this greed, a new workers' movement gradually emerged to request, demand, and sometimes fight for a more just compensation. The workers' movement was vigorously opposed by the capitalists using the force of law. The workers were eventually able to establish their own political organizations to challenge the capitalists, leading to various labour laws to guarantee better pay, job security, and other benefits. In Russia, the workers were able to challenge and ultimately topple the tsarist political regime, leading to the first large government controlled exclusively by communists as representatives of the working class.

The workers' movement strove throughout the twentieth century to establish greater social equality between those who controlled and those who used industrial capital. The strength of the workers' movement was associated with the number of workers involved in industrial production; in some industrial nations nearly half the adult working population was associated with the movement, while in others, such as the USA, less than a quarter joined. These numbers tended to peak by the mid-twentieth century and thereafter the political agenda of the workers' movement also began to falter.

During the Second World War the ultimate possibilities of the applications of modern physics were realized in the design of the nuclear bomb. Meanwhile, other scientists were working on an entirely new range of innovations aimed at reducing, rather than expanding, the energy required to accomplish work. This new innovation, based in mathematics and termed cybernetics, sought to improve the control of social processes by providing human decision-makers with dependable computational routines carried out by a new machine, the computer.

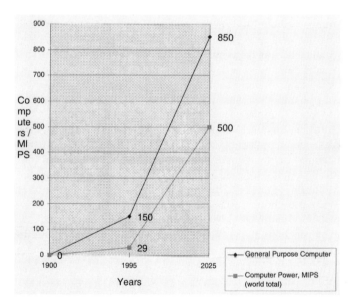

Figure 10.2. Increase in computers and computer power (millions).
Source: Kurian & Molitor (1996). *MIPS: million instructions per second.

At first, the computers were vast and housed in large vacuum tubes that occupied many rooms of a building. Today the essence of vastly more powerful computers can be stored in the head of a pin. And the applications are rapidly expanding. Robert Reich (1991) observes that the modern labour force is composed of three kinds of workers: those who do manual work and may be represented by the classical workers' movements, those who do service work, and those who manipulate symbols (often associated with computers). Reich notes that the educational requirements of these three groups differ significantly, with manual workers requiring no more than a basic education whereas symbol manipulators require a broad and extensive education so that they can carve out a unique niche in the world of symbols, whether it be as a programmer, an advertiser, an inventory manager, or an artist. The rewards to these three groups diverge; those associated with symbol manipulation have promising prospects, whereas those associated with the earlier modes of production can expect less.

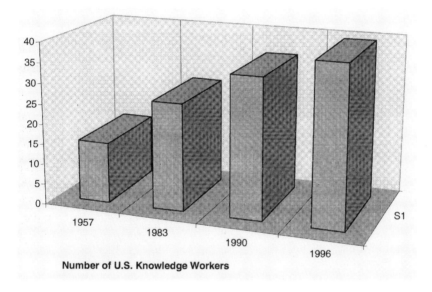

Number of U.S. Knowledge Workers

Figure 10.3. Increase in knowledge workers 1957-1996.
Sources: Cohen (1996); *US News and World Report*, 120.

One great uncertainty is the number of workers that will be required for the future of cybernetic workplaces. Cybernetics seeks to reduce the energy involved in work, including the energy provided by workers. There is the real possibility that the labour force, in the age of cybernetics, will decline in size as it increases in quality. Or alternatively, some members of the labour force will work at jobs with longer hours while others will work for shorter and less predictable periods.

Reich (1991) argues that the major constraints on the employment potential of cybernetic workplaces are the imagination of the workers and

221

their supply. The implication is that those areas of the world that seek to gain the greatest benefits from the cybernetic revolution should increase their supply of appropriately trained workers. The future employment prospects of localities and of nations are seemingly tied to the future of education.

Instant and Infinite Information

The intended purpose of cybernetics was to help in decision-making, and many observers assumed it would strengthen the hands of central managers. Indeed, the early applications were in central planning exercises, drawing on complex data about employees, customers, distances, and costs. The data were combined in systemic models proposing an array of options for managers to choose from. Other applications included the programming of production routines to enhance efficiency and reduce the fallibility of the human factor. Indeed, in the early years, cybernetics seemed to strengthen the hand of central managers.

As time passed, computers became ever more powerful while at the same time their operating costs declined. Moreover, new techniques emerged for linking the information stored in one computer with that in another. With the emergence of networks and the liberating impact of a boundless ownerless Internet, users from any computer terminal found they could gain access to an astounding array of information.[1] In an organization, for example, lower level employees could gain access to essentially the same information as their managers. Thus, the ultimate effect of the cybernetic revolution may be to democratize social relations.

Whatever the impact there is no denying that a great divide has emerged in modern life between those born before the age of computers and those afterwards (BC and AC). In roughly the year 2000 the ACs began to outnumber the BCs in the adult population. The ACs will move into key decision-making roles in work settings, communities and families, with their understanding of the possibilities associated with the information revolution. One example is already evident in the world of work, as discussed below, and in the next chapter we will consider some possible implications for education.

The initial benefits of cybernetics were evident in the computation of figures for accounting, personnel, sales, inventory in business or for the prediction of trajectories in outer space; the recent passage of a spaceship through the atmosphere of Pluto some five years after it was launched is an extraordinary illustration of the computational magic enabled by the cybernetic revolution. But the future possibilities of cybernetics are only beginning to be unveiled. Vast DNA chains are plotted and analyzed with modern computers. The movements of ancient animals are simulated for Hollywood movies. The scores of unfinished symphonies of great composers are projected forward, and new music is composed through linking synthetic performances in high-tech software. The joining of these various possibilities will lead to what Naisbet (1982) describes as a whole new array of High

Tech–High Touch possibilities that challenge our senses and our sensibilities. Thus, many regard the cybernetic revolution as the foundation of a new revolution for humanity, equal in scale to the agricultural and industrial revolutions of the past.

From the Organization that Knows it All to the Learning Organization

The modern factory concentrated raw materials and machinery in a limited physical area so as to reduce the time and motion required for the production of goods that the consumers would presumably want, such as Henry Ford's Black Model-T. Correspondingly, workers were expected to gather in this limited area to carry out their tasks. Typically, the tasks assigned to each worker were highly specific and repetitive, and often the faster the worker could perform the task (such as stitching a seam or turning a wrench), the greater the pay. In other instances the workers were arrayed on an assembly line to make small additions to the work required to build an automobile, a truck, a television, or some other product. The speed of the conveyor belt determined the wage of the work group. Workers were below foremen who in turn were below factory managers who in turn were below production managers and so on in a strict hierarchy. Jobs were defined from above to be performed below, with little or no communication back up the ladder. The major requirements for workers were good health, loyalty, obedience and steadiness. It is often said that the modern school was designed to train a nation of workers.

At the top of the modern factory were the managers and professionals who made the big decisions on what was to be produced, how it was to be produced, how advertised, how sold (Whyte, 1956). These positions required a different type of education, provided in elite colleges and graduate schools. To some degree, those at the top enjoyed autonomy and discretion in the work, and to the extent that they proved clever they were rewarded. The boss at the top decided how much.

Whereas the hierarchical organization will continue to prevail for many decades to come, the advent of cybernetics suggests the possibility of a new approach to organizing work that is much flatter, more collegial, more interactive. The great majority of the employees associated with this organization are professionals, symbol manipulators seeking collectively to apply knowledge and solve problems. Peter Senge (1990) calls it the Learning Organization, exemplified by the university or the hospital. While the factory required its employees to gather at a common worksite, the learning organization is more flexible. Some work is best done at the site, some off the site. The links of email, Internet, and the cellular phone enable team workers in dispersed locations to keep in touch. Thus, along with the diminution of hierarchy may also come an alleviation of population concentration as employees of a common organization work from dispersed sites, sometimes even from their homes.

Just as work–home boundaries are dissolving, so may the boundaries of school and home disappear. It is now possible for children to spend part of their learning time at home, using the Internet to pursue their lessons and projects. The Internet has the potential of reducing and/or transforming the work of teachers. Families dissatisfied with what takes place in school may seize the initiative through expanding the role of homes in education.

The Institutionalization of Innovation

The modern factory required considerable capital to convert simple technical ideas into an effective industrial process. Relatively few individuals had the ingenuity or wealth to assemble the required capital. At first, the capitalists were looked down upon by the landed classes. But as the capitalists increased their wealth, they were extended more respect and power. Among their concerns was to establish laws to preserve their success; these included patent laws to protect their technical innovations and labour laws to limit the rights of workers.

As the industrial system advanced, the challenge to develop new, more promising technical innovations increased. Whereas gentlemen inventors were the source of many of the earlier ideas, over time the industrial concerns came to place increasing importance on the innovation process by setting up their own research laboratories to foster innovation. In this manner, particular firms came to command a critical edge in certain techniques that could not be easily challenged by competitors. This dominance of key industrial processes was most evident during the so-called phase of heavy industry centred in the production of petroleum, steel and motor vehicles.

With the shift to heavy industry and the symbiotic role that developed between industry as the producer of complex products and the state (notably the military) as consumer, the state was drawn into the process of innovation. The state participated through the support of the training of scientists and engineers at universities and through the provision of extensive funding for research and development, both in university and corporate settings. With these public commitments, the process of innovation and permanent change came to be institutionalized. Product cycles became shorter and shorter as this process accelerated. The process of technical change has tended to spill over into other spheres of modern life with so many other routines challenged.

But this government–industrial complex, whether justified for national defence or competitiveness, was not to endure. East Asian nations provided the lead, with the government share of research and development (R & D) progressively declining relative to the innovation directly funded by industry (World Bank, 1993a). A similar pattern emerged in Europe from the late 1980s, and in the USA in 1995, for the first time in forty years, over half of all R & D was funded by the private sector.

Large firms were the major players in R & D for much of the twentieth century, but in recent years it seems that the technical monopoly of large firms is collapsing. Among the contributing factors is the global diffusion of information and a shift in the scientific basis of innovation from big science chemistry and physics to small science biology and mathematics/computers. Whatever the reason, more and more localities find they have a chance to make a difference in technical competition, providing they have the will and are prepared to make appropriate investments. With the opening of the opportunities for technical innovation comes a new invitation for local communities, that of supporting local efforts to participate in global technical competition.

Whatever the source of R & D funds, contemporary nations are committed to devoting from 2 to 3 per cent of their gross national product for this purpose. Figure 10.4 illustrates the recent experience of the core nations. All except Russia are in this range.

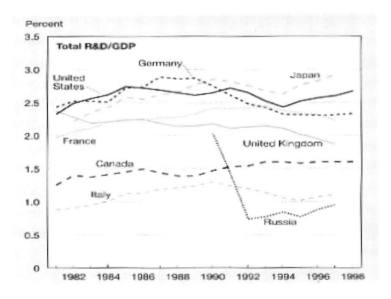

Figure 10.4. Total R & D as per cent of GDP for selected countries, 1982-1996.
Source: National Sciences Board (2000).

The Prospect for the Natural Environment

Humanity's demand for fossil fuels to feed the engines of modern industry raced forward through the mid-twentieth century, leading many to fear that the world's reserves would soon be exhausted. The shift in the nature of work and the growing reliance on low-energy production processes has slowed the consumption of fossil fuels in the most advanced societies to an increase of only 1 per cent annually, though in industrializing Asia the increase currently is at 4 per cent (see Figure 10.5).

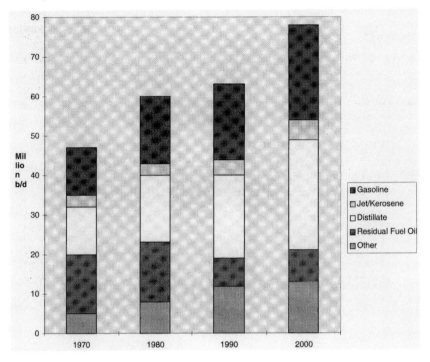

Figure 10.5. Trend in world demand for petroleum products.
Source: Kurian & Molitor (1996, p. 706).

There was once a dream that new destinations would be found in space for the human race to move to so that the earth's environment could be thrown away much as a Coca Cola bottle is carelessly thrown out of a moving car. But the expectation at the turn of the twenty-first century is that we will remain on spaceship earth for as many decades or centuries as we can abide it, and there are no other likely options. And so there should be increasing pressure to make better use of resources, to stress sustainability and replenishment.

While logic might compel in that direction, the signs of a unified global plan are yet to emerge. The world's forests are disappearing at a rate of 2 per cent annually, and desalination is threatening large areas of Africa and Asia. The quality of oceanic waters is progressively declining. And while scientists and politicians debate over the probability of global warming and whether this is a natural or man-provoked development, the level of carbon dioxide in the atmosphere becomes ever more unstable. Doubtless one of the greatest challenges of the next century will be to come to terms with the natural environment which enables human existence.

Table 10.1 summarizes the patterns of use of oil in the six core societies as well as the level of carbon dioxide emissions per capita. Concerning both indicators, the US level is about twice that of the other societies. And concerning CO_2 emissions, whereas the other core societies have signed the Kyoto Accord and committed themselves to a substantial reduction of these emissions, the USA has decided not to be a signatory.

	Kg of oil equivalent per capita			Carbon dioxide emissions per capita	
	1980	1999	Average annual growth (%)	1980	1999
Germany	4602.0	4108.0	-0.5	n.d.	10.1
France	3485.0	4351.0	1.5	9.0	6.3
UK	3573.0	3871.0	0.7	10.3	9.2
USA	7973.0	8159.0	0.4	20.4	19.8
Japan	2967.0	4070.0	2.3	7.9	9.0
Russia	n.d.	4121.0		n.d.	9.8

Table 10.1. Energy use in the core societies. Source: World Bank, *World Development Indicators 2002*. Table 3.7. Energy production and use.

Demographic, Social and Cultural Change

The Demographic Transition

Among the many areas of innovation have been the remarkable advances in health and medical care. At the turn of the twentieth century, the average global life expectancy was less than forty while today it exceeds sixty-five. In several of the more advanced societies it now approaches eighty. The life expectancy for Japanese women in 1995 was eighty-four.

The initial impact of modern medicine was to improve the likelihood that a young baby would survive, and this led to a rapid increase in the size of populations. In the early stages of industrialization some leaders welcomed population growth as it expanded the numbers available for work and war; large populations also mean many consumers. But there is a downside to rapid population growth both for parents who bear the cost of child-rearing and for governments who need to provide educational facilities and other social services. The costs of rapid population growth tend to outweigh the benefits. Thus, in those societies that have become familiar with higher rates of infant survival, there has been a tendency to control the number of births so that all young people can gain the benefits of careful nurturing and education. This tendency was first evident in the more industrial societies, many of which have achieved essentially stable populations.

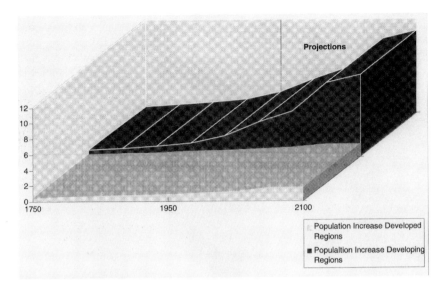

Figure 10.6. World population increase (billions). Source: Kennedy (1993).

Table 10.2 compares the demographic structure of the six core societies; the USA is the only core nation predicted to experience steady population growth over the next fifteen years. In all of the core societies excepting the USA and Russia, at least 15 per cent of the population is sixty-five years or older.

In contrast are the less developed nations of the world where, in many instances, populations continue to grow at a rapid rate. Because of these differences in population growth patterns, the balance of the world's population is gradually shifting from North to South and from West to East. In the year 2000, one half of the world's population resided in India and China.

The trend towards stable populations means that increasing proportions of the world's population will be adults. In those countries that have been able to stabilize population growth for several decades, the proportion of the population over the age of sixty-five is rapidly increasing. By the year 2000 over 15 per cent of the population in most of the advanced industrial countries was over sixty-five.

	Age composition (2000)			Average annual population growth rate 2000-2015
	Age 0-14 %	Age 15-64 %	Age 65+ %	
Germany	15.5	68.1	16.4	-0.2
France	18.7	65.3	16.0	0.3
UK	19.0	65.3	15.8	0
USA	21.7	66.0	12.3	0.8
Japan	14.7	68.1	17.2	-0.5
Russia	18.0	69.6	12.5	-0.5

Table 10.2. Demographic structure and growth in the core societies.
Source: World Bank, *World Development Indicators 2002*,. Table 2.1. Population dynamics.

In past centuries a much smaller proportion of the population lived so long and thus little thought was given to the style of life of older people. Even today, our imagination is limited, focusing on such issues as the costs of medical care and of pensions. It is certainly the case, given the nature of modern social programmes, that the expansion of the old age cohort will lead to large and often unanticipated expenditure in these areas. But the challenge of an aging population has far more complexity.

Put simply, old people seek to live, not to die. What needs to be done to provide older citizens with their right to live? A major area for reform is in the realm of work. The USA has pioneered by challenging the legality of arbitrary retirement ages, asserting that citizens should be allowed to work for as long as they are able.

When life was short, women were often looked to as specialists in child-bearing and family-building. Many women also worked in family enterprises in the time they had free from their maternal responsibilities. There were always exceptional women who broke with these expectations and achieved success in the man's world of education and career. A major development of the latter half of the twentieth century, outlined by Stromquist (1997), has been to challenge the traditional pattern of patriarchal domination and to strive for a new equitable order in gender relations.

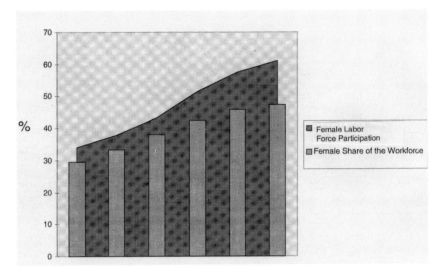

Figure 10.7. Women share of the labour force 1950-2000. Source: Person (1993).

With changes in demography and social values, increasing numbers of young women have come to set their sights on fulfilment outside of the home. Debates go on about the consequences for child-rearing when women aspire to work. On the other hand, the demands of modern life often require that couples who seek to raise young children find they need two incomes to cover the expenses. Moreover, there is compelling evidence that the best parents are educated parents who maintain affluent homes.

	1980	2000
Germany	40.1	42.3
France	40.1	45.1
UK	38.9	44.1
USA	41.0	46.0
Japan	46.3	46.2
Russia	49.4	49.2

Table 10.3. Female percentage of the labour force in the core
societies. Source: World Bank, *World Development Indicators 2002*.
Table 2.2. Labor force structure.

Today in several of the more advanced societies, more women attend tertiary educational institutions than men. And in the case of Sweden, women have

230

achieved virtual parity with men in occupational advancement and earnings. While women are making advances in most parts of the world, elsewhere they encounter many obstacles. These will remain as a challenge for the next century.

Winner Takes All

Among the factors eroding the stability of modern institutions is a new economic climate and context known as 'Winner Takes All' (Frank & Cook, 1995). This phenomenon is most visible in the world of sports and entertainment where star celebrities receive unbelievable prize money or salaries, primarily because they have the glitter to attract attention and viewers or listeners. Before the era of television the prize money at professional tennis and golf matches was modest, at best in the tens of thousands. Today the prize money for a single contest is easily ten times as great. More importantly, the disparity between the winner and the rest of the field has become magnified, and this extends to other benefits:

> *Although thousands of players compete each year in professional tennis, most of the industry's television and endorsement revenues can be attributed to the drawing power of just the top ten players. For example, the Australian Wally Masure, among the top fifty players in the world for many years, in 1993 was a semifinalist at the US Open. At no time in his career, however, did manufacturers offer tennis shoes or racquets bearing his signature. (Frank & Cook, 1995, p. 4)*

The same phenomenon of the top stars gaining an increasingly disproportionate share of the rewards can be extended to other arenas such as music, cinema, and even the corporate and professional world. Top lawyers, doctors, engineers and consultants can command exorbitant fees because they are believed to be able to get the job done, as much by their image as by their efficacy. And in the corporate world, for selected tasks such as takeovers and mergers or the design of a new product, a relatively small group of high-profile specialists has emerged who are hired, at enormous fees, to help a company perform a key action.

While there are many advantages to this trend, the authors of a recent study point out some of the less attractive features.

> *Winner-take-all markets have increased the disparity between rich and poor. They have lured some of our most talented citizens into socially unproductive, sometimes even destructive, tasks. In an economy that already invests too little for the future, they have fostered wasteful patterns of investment and consumption … And winner-take-all markets have molded our culture and discourse in ways many of us find deeply troubling. (Frank & Cook, 1995 pp. 4-5)*

This pattern is as noticeable outside of the USA as in. Both Europe and Japan have their popular icons in the worlds of music, sports, the media and the professions. In Japan, the glamour even extends to the political arena where media stars known as talents are regularly elected to the national Diet, based solely on name recognition.

In view of the increasing pay-offs to entering the circle of the selected few in a given career line, individual common sense dictates increasingly the planning of a career that maximizes the possibility of getting into the favoured group. For those seeking fame in sports this may mean full-time devotion to sports at the neglect of other pursuits such as attention to learning. For those seeking success in the professional and managerial arena this means it is essential to gain access to the gateway of top colleges and graduate schools. Thus, according to the authors, the winner-takes-all markets:

> *have led indirectly to greater concentration of our most talented college students in a small set of elite institutions. They have made it difficult for 'late bloomers' to find a productive niche in life. (Frank & Cook, 1995 p. 5)*

And so widening disparities in education are destined to parallel those in the economy. As the talented and ambitious strive to enter the elite private institutions, the legitimacy of the modern era's common school is eroded.

The Prospects for Justice and Equality

The early stages of industrialism led to the rise of a new capitalist class which came to command ever larger shares of the wealth of nations. In response to the power and practices of this class, an opposition movement of organized labour emerged. And after long struggles parity was achieved in legal provisions and social policies to guarantee a certain level of equality for all – in rights to organize, to vote, to work, to own property, and in provisions for a minimum wage, unemployment insurance and social security.

The great struggle for social equality was transplanted to the international stage after the Second World War, leading to the liberation of many colonial territories and a loose agreement among the United Nations to work for the alleviation of world poverty and the progress of all mankind. Over the subsequent decades, some progress has been made towards these ends, with some of the poorer parts of the world advancing on a trajectory towards sustainable growth and with human rights becoming a matter of important concern in international discourse.

But just as progress is gaining momentum on these national and international fronts, the principal actors are experiencing decay. At the national level, governments are losing power. And as governments weaken, the equitable policies they have launched and supported are also coming under attack. Common to virtually every advanced industrial nation is a political movement to weaken the welfare state, to weaken the safety net, to introduce cost recovery into programme after programme that the ordinary citizen has come to take for granted. Similarly, at the international level most of the major multilateral organizations that had pioneered in the wars on poverty, hunger and illiteracy are encountering increasing difficulty in securing funding and support.

Replacing the old order of justice is a new culture of instability and individual ambition captured in the 'winner-takes-all' imagery that is destined to generate new inequalities and injustices, unless checked. The hope is that new alliances will emerge of grass-roots organizations or of enlightened corporations to define a new vision for the future. But at the dawn of the twenty-first century there was still little sign of this new countervailing movement to the mounting assault on a fair deal for all.

	Gini index		% Share of income or consumption – highest 10%	Year	% Share of income or consumption – highest 10%
	Year	Gini index			
Germany	1994	30.0	23.7	1978.0	24.0
France	1995	32.7	25.1	1975.0	30.5
UK	1995	36.8	27.7	1979.0	23.4
USA	1997	40.8	30.5	1980.0	23.3
Japan	1993	24.9	21.7	1979.0	22.4
Russia	1998	48.7	38.7	n.d.	n.d.

Table 10.4. Comparative trends in income equality for the core societies. Source: World Bank, *World Development Indicators 2002*. Table 2.8. Distribution of income or consumption; World Bank, *World Development Report 1985*. Table 28. Income distribution.

The recent developments have had a complex impact on the core societies. Income inequality in the five core societies for which data were available was about the same (presented in Table 10.4). Over the past two decades, income inequality sharply decreased in France, remained essentially stable in Germany and Japan, appreciably increased in England, and sharply increased in the USA.

The Age of Discontinuity

The American Dream at the midpoint of the twentieth century involved a happily married couple raising a family in a tidy home located in a safe neighbourhood. The wife took care of the home front while the husband pursued a steady job culminating after thirty years in a golden watch and a nice retirement package (Whyte, 1956). The Japanese corollary is lifetime employment in one of Japan's powerful multinational corporations or in government service.

233

These dreams were possible when the labour force was young, the corporations were stable, and the governments were strong. But in the twenty-first century, the foundations for this old dream are weakening. Shake-ups in the world of work provide, perhaps, the greatest challenge. Through much of the twentieth century, corporations and governments grew in scale and seemed to improve in stability. But now that trend is reversing. The extensive downsizing of both public and private employers is causing large numbers of people to lose jobs they expected to keep for life.

Adding to the employment dilemma is the reality of longer life-spans. Whereas the average worker once expected to slow down in their fifties, many today discover that life is just beginning at fifty, with at least twenty or thirty more years of vigorous life ahead. The reality of longer life-spans is leading healthy adults to think of new ways to build their careers. Whereas a single job was once sufficient, multiple jobs in serial careers now become attractive. Starting as a schoolteacher, a young mathematician can consider shifting to accounting, then to management, and then to a career as a financial manager or computer systems consultant. Adding urgency to these career plans is the new turbulence of occupational life where governments expand and contract and corporations engage in aggressive takeovers and restructuring that leave the jobs of many employees in jeopardy.

Greater flexibility in career building can lead to rethinking in other areas. Lives begun with one romantic partner who complemented the needs associated with a first job may prove less fulfilling as jobs change. Adding to the strain of new job requirements may be the need to relocate. Where both partners work, sometimes only one relocates, leading to long-distance marriages or dissolution. Thus, serial jobs may be accompanied by serial marriages. Peter Drucker (1992) has suggested that we are entering an Age of Discontinuity.

Education will take on increasing importance for individuals as they seek to navigate the different stages of their lives. First degrees at conventional universities and colleges will provide the foundation while more specialized institutions will be needed to respond to the career-bridging challenges.

The Search for the Best Place

Among the more celebrated discontinuities of the late twentieth century was the reversion in the control of Hong Kong to mainland China. With this shift, many Hong Kong citizens sent their children overseas to study and gain citizenship; others purchased homes and established businesses in foreign locations with the expectation of moving later to these sites. Hong Kong investments are notable in such far flung sites as Los Angeles, Vancouver, Perth and Penang.

While the Hong Kong example may be extreme, it sometime seems that nearly everyone has a dream of some other place that is better, that may meet their needs for better weather, safer neighbourhoods, better employment opportunities, lower taxes and greater freedom.

In addition to those who seek mobility by choice there are the increasing numbers of political refugees who are pushed out of particular locales. Notable examples in recent years are Tibet, South Africa, Vietnam, China, Rwanda and the former Yugoslavia. Increasing numbers who are on the wrong side of a political escalation or an ethnic fence find they no longer have a home (see Figure 10.8). As nation states weaken and embedded ethnic rivalries rekindle, the flow of political refugees is sure to increase.

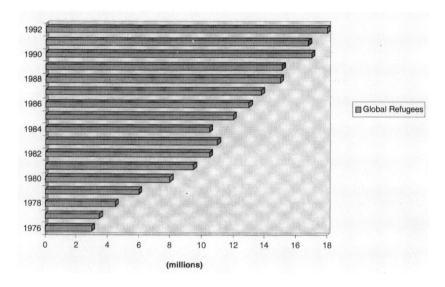

Figure 10.8. Global refugees, 1976-1992. Source: Institute for National Strategic Studies (1995).

The USA has been a favoured destination for these mobile citizens and will continue to be so for some time. But other nations are beginning to see the benefits of opening their doors, including Canada, Australia, South Africa, Israel, Brazil and Mexico. In the future other large nations such as Russia, Germany, Malaysia and Indonesia may welcome the world's adventurers. Strong and flexible higher educational institutions were a major factor in America's welcoming mat. Already, many of these other destinations are liberalizing their educational systems.

The spread of the world's population will lead to a growing diversity in the values and lifestyles of those living within the respective national boundaries of the preferred places, with all of the attendant complications in terms of education, communication, commerce and governance. The challenge will be to cultivate a new language of tolerance.

While some centres of the world will be preferred and will attract those with ambition, education and capital, other areas will experience a drain of their talent and resources. There is the risk in this new mobile world that the geographical stratification of the haves and have-nots will be accentuated. And there may be no will to address the differences.

The Quest for Community

At the same time that mobility is increasing, those who move to new places yearn for stability and a sense of belonging. In the USA of times past this was a familiar dilemma and led to the American art of instant community. Daniel Boorstin (1965) has described how those who moved westward developed a time-worn formula of building a church, a country store, a court and most important of all a local school with its school ground for community sports and picnics. Americans became joiners and boosters to get to know each other and to attract others to their newly established home.

In the post-war rush for affluence Americans may have lost their devotion to community building. As Robert Putnam (1996) observed, more and more in recent times people go 'bowling alone'. But in the world of the future these talents need to be rediscovered. Amitai Etzioni (1993), an Israeli-born sociologist familiar with the life of the kibbutz, has become an international leader in promoting the 'spirit of community'. He, like many of today's politicians, argues that the foundations of community begin with the family and the school. It will be important to teach future generations the lessons of the past: that we all have responsibilities as well as rights, that the good life may be God-given but it has to be made by man. The restoration of solid foundations where we live may be the best answer to the discontinuities and dislocations that will characterize the places where we work and govern.

The interest in strengthening community has led some service sector pioneers to propose a new form of social organization where a community centre is established that combines the services of the school, the library, the clinic, the welfare office, and certain other government functions. This approach is already being piloted in many inner-city areas in the USA and may have broader application. It implies a new kind of educational system where the school reaches beyond cognitive development to whole-person education throughout the life cycle.

Political Change

The Decline of the Strong Nation State

Paul Kennedy (1993) concludes his thoughtful survey, *Preparing for the Twenty-first Century*, by observing that recent accomplishments in economic organization seem to be outpacing progress in the organization of governments. At the time of writing, Jacques Chirac and Tony Blair are the only leaders of core nations who command the support of a solid majority.

With increasing frequency governments, at least those in charge of the major industrial nations, seem to collapse before they can complete their terms. Moreover, nations themselves seem to be collapsing with remarkable rapidity. Fundamental forces are eroding the foundations of the modern nation state. And as the modern state goes, so do its various institutions established for the modern citizen, including the provision of public education and the welfare state's safety net.

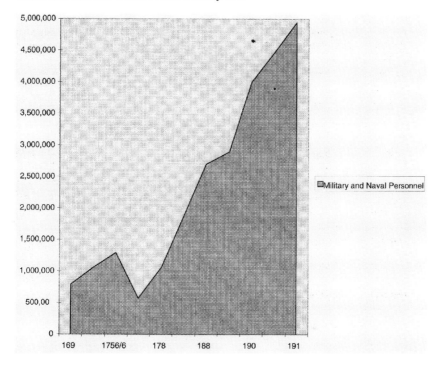

Figure 10.9. Increase in size of armies/navies, 1690-1914. Source: Kennedy (1987).

A major corollary of the revolution in physics that gave birth to modern industrialism was the new potentiality for military conflict. Not only was energy harnessed to produce new civilian products, it was also harnessed to produce ever more powerful tools for warfare. Rifles shot further, machine guns expanded the potential of rifles, artillery increased in power and range, aircraft evolved to conduct long-distance bombing. Railways intended for industrial goods also transported troops and equipment. The cars and trucks used for industrial goods also proved useful in transporting soldiers, and with heavier armour and a rotating turret they became tanks to provide the advance guard for the more conventional vehicles.

Whereas historians once viewed the medieval era as a static age to be followed by the birth of democracy and modernism, Brian Downing (1992)

237

suggests that the medieval period was relatively tranquil and allowed for considerable expression of popular will. But over the course of the modern period military aggression in some areas led to a suppression of popular will. In the more peripheral areas of Europe, the medieval institutions of governance gradually and peacefully evolved into modern institutions of democracy such as the English parliament or the Swedish constitutional monarchy. In contrast, in the heart of Europe warfare became a constant preoccupation and increasing proportions of the population were mobilized to deploy the new military technology to satisfy the pleasure of their princes.

Charles Tilly (1975) notes that there were some 500 principalities in continental Europe at the close of the fifteenth century. Following three centuries of war, there were some twenty winners and many losers. The military revolution reduced continental Europe to French absolutism (followed after the Revolution by Napoleon and the centralized French state), the German Empire, the Austro-Hungarian Empire, Poland, Russia, Spain, Italy, and a scattering of lesser states. Meanwhile, the USA rose across the Atlantic and Japan became the dominant Asian power.

Concurrent with the consolidation of modern Europe, the strongest Western powers deployed their military might overseas in the conquest of Africa and Asia. The United Kingdom, which had been least involved in the European wars, was the biggest winner. Spain, weakened by the conflicts, eventually had to surrender its conquests in Latin America. France and Germany as imperial latecomers enjoyed extensive holdings in Africa and Asia. The European imperial powers were to hold on to their colonies through the Second World War. Japan at the close of the nineteenth century decided to imitate Europe by using its new military might to colonize portions of China, Korea and Russia. As with much of Europe, Japan gave up these colonies after the Second World War.

Military power enabled the formation of strong states with large armies. In many modern nations these were standing armies that required a continuing supply of new recruits. Through the eighteenth century the armies were not notably selective, but at the conclusion of the Franco-Prussian War the French leadership concluded that its greatest threat was the Prussian schoolmaster. Perhaps for the first time in modern history, a central state government launched a major programme of educational improvement to elevate the intellectual capability of the masses. At various points over the subsequent course of modern history this example was repeated. Military preparedness was a major consideration in Japan's modern educational reform of 1872, and it became a preoccupation in the USA from the time of the First World War.

To motivate youth to serve the state, youth's loyalty to other institutions had to be weakened. Thus, as modern nations came to depend on youth for military service, they introduced requirements of free compulsory education, and they placed youth in school settings where they were exposed to a curriculum that stressed the virtues of the state and

238

(except for England and Germany) avoided, even prohibited, attention to the virtues of rival institutions claiming youth's allegiance such as local churches or ethnic communities. The school sought to direct allegiances away from primordial and local ties and towards the rewards of national citizenship.

An important stimulus to the strong state was the triumph in Russia of the Bolshevik Revolution. As the new communist regime consolidated its control, it began a radical programme to reform the Russian economy. Whereas the Western capitalist states provided minimum security to the masses, the Russian state offered full security. Workers were to work for the state, and in return the state would work for the workers. Russia devised a system of public health and social security that became the envy of labourers around the world.

The Western nations were stimulated to match the socialist challenge. Thus, the strong modern states devised various programmes to look after the interests of the common man. Legislation emerged to cover war and work-related injury, for general health, for unemployment, and even for social security in old age. By the middle of the twentieth century, these provisions were so extensive as to earn most European governments the label of the welfare state. Citizens were to be guaranteed benefits from the cradle to the grave.

The rush to devise the most generous and comprehensive safety net occurred in a context of global competition between two great ideological blocs, the so-called East and the West. But the burden of the combined expenses of military preparedness and a comprehensive safety net was enormous, and eventually proved excessive. Towards the end of the twentieth century, the East, led by Russia, acknowledged this with a wholesale programme of reform beginning with glasnost and still evolving at the time of writing. A major thrust of these reforms has been the abandonment by the central state of many of its responsibilities in the areas of employment and welfare. The state has urged local governments and individual citizens to assume the burden. Parallel with the Russian initiative, some of the Western states have taken similar steps to dismantle and/or devolve their welfare systems.

The End of the Cold War

The largest expense of the strong state was for defence and national security, typically absorbing one half of all government expenditure and about 10 per cent of gross national product. Fifty years of mutual stand-off in the Cold War finally convinced the leaders of the Soviet Union and the USA that there was little point in continuing this stubborn struggle, especially as it was diverting their nations from other important tasks. Thus, in 1991 the Soviet Union and the USA signed the first of several documents pledging to reduce their intercontinental aggressive capabilities. The Cold War was to be concluded.

In the years since, the major powers have taken measures to dismantle their military apparatus or at least to slow the pace of military preparedness. In the case of Russia, the budget for defence has been sharply reduced. In most of the states of the Western nations the budget has levelled off or been modestly reduced. Table 10.5 presents relevant data for the core societies.

	Military expenditures (% of GNI)		Armed forces personnel (% of labour force)	
	1992	1999	1992	1999
Germany	2.1	1.6	1.1	0.8
France	3.4	2.7	2.1	1.6
UK	3.8	2.5	1.0	0.7
USA	4.8	3.0	1.5	1.0
Japan	1.0	1.0	0.4	0.4
Russia	8.0	5.6	2.5	1.2

Table 10.5. Recent trends in military preparedness of the core societies. Source: World Bank, *World Development Indicators 2002*. Table 5.7. Defense expenditures.

Just as the strong state has begun to curtail its preparedness, various private groups have moved to increase their military capability. Gaining the greatest publicity is the tendency for lone individuals or small local gangs to stock up on arms and terrorize neighbourhoods. In virtually every major city of the industrial world, certain sections have become known as war zones where it is no longer safe to walk at night and where even random shootings occur in the day. Often, the individuals who stalk these areas have weapons superior to those possessed by the local police.

Less publicized is the emergence in various parts of the world of local warlords who have totally neutralized the authority of the nation state. In Burma for thirty years the famed opium dealer, Khun Sa, has been able to operate a separate fiefdom through his command of military weaponry superior to that of the Burmese army. Similarly, the drug lords of the Medeine Valley in Colombia have established an independent empire for themselves. Other dissident groups operate with impunity in Afghanistan, the Middle East, Russia, Sri Lanka, the Philippines, and even the Midwest of the USA. Declining nation states often lack the resources to match the weaponry that these groups can purchase on the open market.

The strong state depended both on the stick of coercion and the carrot of the safety net. With the decline of these two props, the influence of the centre is waning. In the case of Russia this has become especially apparent as many republics have formally seceded. Elsewhere in the world there are similar signs of state decline: Mindanao in the Philippines, the Tamil area of Sri Lanka, the Punjab and Kashmir in India, Quebec in Canada. While such drastic signs are not evident in the USA, the United Kingdom, France and Japan, nevertheless, all have taken steps to reduce the role of central government. In these cases, the era of the strong central state may be passing.[2]

September 11, 2001 may, however, have revitalized the position of those who favour a strong state and a colder world. The destruction targeted at American citizens has provoked a sharp reaction involving a rapid build-up of US security and defence forces that has every appearance of reversing the recent American trend towards a smaller state. The American reaction has not, however, been mirrored by similar build-ups of the other core societies. Thus, the twenty-first century begins with one pre-eminent power that seemingly seeks to assert its will on the world with little regard for the views of its former allies.

Samuel Huntington (1993) reminds us that the conflict now at the forefront of American policy may be an early sign of the 'clash of civilizations'. A great war may yet arise in the Middle East. Huntington suggests that yet other civilizational conflicts may surface in the decades ahead, notably in East Asia and possibly in Africa. However, the will of the core nations to cooperate in containing future aggression is seemingly waning, as reflected in the decline of the United Nations.

Conclusion: how we think about ourselves

The opening of the twenty-first century sees a new and surprising world. Table 10.6 seeks to summarize several of the mega-trends and their differential development in the six core societies. The increased level of international trade and the rise of cybernetics seems to cut across the core societies and the decline of the superstate is a trend in all settings except possibly the USA. Clearly, an unknown for the near future is the duration of America's self-proclaimed war against international terrorists and the impact this war has on the previously apparent trend towards the downsizing of imperial America. On the other hand, the core societies differ in terms of their population growth and structure, their openness to immigrants, their energy policies, the strength of their safety net, and income inequality.

Whereas the dream at mid-century was of stable change and security following a long period of war and depression, the future is an age of uncertainty. Big Brother was a threat scheduled for 1984, but he proved weak against the onslaught of cybernetics and the countervailing stalemate of too many nations having too many guns: war and regimes of organized terror and control may become outdated.

While Big Brother threatened humanity's freedom, he nevertheless promised a solution to the basic wants of home, food, safety, and

241

environmental preservation. With the passing of Big Brother, so also passes the predictability and security dreamed of at mid-century. Indeed, in many places of the world, far too much seems lost. It is shocking to admit that many places on Earth are not safe after dark and that uncontrolled industrial pollutants as well as new epidemic diseases are shortening the lives of large numbers of people.

Trend	Germany	France	England	USA	Japan	Russia
Trade as % of GNP	Moderate to high	Moderate to high	High	Moderate	High	Low
Population growth rate	Negative	Moderate	Zero	High	Negative	Negative
Age structure	Standard age distribution	Standard age distribution	Standard age distribution	Young population	Old population	Standard age distribution
In-migration	Moderate	Low	Moderate	High	Zero	Zero
Women in labor force	High	High	Increasing	High	Increasing	High
Use of natural fuels	Stable	Stable	Moderate increase	Increasing	Declining	Increasing
Trend in economic inequality	Stable	Stable	Moderately up	Sharply up	Moderate decline	Sharply up
Reliance on computers	Moderate but increasing	Moderate but increasing	Moderate but increasing	World leader	High	Moderate
R & D as % of GNP	High	Moderate	Moderate	Moderate to high	High	Low
State safety net	Stable	Stable	Down	Down	Stable	Sharply down
Favors military solutions	Pacifist	Neutral	Yes	Yes	Pacifist	Neutral

Table 10.6. Comparing trends in the core societies.

In the face of uncertainty, the responsibility rests heavily on each individual to navigate the next century. The first challenge individuals face is to build a network of affection, through establishing deep and true relations with others, and developing strong friendships that last over time, sustained by a new level of commitment out of recognition that friendship is one of the greatest assets in a time when nothing else is known. Personal responsibility also will turn inward, telling each and every individual that it is up to themselves to prepare for the future through acquiring a solid educational foundation, and through building on that foundation throughout life. Those who do best will be those who become both open to change and who have the vision to create change in all areas, ranging from the things they do to the data they use and the way they relate to others. Thus, openness, creativity and commitment may be the watchwords for personal solutions.

In the absence of a Big Brother in some far-off capital, individuals will recognize the value of fostering stronger ties nearby. One approach is to foster a new spirit of community in the neighbourhood and at the workplace. Thus, it will become prudent to devote more time to local activities such as youth sports, community clean-ups, meeting neighbours, helping those who cannot help themselves.

In the economic sphere, the new worker will have to work smarter if not harder. More individuals may work on their own providing special services to network-like collaborations that act like companies but are not as permanent as the companies of old. A key element in the success of these new entities will be their awareness of global trends and their ability to sponsor opportunities anywhere and everywhere. National boundaries will be lowered and transportation will be cheaper. And so the successful worker will be the globally oriented worker, wherever he or she might be located.

In support of this new reality will be a new culture of flexibility and tolerance. The culture will encourage deep commitments, at both a personal and spiritual level. But it will not insist that all make the same commitments, or that an individual stick forever to a particular commitment. Rather, the culture will encourage multiple views of what is right and true, and the continual creation of new solutions to the challenges humankind will encounter.

Notes

[1] The Mark Loter Domain Survey reports an increase from four networks in 1989 to 25,210 in 1994. By the end of the decade it is predicted that 120 million machines will be connected to the Internet. The World Wide Web (WWW) was introduced in 1992; by June of 1995 some 38,796 servers were involved.

[2] However, as Gopinathan (1997) reminds us, there are other areas of the world where the central state remains essentially unchallenged as the pre-eminent force in national organization. The states of several of the Eastern Asian nations are most remarkable in this regard. In terms of a commitment to military muscle most of the Eastern Asian states resemble the formerly strong states of the West; however, the Asian states have been much more conservative in the promise of social security to their people, believing that such promises tend to erode the work ethic. Thus, the Asian states do not carry as heavy a burden and so may be able to endure for a longer period.

CHAPTER 11

Imagined Futures

We should all be interested in the future because we will have to spend the rest of our lives there. (Charles F. Kettering)

The close of the twentieth century witnessed an extraordinary array of changes that some claim will lead to a fundamental reordering of the way humanity lives, and to the fabled apocalypse. If so, modern education will certainly change. Educators are inclined, when looking to the future, to speak of dilemmas that need to be considered. Each dilemma invites multiple solutions, appropriate for distinctive contexts. In this concluding chapter, eight dilemmas facing modern education are identified and then four possible future scenarios for addressing these dilemmas are outlined.

The Contemporary Dilemmas of Modern Education

What is the Purpose of Education?

The future direction of society is always in question. The founders of modern education recognized that the school was a powerful means for shaping that future through its role in shaping the hearts and minds of each new generation. The state focused on the goals of fostering loyal subjects, disciplined workers and good parents. These same goals will certainly continue to influence the direction of much future education. But at the turn of the twenty-first century the state was less dominant than in its heyday, and many see a need for education to foster a more autonomous generation that raises questions about what they confront, whether in the classroom, the community, the polity or the workplace.[1] In this way, it is hoped that the future generations will be more creative and critical.

Who Will Sponsor Education?

Whereas public spending for education increased in most nations through most of the twentieth century, a tendency towards levelling or even a decline was evident by the turn of the century. Many of the modern rationales for central state funding of education are eroding; concurrently the state's

245

capacity for supporting education is weakening. And so new funders of education need to be identified.

The future beneficiaries are seen to be employers, who make use of the skills and perspectives of the educated, the educated, who are rewarded in relation with how well they manipulate symbols, and the local areas where the employers and the educated locate. The question becomes, who will pay and how?

Among the possibilities is a transfer of responsibility from central and regional to local authorities, and that trend is well under way in several of the advanced societies, notably France and Russia, and it is well established in England and the USA. Michael Fullan (1993), a leading observer of the educational reform movement, argues that a radical shift to local autonomy is the only option that will work.

A dilemma that emerges with local responsibility is that some localities are more affluent than others. The richer areas are likely to provide better education, which will rebound in terms of attracting better employers who will enhance private incomes. Thus, the schools in the rich locales will get richer while the poor locales will fall further behind. Indeed, in many contemporary nations most local governments do not have the capability to support education.

Some commentators point to the possibility for schools of building partnerships with interested local bodies such as Rotary Clubs, the media, or major employers. Solutions of this kind may bring in a new kind of teaching and additional resources, but they may also allow partners to exert undue influence on the curricula of the partnered schools.

Yet another possibility is for parents to assume full responsibility for their children's education, bypassing the traditional school. The movement towards home education seems to be accelerating in the USA and England. Correspondence courses have always been available for home education, and as time goes on the Internet and media will supply new material. This option is perhaps the least expensive option of all those considered above, and it may open the greatest scope for creativity.

Everything that is covered above applies with even greater force to the advanced stages of education. Whereas in the past higher education was blessed by the state, recent analysis portrays higher education as a consumer good whose primary benefits accrue to the individual. And so the individual should pay. Philanthropy which was once directed to higher education may in the future be directed to lower levels in the educational cycle. New, less costly and more flexible approaches to higher education are sure to evolve. Alongside these will be others of high quality and cost paid for those who can afford a Mercedes.

Who Wants to be Educated?

Whereas the modern school took in youth at a malleable age and sought to shape them in such a way as to fit a new emerging society fostered by the state, the school of the future faces a new challenge. Forces beyond the control of the state and which are proceeding at such a rapid pace as to require continuous adaptation are shaping the rhythm of life.

The modern school has tended to shut out these external developments, restricting its mission to the cognitive curriculum. Meanwhile, many young people find they cannot endure the mindless routine of the modern school, and they drop out and drop in again. These young people seek not just cognitive education but guidance on how to cope with life in a new social environment where they often have only one parent or where parents and siblings are so heavily involved in other commitments that they do not communicate life's lessons.

In addition to youth there are many working adults and older people who seek continuing education both to prepare them for new jobs and to enrich their understanding of life. The clients for the school of the future are numerous. Many of these clients, while diverse in age or other attributes, have common learning needs. And so there are likely to be schools of the future that rely on mixed aged classes. Other options opened by the expansion of clients will include the extensive use of students as tutors. The hierarchy of teacher and student may be replaced by new modes of mutual exchange of different spheres of knowledge and experience.

Where Will Education Take Place?

The great accomplishment of the modern period was to shift most educational activity from the home and church to the state-controlled common school, physically separate from these former locales. At the school state-supported officials teach a curriculum over which parents and the church have little influence. Having lived with these innovations for over one hundred years, it is difficult to imagine any other option. But as the state pulls back on its support and schools begin to fold, it will become necessary to consider new physical settings for education.

One option is to move the school closer to other public or private institutions and mobilize the members of these institutions to assume part-time instructional roles. Thus, officials in a government office might enlarge their jobs to rotate in and out of classrooms. Or employees in a commercial mall might expand their jobs to take on part-time teaching.

Religious institutions, which tend to be underutilized during weekdays, might also be mobilized for education, with senior citizens and other volunteers assuming various instructional roles. Another option is to shift education back to the home. Greater flexibility in the location of education becomes possible with the new discoveries in the what and how of education to be discussed below.

What Should be Taught?

Modern education was created to foster loyalty to the state and provide the skills and work habits required by the corporate sector. The decline of the state and the diversification of work necessitate a fundamental re-examination of what needs to be taught.

The modern curriculum has remained essentially unchanged since the late nineteenth century. It takes children grade by grade in uniform classes of 20-40 through a common sequence of courses focusing on language, history, mathematics and science, with some attention to health/physical education and aesthetics. While every child is exposed to the same material, few of these children will be working in a common workplace. Some will be working largely with material objects, and they would be well served by knowing more about nature and matter. Others will be working largely with people, and they will need to know more about human nature. Yet others will be working with computers, sounds, or symbols. One option for the future curriculum is to foster greater diversification in line with the growing complexity of our lives.

Moreover, as James P. Byrnes & Judith Torney-Purta (1997) remind us, the learning needs of pupils are far more complex than once believed. Children have not a single but, rather, multiple intelligences, and in particular children there is often a differential development of these intelligences. In other words, children differ in their talents and a more diversified curriculum would allow for more children to realize their potential.

The rhythm of the modern school, with its break-up of the day into carefully defined periods, was designed in imitation of the clock-determined work routines of the modern factory and office. In the future, a decreasing proportion of the labour force will work under those conditions. Most workers will have considerable control over their schedules, sometimes working alone and sometimes working in more or less autonomous teams. As the rhythm of work changes, there is reason to change the rhythm of schools.

Yet another possible option for the future is a re-examination of the sequencing of educational material. It has long been assumed, especially in the sciences, that there is a natural sequence to subjects. If a student ever abandons this sequence, there is no coming back. Such assumptions are discouraging for those who experience broken careers or disappointment in work, and want to come back to school to discover a new direction. Moreover, there is increasing evidence that the assumptions are ill supported.[2] While not all students can make their way through identical material at the same pace, careful teaching that gives proper attention to the mastery of individual units enables students to master material they are interested in. The major constraint to learning is with the educational process and not with the student.

Thus, there will be a move to customize the curriculum. In the past the subjects of mathematics, science and national language were taught the same way for all students. In the future these subjects will have to be adapted both to the intellectual strengths (and weaknesses) of learners as well as to their occupational goals. Thus, there will be a mathematics course for those strong in computation as well as for those strong in music or social intelligence. There will be English for those interested in literature as well as business English. Individuals, based on their own needs, can select the curriculum of their choice from a learning bank. Each of these modular curricula will be designed in such a way that students can make their choices and proceed at their own pace

How Will Values be Cultivated?

Most current pedagogical thinking focuses on the cognitive curriculum, but in the meantime society faces an increasing sense of moral uncertainty in the face of rapid change. With the rapid shift in family structure, many children come from reduced families that may not provide sufficient guidance. Schools will be asked to assist in filling this void. There are different approaches to values education. The most controversial is the contrast of a more directive approach with a reliance on cognitive reasoning. While this distinction is useful for education at the lower grade levels, as children mature more innovative approaches are attractive. Among the promising options are value-shaping experiences such as community service.

How Might Students Learn?

Despite major advances in communications and information technology, teacher-centred lectures and discussion are still the dominant mode of teaching in the modern school. But as several of the chapters in this section indicate, there are many new possibilities for learning.

Among the most extensively utilized is instructional technology relying on carefully developed modules which teachers can use in guiding the learning of students or even which students can use on their own. Ernesto Scheffelbein (1997) reviews the possibilities for this medium, pointing out how they keep students engaged, provide greater flexibility in the use of school facilities and in the scheduling of instruction, and are often less costly than traditional methods.

Radio and television are other options for instruction that may assume a greater role in future education. Orozco-Gomez (1997), who has reviewed the evidence, proposes that a new alliance should be formed between the media and the educational sector that promotes the mutual reinforcement of important lessons.

Yet another possibility receiving much attention in recent years is the use of computers. An extraordinary amount of material can now be accessed on computers and that is certain to increase in the years to come. Under current development are a variety of instructional materials that are being tried out in controlled settings. In general, these materials seem to have outstanding potential for retaining the interest of students. With the advent of the Internet, they have the advantage of being accessed wherever there is a computer with a modem. In addition, the format for instruction can incorporate a seemingly unlimited range of options. The programmes can be self-instructional, they can involve limited interaction, immediate interaction, and even interaction with facial images and voice transmission. As with other of the new instructional options, the computer-based options also allow flexible schedules.

How to Assess Development?

Among the most arbitrary inventions of the modern school was the pencil and paper test administered under conditions of high stress to determine the progress of students in developing their minds and dispositions. There was a certain logic to this testing procedure as many working situations approximated to this high stress condition. But the shift to cybernetic workplaces may enable new working situations that are more individualized, with more flexible schedules and work sites. The emphasis will be on the range and quality of accomplishment, and often creativity will be valued. Tests that measure the ability of individuals to replicate time-worn solutions to classical problems may be less appropriate in these situations.[3]

Just as evaluation in work will change, so may evaluation in education. Linda Bond (1997) and her colleagues discuss the advantages of one possibility for evaluation, the portfolio, which is gaining increasing attention in the USA and England. Artists typically compile portfolios of their work to share with clients and employers. The same principle is now being utilized in a wide variety of educational settings. Portfolios seem to stimulate greater energy among students as well as to promote experimentation with new approaches.

Divergence within Societies

It may be, given the new diversity and complexity of life, that the most important change within the respective societies will be from the 'one best system' design of the common school to multiple designs appropriate for the diversifying challenges of the future.

The more decentralized societies of the USA and England have already gone a long way down this road. In the USA, there are significant differences in the approaches across school districts and especially across states. Within most of the larger districts, a magnet school system has been introduced which enables the several schools of a common grade level to develop distinctive educational programmes, with, for example, one school focusing on international studies, a second on science, a third on the creative arts, and so on. Amplifying this trend to diversification is the movement to establish charter schools and the programme to encourage schools to adopt comprehensive school reform models.

While European societies have been more reluctant to experiment with major diversification of the schools in the academic track, they have been highly creative in the development of distinctive vocational schools oriented to different sectors of the modern economy. Vocational schools have been established for professions as diverse as restaurant service and computer technical service. Germany is especially well regarded for its system of linking vocational training with internships at the factories of prospective employers, who in turn pay for part of the cost of the training; this model has been adapted to a wide spectrum of industries.

Convergence across Societies

This discussion of the respective modern systems suggests that in each of the core systems schools at particular levels stand out as having a world-class approach: the Japanese and Russian primary schools, the German vocational school, the English or French upper secondary academic school, the American university and graduate school, and, finally, the Russian talent school for the development of exceptional musicians, artists and athletes.

A popular proposal favoured by global thinkers is to take the best from each of the core societies and integrate these world-class school models in a single system to be shared by all modern societies. To some degree the history of modern education is the history of converging reforms. The French studied the Prussian example in strengthening their normal schools and primary schools. The American common school was imported from the European continent. The Japanese carefully studied the systems of Europe and the USA prior to launching the Meiji reforms. And the early Russian reformers admired John Dewey. Yet, despite the inclination to look abroad for best practices, each of the systems of the six core societies has many distinctive elements.

Should there be a new wave of cross-national borrowing to create the perfect convergent system? Phillips (1989) reminds us that educational practice is not easily 'borrowed' or 'lent'. In the words of Michael Sadler (1900, p. 49):

> *We should not forget that the things outside the schools matter even more than the things inside the schools, and govern and interpret the things inside. We cannot wander at leisure among the educational systems of the world, like a child strolling through a garden, and pick off a flower from one bush and some leaves from another, and then expect that if we stick what we have gathered into the soil at home, we shall have a living plant. A national system is a living thing, the outcome of forgotten struggles and 'of battles long ago'. It has in it some of the secret workings of national life.*

Yet, some parents today actually implement this convergence principle as they intentionally move their children from place to place. Approximately 100,000 children from around the world are sent to British public schools. Even more remarkable are the 600,000 young people from around the world who attend American colleges and universities.

At the same time that children move to the best schools in foreign locations, some entrepreneurs are moving their schools to the home places of interested children. This tendency is especially notable at the university level where the USA, England and Australia have mounted a vigorous effort to set up branch campuses throughout the world. Similarly, a hybrid group of international high schools is now established in most major cities around the world. Over the past decade, Kawai Juku has pioneered in the export of its supplementary educational approach to Europe, the USA, and East Asia. With the export of these educational opportunities, a young person in Geneva, Switzerland can attend a supplementary *juku* to buttress their initial studies, attend a British-style secondary school, and enter the branch campus of an American university without ever leaving his or her home town.

Thus, we see some evidence of a convergence of modern educational systems or at least an incipient pattern of certain young people undergoing educational experiences that draw on the best aspects of several of the core modern systems. But these discriminating consumers tend to come from affluent and well-informed families that can afford the high costs associated with these peak experiences. The convergent journey through youth may work for the few, but the prospect for expansion is limited.

New Schooling Models

We might recall that the seeds of the modern educational revolution were first sewn in the periphery of the modern world, in Scandinavia and Northern Germany, rather than in the French and English centre. It may be that the seeds of the next major educational revolution, likewise, are already planted in a peripheral site.

One such area deserving consideration is the South-east Asian axis where Singapore and Malaysia are facing off in a major development duel to leap beyond the examples of the First World. In 2001, Malaysia finished its construction of the twin towers of Kuala Lumpur that, reflecting Malaysia's development aspirations, are the tallest buildings in the world. The per capita incomes of these two nations have now passed that of most European societies. And the average educational attainments of their populations are impressive.

Both of these nations have made major commitments to the development of their computer industries and to the emphasis of computer literacy and computer education in their schools. According to Malaysia's Vision 2020, within two decades every seat in a Malaysian primary school will be equipped with a computer terminal and a substantial portion of each day's education will be computer based. Young people will complete all of their exercises on computers and receive, when appropriate, instant feedback as they advance through these exercises. Computers will be used to analyse student learning difficulties and to provide guidance to teachers on the strengths and weaknesses of each of their students. Singapore has similar aspirations.

Another Eastern Asian educational system to watch is that of South Korea, a nation that recently joined the Organization for Economic Cooperation and Development. South Korea currently has the highest tertiary-level enrolment ratio in the world, surpassing even Japan and the USA, and it is spending an exceptionally high proportion of its gross national product on research and development. Over the past decade, Korean scientific publications have rapidly emerged as contenders (with a growing share of publications) in the recognized journals for scientific discourse.

It should be recalled in the recent international achievement tests known as TIMSS (Third International Mathematics and Science Study) and PISA (OECD's Programme for Individual Student Assessment) that the young people from Singapore scored at the top of the scale on just about every test they took. In the tests where Singapore was not number 1, Korea was. Clearly, at least in terms of the criteria of academic achievement something positive is occurring in these Eastern Asian educational systems.

New Educational Models

The modern school was a new educational innovation, replacing the former tradition of home schooling and self-study. Children were now placed in schools some distance from their homes where trained teachers taught them a prescribed curriculum organized in terms of sequential grades. Each component of the modern school – the schoolhouse, the curriculum organized in grades and conveyed through textbooks, the trained teacher – while introduced to enhance learning, also added substantial costs. In an age of rising educational costs that are not matched with rising accomplishments, it is inevitable that critics will question the value of these components and ask if some cannot be modified or even dispensed with.

At the primary level, one interesting proposal developed in South-east Asia over a quarter of a century ago was the modification of the curriculum to allow for individual self-pacing and the modification of the teacher's position so that teachers served as instructional managers of the individualized learning experiences. These two modifications enabled a substantial reduction in costs while realizing equivalent educational results.

Teachers' salaries are the major expense of the modern school, and so any reduction of the modern school's dependence on teachers is likely to lead to a more affordable school. One vision possible in the cybernetic era is to shift a significant part of the teaching challenge over to computer-assisted technology, such as the presentation of materials, the presentation of exercises, the evaluation of student performance on exercises, and the analysis of student learning difficulties. Teachers might serve in a new role of coordinating these technical tasks, while intervening to introduce new concepts and to stimulate higher-level thinking. Considerable technology is now being developed to accomplish these various tasks. Ironically, this technology currently has its highest applicability at the tertiary level for adult learners rather than at the primary level where the educational challenge is most pressing. The shift to educational technology also reduces the reliance on school buildings as a site for learning; students can complete most of their learning assignments at home or at a nearby computer centre or learning station. Where good instructional technology is in place, teachers' contact hours are reduced and so are educational expenses.

Distinct from cost is the challenge of motivating students. In the early decades of the modern era, the school was an exciting place for most children – or at least a more attractive option than working in the fields. In today's information society, the school encounters potential competition from many teachers, and often loses. Young people, especially as they reach their teens, frequently express boredom with their schooling. Yet these same young people have dreams of becoming successful adults with interesting careers and a full package of material possessions. To help children make the transition from youth to adulthood, some societies are beginning to organize internships in workplaces as an alternative to formal schooling. Germany perhaps pioneered in this regard with its unique programme of industry-based vocational schools. This same principle could easily be applied to other occupational areas such as internships in commercial and industrial corporations, internships in museums and other aesthetic activities such as architectural firms or the music industry, and internships in the media and sports and leisure organizations. Societies might propose to offer to every middle school graduate an opportunity over the coming years to participate in a minimum of three internships. Upon the completion of the internship phase, the young people would have a clearer sense of their occupational aspirations and a stronger determination to commit to the studies appropriate for realizing those aspirations. Boredom might be replaced by purposeful motivation. As these internships would benefit the host sites as much as the youth, the host sites would cover most of the costs – thus relieving the educational sector of many of the expenses currently devoted to high school education.

In sum, there are ways to design education that reduce dependence on the modern props of school buildings, the uniform curriculum, textbooks, trained teachers, and one-time national examinations. Focusing on the goals of education as contrasted with the modern means is the key to the elaboration of these possibilities. Educational technology opens up many of these possibilities. Will the twenty-first century, drawing on the power of the cybernetic revolution, launch the third educational revolution?

Notes

[1] A recent comparative survey (Cummings et al, 2001) of the values education priorities of educational elites in twenty-two settings around the world found that the fostering of autonomous personalities was the most common choice out of nineteen value options, and for most of the settings it was the first choice.

[2] Schmidt et al (2001) report considerable variation in the sequencing of the middle school mathematics and science curricula of some forty-five societies, but they do not link these sequencing differences as such to learning outcomes. In the USA, at the high school level there is an interesting debate concerning the wisdom of teaching physics or biology first. In many societies, high school science is provided as an integrated curriculum.

[3] Also, as students begin to focus on diverse educational objectives and individualize their educational experience, the expectation now typical in international assessments of educational achievement, as well as the accountability exercises of many modern educational systems, that each child should do equally well on all tests for a common array of subjects, will be challenged.

Bibliography

Alexander, Robin (2001) *Culture and Pedagogy: international comparisons in primary education.* Oxford: Blackwell.

Almond, Gabriel & Sidney Verba (1963) *The Civic Culture: political attitudes and democracy in five nations.* Princeton: Princeton University Press.

Alston, P. (1969) *Education and the State in Tsarist Russia.* Stanford: Stanford University Press.

Altbach, Philip (1987) The Oldest Technology: textbooks in comparative context, *Compare*, 17, pp. 93-106.

Altbach, Philip (Ed.) (2001) *International Higher Education: an encyclopedia.* New York: Garland.

Amano, Ikuo (1990) *Education and Examination in Modern Japan*, trans. William K. Cummings & Fumiko Cummings. Tokyo: University of Tokyo Press.

Ambrosius, G. & W.H. Hubbard (1989) *A Social and Economic History of Twentieth Century Europe.* Cambridge, MA: Harvard University Press.

Anderson, Benedict (1983) *Imagined Communities: reflections on the origin and spread of nationalism.* London: Verso.

Anderson-Levitt, Kathryn M. (2002) Teaching Culture as National and Transnational: a response to teachers' work, *Educational Researcher*, 31(9), pp. 9-21.

Anderson, Margo J. *The American Census: a Social History.* New Haven: Yale University Press.

Apple, Michael W. (1979) *Ideology and Curriculum.* Boston: Routledge & Kegan Paul.

Apple, Michael W. (1986) *Teachers and Texts.* New York: Routledge.

Archer, Margaret (1977) *Social Origins of Educational Systems.* Beverly Hills: Sage.

Ashby, Eric (1966) *Universities: British, Indian, African. A Study in the Ecology of Higher Education.* Cambridge, MA: Harvard University Press.

Ashton, David & Francis Green (1996) *Education, Training, and the Global Economy.* Cheltenham: Edward Elgar.

Baker, David P. (1999) Schooling All the Masses: reconsidering the origins of American Schooling in the postbellum era, *Sociology of Education*, 72, pp. 197-215.

Baker, David P., Brian Goesling & Gerald K. Letendre (2002) Socioeconomic Status, School Quality, and National Economic Development: a cross-national analysis of the 'Heyneman–Loxley Effect' on mathematics and science achievement, *Comparative Education Review*, 46, pp. 291-312.

Bain, Olga (2001) *Russia: towards autonomous personalities*, in W.K. Cummings, M.T. Tatto & J. Hawkins (Eds) *Values Education for Dynamic Societies: individualism or collectivism*, pp. 21-58. *Comparative Education Research Center Series*. Hong Kong: Hong Kong University Press.

Bain, Olga (2003) *University Autonomy in the Russian Federation since Perestroika*. New York: RoutledgeFalmer.

Banfield, Edward (1958) *The Moral Basis of a Backward Society*. New York: Free Press.

Baran, P. & P. Sweezy (1968) *Monopoly Capital: an essay on the American economic and social order*. New York: Monthly Review Press.

Barnard, Henry (1851) *Normal Schools and Other Institutions, Agencies, and Means Designed for the Professional Education of Teachers*. Hartford, CT: Case, Tiffany.

Barnard, Howard. C. (1922) *The French Tradition in Education*. Cambridge: Cambridge University Press.

Beare, H. & W.L. Boyd (Eds) (1993) *Restructuring Schools*. Washington, DC: Falmer Press.

Beeby, C.E. (1962) *Quality of Education*. Cambridge, MA: Harvard University Press.

Bellah, Robert N. (1975) *The Broken Covenant: American civil religion in time of trial*. New York: Seabury Press.

Bendix, Reinhard (1956) *Work and Authority in Modern Industry*. New York: John Wiley & Sons.

Bendix, Reinhard (1969) *Nation-building and Citizenship*. Garden City, NY: Doubleday & Co.

Bereday, George Z.F. (1964) *Comparative Method in Education*. New York: Holt, Rinehart & Winston.

Bereday, George S.F., William W. Brickman & Gerald H. Read (Eds) (1960) *The Changing Soviet School*. Cambridge: Riverside Press.

Berlak, A. & Berlak (1981) *Dilemmas of Schooling*. London: Methuen.

Black, C.E. M.B. Jansen, M.J. Levy Jr., G. Rozman, H.D. Smith II, S.F. Starr, H. Rosousky, & H.S. Levine (Eds) (1975) *The Modernization of Japan and Russia: a comparative study*. London: Macmillan

Bloom, Benjamin (1985) *Developing Talent in Young People*. New York: Ballantine.

Bloom, B.S., Hastings, J.T., & Madaus, G.F. (1971). *Handbook on Formative and Summative Evaluation of Student Learning*. New York: McGraw-Hill.

Boli, J., F.O. Ramirez & J.W. Meyer (1985) Explaining the Origins and Expansion of Mass Education, *Comparative Education Review*, 29, pp. 45-170.

Bond, Linda Ann (1997) Reforms in Evaluation. Does American Educational Assessment Pass the Test? in William Cummings & Noel McGinn, (Eds) *The*

International Handbook of Education and Development: preparing schools, students, and nations for the twenty-first century. Oxford: Pergamon.

Boorstin, Daniel J. (1958) *The Americans: the colonial experience.* New York: Random House.

Boorstin, Daniel J. (1965) *The Americans: the national experience.* London: Penguin.

Boorstin, Daniel J. (1974) *The Americans: the democratic experience.* New York: Random House.

Boorstin, Daniel J. (1983) *The Discoverers.* New York: Random House.

Boudon, Raymond (1973a) *Education, Opportunity and Social Inequality: changing prospects in Western society.* New York: John Wiley & Sons.

Boudon, Raymond (1973b) *Mathematical Structures of Social Mobility.* San Francisco: Jossey-Bass.

Bowles, S. & H. Gintis (1976) *Schooling in Capitalist America.* New York: Basic Books.

Boyd, David (1973) *Elites and their Education.* Slough: National Foundation for Educational Research.

Boyer, Ernest L. (1983) *High School: a repeat on secondary education in America.* New York: Harper & Row.

Braudel, Fernand (1985) *The Structures of Everyday Life.* Volume 1 of Civilization and Capitalism: 15th-18th century. London: Fontana.

Brint, Steven (1998) *Schools and Societies.* Thousand Oaks: Pine Forge Press.

Broadfoot, P. & M. Osborn (1988) What Professional Responsibility Means to Teachers: national contexts and classroom constants, *British Journal of Sociology,* 9, pp. 265-287.

Broadfoot, Patricia & Marilyn Osborn with Michel Ciilly & Arlette Buchée (1993) *Perceptions of Teaching: primary school teachers in England and France.* London: Cassell.

Bronfenbrenner, Urie (1970) *Two Worlds of Childhood.* New York: Russell Sage Foundation.

Bryant, Seymour (1917) *The Public School System in Relation to the Coming Conflict for National Supremacy.* London: Longmans, Green.

Burke, Edmund (1989) *Reflections on the Revolution in France,* in Paul Langford, P.J. Marshall & John A. Woods (Eds) *The Writings and Speeches of Edmund Burke,* vol. 3. Oxford: Clarendon Press.

Byrnes, James. P. & Judith Torney-Purta (1997) Understanding the Learning Process: three theoretical perspectives, in William Cummings & Noel McGinn (Eds) *The International Handbook of Education and Development: preparing schools, students, and nations for the twenty-first century.* Oxford: Pergamon.

Canton, Norman E. (1993) *The Civilization of the Middle Ages.* New York: Harper Collins.

Carnoy, Martin (1974) *Education as Cultural Imperialism*. New York: D. McKay.

Carnoy, Martin & Joel Samoff (1990) *Education and Social Transition in the Third World*. Princeton: Princeton University Press.

Cha, Yun-Kyung, Suk-Ying Wong & John W. Meyer (1988) *Values Education in the Curriculum: some comparative empirical data*, in W. K. Cumming, Gopinathan & Y. Tomoda (Eds) (1988) *The Revival of Values Education in Asia and the West*. New York: Pergamon.

Chisick, H. (1981) *The Limits of Reform in the Enlightenment: attitudes towards the education of the lower classes in eighteenth-century France*. Princeton: Princeton University Press.

Clark, Burton (1983) *The Higher Education System*. Berkeley: University of California Press.

Clark, B. (Ed.) (1984) *School and University*. Berkeley: University of California Press.

Cohen, W. (1996) Why the Chip is Still the Economy's Champ, *US News and World Report*, 120(12), pp. 55-56.

Collins, Randall (1979) *The Credential Society: an historical sociology of education and stratification*. New York: Academic Press.

Commission on Excellence in Education (1983) A Nation at Risk. Washington, DC: US Government Printing Office.

Cookson, P.W. Jr & C.H. Persell (1986) English and American Residential Schools: a comparative study of the reproduction of social elite, *Comparative Education Review*, 30, pp. 260-270.

Coombs, Philip H. (1968) *The World Educational Crisis; a systems analysis*. New York: Oxford University Press.

Coombs, Philip H. (1985) *The World Crisis in Education: the view from the eighties*. New York: Oxford University Press.

Cornbleth, C. & D. Waugh (1993) *The Great Speckled Bird*, Educational Researcher, 22(1), pp. 31-37.

Craig, J. (1981) The Expansion of Education, *Review of Research in Education*, 9, pp. 151-213.

Cremin, Lawrence (1951) *The American Common School*. New York: Teachers College.

Crozier, Michel (1964) *The Bureaucratic Phenomenon*. Chicago: University of Chicago Press.

Cuban, L. (1992) Managing Dilemmas While Building Professional Communities, *Educational Researcher*, 21(1), pp. 4-11.

Cummings, W.K. (1980) *Education and Equality in Japan*, pp. 14-76. Princeton: Princeton University Press.

Cummings, W.K (1985) *Japan*, in B.R. Clark (Ed.) *The School and the University*, pp. 121-159. Berkeley: University of California Press.

Cummings, W.K. (1987) *Samurai Without Swords: making of the modern Japanese,* in Edgar B. Gumpert (Ed.) *In the Nation's Image.* Atlanta: Center for Cross-Cultural Education, Georgia State University, pp. 15-38.

Cummings, W.K. (1990a) *Who Teaches? An International Analysis, in Val Rust & Per Dalin* (Eds) *Teachers and Teaching in the Developing World,* pp. 3-22. New York: Garland.

Cummings, W.K. (1990b) Examinations and Evaluation, in M. Thomas (Ed.) *International Comparative Education: practices, issues and prospects,* pp. 87-106. Oxford: Pergamon.

Cummings, W.K. (1992) *Examining the Educational Productional Function: UK, US and Japanese Models,* in Herbert Walberg & David W. Chapman (Eds) *International Perspectives in Educational Productivity,* pp. 4-21. Greenwich: JAI Press.

Cummings, W.K. (1996) *Private Education in Asia,* in William K. Cummings & Philip G. Altbach (Eds) *The Asian Educational Challenge: implications for America.* Albany, NY: SUNY Press.

Cummings, W.K. (1999) The InstitutionS of Education: compare, compare, compare, *Comparative Education Review,* 21, pp. 413-437.

Cummings, W.K. & Atsushi Naoi (1974) *Social Background, Education and Personal Advancement in a Dualistic Employment System, Developing Economies,* pp. 250-274.

Cummings, W.K. & Riddell, A. (1994) Alternative Policies for the Finance, Control and Delivery of Basic Education, *International Educational Research,* 21(8), pp. 751-776.

Cummings, William K., Maria Teresa Tatto & John Hawkins (Eds) (2001) *Values Education for Dynamic Societies: individualism or collectivism.* Hong Kong: Comparative Education Centre, University of Hong Kong.

Custance, Roger (Ed.) (1982) *Winchester College: sixth-centenary essays.* Oxford: Oxford University Press.

Dore, R. (1965) *Tokugawa Education.* Berkeley: University of California Press.

Dore, R. (1973) *British Factory, Japanese Factory; the origins of national diversity in industrial relations.* Berkeley: University of California Press.

Dore, R. (1976) *The Diploma Disease.* Berkeley: University of California Press.

Downing, Brian (1992) *The Military Revolution and Political Change: origins of democracy and autocracy in early modern Europe.* Princeton: Princeton University Press.

Drucker, P.F. (1992) *The Age of Discontinuity: guidelines to our changing society.* New Brunswick: Transaction.

Duke, Benjamin (1973) *Japan's Militant Teachers.* Honolulu: University of Hawaii Press.

Durkheim, Emile (1951) *Suicide.* New York: Free Press.

Durkheim, Emile (1953) *The Rules of Sociological Method.* New York: Free Press.

Durkheim, Emile (1969) *The Evolution of Educational Thought:* lectures on the formation and development of secondary education in France, trans. Peter Collins. London: Routledge & Kegan Paul.

Easterlin, Richard A. (1981) *Why* Isn't the Whole World Developed? *Journal of Economic History*, 41, pp. 1-19.

Eckstein, M. & H. Noah (1989) Forms and Functions of Secondary School Leaving Examinations, *Comparative Education Review*, 33, pp. 295-316.

Eckstein, Max A. & Harold J. Noah (1993) *Secondary School Examinations: international perspectives on policies and practice.* New Haven: Yale University Press.

Eklof, Ben (1986) *Russian Peasant Schools: officialdom, village culture, and popular pedagogy, 1864-1914.* Berkeley: University of California Press.

Eklof, Ben (Ed.) (1993) School and Society in Tsarist and Soviet Russia: selected papers from the *Fourth World Congress for Soviet and East European Studies,* Harrogate, 1990. New York: St Martin's Press.

Eklof, Ben & Edward Dneprov (Eds) (1993) *Democracy in the Russian School: the reform movement in education since 1984.* Boulder: Westview Press.

Eraut, Michael (2001) *Developing Professional Knowledge and Competence.* London: RoutledgeFalmer.

Etzioni, A. (1993) *The Spirit of Community.* New York: Touchstone.

Evans, K. (1985) *The Development and Structure of the English School System.* London: Hodder & Stoughton.

Fägerlind, Ingemar & Lawrence J. Saha (1989) *Education and National Development: a comparative perspective,* 2nd edn. Oxford: Pergamon.

Finckenauer, James O. (1995) *Russian Youth: law, deviance, and the pursuit of freedom.* New Brunswick: Transaction.

Fitzpatrick, Sheila (1970) *The Commissariat of Enlightenment: Soviet organization of education and the arts under Lunacharsky, October 1917-1921.* Cambridge: Cambridge University Press.

Frank, R. & P. Cook (1995) *The Winner-Take-All-Society.* New York: Free Press.

Fullan, M. (1993) *Changed Forces: probing the depths of educational reform.* London: Falmer Press.

Fuller, Wayne (1982) *The Old Country School: the story of rural education in the Middle West.* Chicago: University of Chicago Press.

Gardner, H. & T. Hatch (1989) Multiple Intelligences Go to School: educational implications of the Theory of Multiple Intelligences, *Educational Researcher*, 18(4), pp. 4-10.

Geertz, Clifford (1963) *Agricultural Involution: the process of ecological change in Indonesia.* Berkeley: University of California Press.

Gemery, Henry A. (2000) *The White Population of the Colonial United States*, in R. Michael Haines & Richard H. Steckel (Eds) *A Population History of North America.* Cambridge: Cambridge University Press.

George, R. (1987) *Youth Policies and Programs in Selected Countries*. Washington, DC: Institute for Educational Leadership.

Gildea, Robert (1983) *Education in Provincial France 1800-1914: a study of three departments*. Oxford: Clarendon Press.

Ginsberg, R. & R. Wimpelberg (1988) *An Assessment of Twentieth Century Commission Reports of Educational Reform*, in C.V. Willie & I. Miller (Eds) *Social Goals and Educational Reform: American schools in the 20th century*, pp. 29-69. New York: Greenwood Press.

Glenn, C. (1988) *The Myth of the Common School*. Amherst: University of Massachusetts Press.

Glenn, C. (1989) *Choice of Schools in Six Nations*. Washington, DC: Department of Education.

Goffman, Irving (1962) *Asylums: essays on the social situation of mental patients and other inmates*. Chicago: Aldine.

Goldstone, Jack A. (1991) *Revolution and Rebellion in the Early Modern World*. Berkeley: University of California Press.

Goode, William J. (1963) *World Revolution and Family Patterns*. New York: Free Press.

Goodlad, John I. (1984) *A Place Called School: prospects for the future*. New York: McGraw-Hill.

Goodson, Ivor, (Ed.) (1986) *International Perspectives in Curriculum History*. London: Routledge.

Goodwin, Jason (2000) *Lords of the Horizons*. New York: Henry Holt.

Gopinathan, S. (1997) Educational Development in a Strong Developmentalist State: the Singapore experience, in William Cummings & Noel McGinn (Eds) *The International Handbook of Education and Development: preparing schools, students, and nations for the twenty-first century*. Oxford: Pergamon.

Gouldner, Alvin W. (1971) *The Coming Crisis of Western Sociology*. London: Heinemann.

Grant, N. (1982) *Soviet Education*. New York: Penguin.

Gumilev, L. N. (1997) *Ethnogez i Bioshera Zemli (Ethnogenesis and Biosphere of the Earth)*. Moscow: Institut DI-DIK.

Guthrie, J.W. (1993) School Reform and the New World Order, in S.L. Jacobson & R. Berne (Eds) *Reforming Education: the emerging systemic approach*. Thousand Oaks: Corwin Press.

Hage, J. & M. Garnier (1992) Strong States and Educational Expansion: France, Italy, in B. Fuller & R. Rubinson (Eds) *The Political Construction of Education: the state, school expansion and economic change*. New York: Praeger.

Hans, Nicholas A. (1963) *The Russian Tradition in Education*. London: Routledge & Kegan Paul.

Hanushek, E. (1989) The Impact of Different Expenditures on School Performance, *Educational Researcher*, 18(4), pp. 45-51, 62.

Harbison, Frederick Harris & Charles A. Myers (1964) *Education, Manpower, and Economic Growth; strategies of human resource development.* New York: McGraw-Hill.

Hartwell, Ash (1997) Scientific Ideas and Education in the 21st Century, in William Cummings & Noel McGinn (Eds) *The International Handbook of Education and Development: preparing schools, students, and nations for the twenty-first century.* Oxford: Pergamon.

Heilbroner, Robert L. (1962) *The Making of Economic Society.* Englewood Cliffs: Prentice-Hall.

Hess, Robert D., S. Y. Lee, J. W. Stigler, S. Kitamura, S. Kimura, & T. Kato (1986) Family Influences on School Readiness and Achievement in Japan and the United States: an overview of a longitudinal study, in Harold Stevenson, Hiroshi Azuma & Kenji Hakuta (Eds) *Child Development and Education in Japan.* New York: W.H. Freeman.

Heyneman, Stephen P. (1987) Uses of Examinations in Developing Countries: selection, research, and education sector management, *International Journal of Educational Development*, 7(4), pp. 251-263.

Heyneman, Stephen P. & I. Fägerlind (Eds) (1988) *University Examinations and Standardized Testing: principles, experience and policy options.* Washington: World Bank.

Heyneman, Stephen P. & William A. Loxley (1982) Influences on Academic Achievement across High and Low Income Countries: a re-analysis of IEA data, *Sociology of Education*, 55, pp. 13-21.

Heyneman, Stephen P. & William A. Loxley (1983) The Effect of Primary-School Quality on Academic Achievement across Twenty-Nine High- and Low-Income Countries, *American Journal of Sociology*, 88, pp. 1162-1194.

Hobsbawm, E. J. (1990) *Nations and Nationalism since 1780.* Cambridge: Cambridge University Press.

Holmes, Brian (1958) The Problem Approach in Comparative Education: some methodological considerations, *Comparative Education Review*, 2, pp. 1-23.

Holmes, Brian & M. McLean (1989) *The Curriculum: a comparative perspective.* London: Routledge.

Holmes, Brian, Gerald H. Read & Natalya Voskresenskaya (1995) *Russian Education: tradition and transition.* New York: Garland.

Holmes, Larry Eugene (1999) *Stalin's School: Moscow's Model School No. 25.* Pittsburgh: University of Pittsburgh Press.

Hong, M. (1992) Japanese Colonial Education in Korea 1910-1945, PhD dissertation, Harvard Graduate School of Education.

Horowitz, Irving Louis (1972) *Three Worlds of Development.* New York: Oxford University Press.

Hosking, Geoffrey (1990) *The First Socialist Society: a history of the Soviet Union from within.* Cambridge, MA: Harvard University Press.

Huntington, S. (1993) The Clash of Civilizations, *Foreign Affairs*, 72(3), pp. 22-49.

Inkeles, Alex (1974) *Becoming Modern. Cambridge, MA*: Harvard University Press.

International Society for Education Information (1986a) The Modernization of Japanese Education. *Thought and System*. Volume 1. Tokyo: Shobi Printing Co.

International Society for Education Information (1986b) The Modernization of Japanese Education. *Content and Method*. Volume 2. Tokyo: Shobi Printing Co.

Institute for National Strategic Studies (1995) *Strategic Assessment 1995: US security challenges in transition*. Washington, DC: Institute for National Strategic Studies.

Jacoby, Susan (1975) *Inside Soviet Schools*. New York: Schocken.

James, E. (1987) The Public/Private Division of Responsibility for Education: an international comparison, in E.H. Haertel, T. James & H.M. Levin (Eds) *Comparing Public and Private Schools*. New York: Falmer Press.

Japanese Government Policies in Education, Science, Sports and Culture 1995: Remaking Universities: continuing reform of higher education. Retrieved on 5 May 2003, from: http://wwwwp.mext.go.jp/eky1995/index-16.html

Johansson, E. (1981) The History of Literacy in Sweden, in H.J. Graff (Ed.) *Literacy and Social Development in the West:* a reader. Cambridge: Cambridge University Press.

Johnson, D. (1987) *Private Schools and State Schools: two systems or one?* Milton Keynes: Open University Press.

Johnson, Paul (1991) *The Birth of the Modern: World Society 1815-1830*. New York: Harper Collins.

Johnson, R. (1989) Thatcherism and English Education: breaking the mould, or confirming the pattern? *History of Education*, 18(2), pp. 91-121.

Jones, Anthony (Ed.) (1994) *Education and Society in the New Russia*. Armonk, NY: M.E. Sharpe.

Judge, Harry, Michel Lemoss, Lynn Paine & Michael Sedlak (1994) *The University and the Teachers: France, the United States, England*. Wallingford: Triangle.

Kamens, David & Aaron Benavot (1992) A Comparative and Historical Analysis of Mathematics and Science Curricula, 1800-1986, in John W. Meyer, David H. Kamens & Aaron Benavot *School Knowledge for the Masses: world models and national primary curricular categories in the twentieth century*. Washington, DC: Falmer Press.

Kaneko, Motohisa (1987) *Enrollment Expansion in Postwar Japan*. Hiroshima: Research Institute for Higher Education, Hiroshima University.

Kelly, Gail (1982) *Franco-Vietnamese Schools: 1918-1938. Regional Development and Implications for National Integration*. Madison: University of Wisconsin-Madison, Center for Southeast Asian Studies.

Kennedy, Paul (1993) *Preparing for the Twenty-first Century*. New York: Random House.

Kennedy, Paul (1987) *The Rise and Fall of the Great Powers*. New York: Random House.

Kerr, Clark, John T. Dunlop, Frederick Harbison, & Charles A. Myers (1960) *Industrialism and Industrial Man; the problems of labor and management in economic growth*. Cambridge, MA: Harvard University Press.

Kinmouth, E.H. (1981) *The Self-made Man in Meiji Japanese Thought: from Samurai to Salary Man*. Berkeley: University of California Press.

Kliebard, Herbert M. (1987) T*he Struggle for the American Curriculum 1893-1958*. New York: Routledge & Kegan Paul.

Klitgaard, R. (1985) *Choosing Elites*. New York: Basic Books.

Korten, David (1995) *When Corporations Rule the World*. West Hartford: Kumarian Press.

Kurian, G.T. & G. Moliter (Eds) (1996) Encyclopedia of the Future. Vol. 1-2. New York: Macmillan.

Labaree, D.F. (1988) *The Making of an American High School*. New Haven: Yale University Press.

Lach, D.F. (1977) *Asia in the Making of Europe*: Vol. 2: *A Century of Wonder*, Book Three: *The Scholarly Disciplines*. Chicago: University of Chicago Press.

Lamberti, Marjorie (1989) *State, Society, and the Elementary School in Imperial Germany*. New York: Oxford University Press.

Lapointe, A.E., N.A. Mead, & G.W. Phillips, (1989) *A World of Differences: an international assessment of mathematics and science*. Princeton: ETS.

Lerner, Daniel (Ed.) (1958) *The Passing of Traditional Society*. New York: Free Press.

LeTendre, Gerald K., David Baken, Motoko Akiba, Brian Goesling, & Alan Wisemann (2001) Teachers' Work: institutional isomorphism and cultural variation in the US, Germany, and Japan, *Educational Researcher*, 30(6), pp. 3-15.

Levy, Daniel (1986) *Higher Education and the State in Latin America*. Chicago: University of Chicago Press.

Levy, Jack (1983) *War in the Modern Great Power System, 1495-1975*. Lexington: University of Kentucky Press.

Lewy, A. (1981) The Scope of Educational Evaluation: an introduction, in A. Lewy & D. Nevo (Eds) *Evaluation Roles in Education*. London: Gordon & Breach.

Livingstone, Ian (1986) Perceptions of the Intended and Implemented Curriculum. *Report on the Second International Mathematics Study.* Washington, DC: US Department of Education, Center for Statistics.

Locke, John (1990) Drafts for the Essay concerning Human Understanding, and other Philosophical Writings, ed. Peter H. Nidditch & G.A.J. Rogers. New York: Oxford University Press.

Long, Delbert H. & Roberta A. Long (1999) *Education of Teachers in Russia.* Westport: Greenwood Press.

Lortie, Dan (1975) *Schoolteacher: a sociological study.* Chicago: University of Chicago Press.

Lubbock, Percy (1929) *Shades of Eton.* London: Jonathan Cape.

Lynch, J. & D. Plunket (1973) *Teacher Education and Cultural Change: England, France, West Germany.* London: George Allen & Unwin.

Mack, Edward C. (1939) *Public Schools and British Opinion (1780-1860).* New York: Columbia University Press.

Mack, Edward C. (1941) *Public Schools and British Opinion since 1860.* New York: Columbia University Press.

Madaus, G. (1988) The Influence of Testing on the Curriculum, in L. Tanner (Ed.) Critical Issues in Curriculum (*87th Yearbook of the National Society for the Study of Education, Part 1*). Chicago: University of Chicago Press.

Madaus, G.F. & Kellaghan, T. (1991) *Student Examination Systems in the European Community: lessons for the United States.* Washington, DC: Office of Technology Assessment.

Mandela, Nelson (1995) *Long Walk to Freedom.* London: Abacus.

Marschalck, Peter (1987) The Age of Demographic Transition: mortality and fertility, in J. Bade Klaus (Ed.) *Population, Labour and Migration in 19th and 20th Century Germany.* New York: St Martin's Press.

Marsh, Robert M. (1967) *Comparative Sociology: a codification of cross-societal analysis.* New York: Harcourt, Brace & World.

Marshall, Byron (1994) *Learning to be Modern: Japanese political discourse on education.* Boulder: Westview Press.

Marshall, T.H. (1964) *Class, Citizenship, and Social Development.* New York: Doubleday.

Marx, Karl & Frederich Engels ([1848] 1955) *The Communist Manifesto.* New York: Appleton-Century-Crofts.

Marx, Karl & Frederich Engels (1957) *Basic Writings on Politics and Philosophy,* ed. S. Lewis. Garden City, NY: Anchor Books.

Maynes, Mary Jo (1985) *Schooling for the People: comparative local studies of schooling history in France and Germany, 1750-1850.* New York: Holmes & Meier.

McClelland, David (1976) *The Achieving Society.* New York: Irving.

McKnight, Curtis C. (1987) *The Underachieving Curriculum: assessing US school mathematics from an international perspective.* Champaign: Stipes.

McNeill, William H. (1963) *The Rise of the West: a history of the human community.* Chicago: University of Chicago Press.

McNeill, William H. (1967) *A World History.* New York: Oxford University Press.

Melton, James van Horn (1988) *Absolutism and the Eighteenth-century Origins of Compulsory Schooling in Prussia and Austria.* New York: Cambridge University Press.

Metzger, Walter P. (1955) *Academic Freedom in the Age of the University.* New York: Columbia University Press.

Meyer, John .W. (1977) The Effects of Education as an Institution, American *Journal of Sociology,* 83, pp. 55-57.

Meyer, John. W. & M.T. Hannah (Eds) (1979) *National Development and the World System: educational, economic, and political change, 1950-1970.* Chicago: University of Chicago Press.

Meyer, John W., David H. Kamens & Aaron Benavot (1992) *School Knowledge for the Masses.* Washington, DC: Falmer Press.

Mills, C. Wright (1951) *White Collar: the American middle classes.* New York: Oxford University Press.

Ministry of Education (MOE) (1980) *Japan's Modern Educational System: a history of the first hundred years.* Tokyo.

Mitch, D. (1992) The Rise of Popular Literacy in Europe, in B. Fuller & R. Rubinson (Eds) *The Political Construction of Education: the state, school expansion and economic change.* New York: Praeger.

Mitchell, B.R. (1981) *European Historical Statistics: 1750-1975.* New York: Facts on File.

Mitchell, B.R. (1982) *International Historical Statistics: Africa and Asia.* New York: New York University Press

Mitchell, J.V. Jr (Ed.) (1985) *The Ninth Mental Measurements Yearbook.* Loncoln: University of Nebraska Press.

Mitchell, Richard (1976) *Thought Control in Prewar Japan.* Ithaca: Cornell University Press.

Miyazaki, I. (1981) *China's Examination Hell: the Civil Service examination of Imperial China, trans. C. Schirokauer.* New Haven: Yale University Press.

Montgomery, R.J. (1965) *Examination.* Pittsburgh: University of Pittsburgh Press.

Moody, Joseph N. (1976) *French Education since Napoleon.* Syracuse: Syracuse University Press.

Moon, B. (1988) Who Controls the Curriculum? The Story of 'New Math' 1960-80, in I. Goodson (Ed.) *International Perspectives in Curriculum History.* London: Routledge.

Moore, B. (1966) *Social Origins of Dictatorship and Democracy*. Boston: Beacon Press.

Morison, Samuel Eliot (1935) *The Founding of Harvard College*. Cambridge, MA: Harvard University Press.

Morison, Samuel Eliot (1936a) *Harvard College in the Seventeenth Century*. Cambridge, MA: Harvard University Press.

Morison, Samuel Eliot (1936b) *Three Centuries of Harvard 1636-1936*. Cambridge, MA: Harvard University Press.

Muckle, J. (1988) *A Guide to the Soviet Curriculum: what the Soviet child is taught in school*. New York: Croom Helm.

Mueller, H.E. (1984) *Bureaucracy, Education and Monopoly*. Berkeley: University of California Press.

Müller, Detlef K., Fritz Ringer & Brian Simon (1987) *The Rise of the Modern Educational System: structural change and social reproduction 1870-1920*. Cambridge: Cambridge University Press.

Murphy, J.T. (1988) *The Paradox of Decentralizing Schools*, Phi Delta Kappa, 70, pp. 808-812.

Naisbet, J. (1982) *Megatrends*. New York: Avon Books.

Nakayma, S. (1984) *Academic and Scientific Traditions in China, Japan, and the West*, trans. J. Dusenbury. Tokyo: University of Tokyo Press.

National Institute of Population and Social Security Research. Page translated by Yuko Hosoya. Retrieved 28 January 2003, from: http://www1.ipss.go.jp/tohkei/Index-tj.htm

National Science Board (2000) *Science and Engineering Indicators 2000*, pp. 2-46.Washington, DC: US Government Printing Office.

Neave, G. (1985a) France, in B.R. Clark (Ed.) *The School and the University*. Berkeley: University of California Press.

Neave, G. (1985b) Elite and Mass Higher Education in Britain: a regressive model? *Comparative Education Review*, 29, pp. 347-361.

Needham, Joseph (1964) Science and Society in East and West, in Maurice Goldsmith & Alan Mackay (Eds) *Society and Science*, pp. 127-149. New York: Simon & Schuster.

Needham, J. (1956) *Science and Civilization in China: history of scientific thought*. Cambridge: Cambridge University Press.

Newman, John Henry Cardinal. *Discourse V*, in Charles Frederick Harrold (Ed.) (1995) *The Idea of a University*, pp. 88-107. New York: Longmans, Green & Co.

Nielsen, H. Dean & William K. Cummings (1997) *Quality Education for All: community-oriented approaches*. New York: Garland.

Nisbet, Robert (1969) *Social Change and History*. London: Oxford University Press.

271

Noah, Harold J. & Max A. Eckstein (1969) *Towards a Science of Comparative Education.* New York: Macmillan.

Nord, Warren A. (1995) *Religion and American Education: rethinking a national dilemma.* Chapel Hill: University of North Carolina Press.

North, Douglass C. (1990) *Institutions, Institutional Change and Economic Performance.* Cambridge: Cambridge University Press.

Nothdurft, W.E. (1989) *School Works: reinventing public schools to create the workforce of the future.* Washington, DC: The Brookings Institution.

Ochs, Kimberly & David Phillips (2002) Comparative Studies and 'Cross-national Attraction' in Education: a typology for the analysis of English interest in educational policy and provision in Germany, Educational Studies, 29, pp. 325-339.

O'Connor, Timothy Edward (1980) *The Politics of Soviet Culture:* Anatolii Lunacharskii (UMI Research Press, c. 1983). A revision of the author's PhD thesis, University of Minnesota.

Organization for Economic Cooperation and Development (OECD) (1995a) *Decision-making in 14 OECD Education Systems.* Paris: OECD.

Organization for Economic Cooperation and Development (OECD) (1995b), (1998), (2000), (2001),(2002) *Education at a Glance.* Paris: OECD.

Ornstein, A.C. (1988) Administrator/Student Ratios in Large School Districts, Phi Delta Kappa, 70, pp. 806-808.

Orozco-Gomez, G. (1997) School and Television: a new rationale for building an alliance, in William Cummings & Noel McGinn (Eds) *The International Handbook of Education and Development: preparing schools, students, and nations for the twenty-first century.* Oxford: Pergamon.

Owen, D. (1985) *None of the Above: behind the myth of scholastic aptitude.* Boston: Houghton Mifflin.

Palmer, Robert R. (1975) *The School of the French Revolution: a documentary history of the College of Louis-le-Grand and its Director, Jean-François Champagne 1782-1814.* Princeton: Princeton University Press.

Parsons, Talcott (1951) *The Social System.* New York: Free Press.

Parsons, Talcott (1960) *Structure and Process in Modern Societies.* New York: Free Press.

Parsons, Talcott (1966) *Societies: evolutionary and comparative perspectives.* Englewood Cliffs: Prentice Hall.

Parsons, Talcott (1967) *The System of Modern Societies.* Englewood Cliffs: Prentice Hall.

Parsons, Talcott, Alfred Kroeber & Edward Shils (1951) *Towards a General Theory of Action.* New York: Harper Row.

Passin, Herbert (1966) *Society and Education in Japan.* New York: Teachers College Press.

Peresedentev, Victor (1999) *Population under Duress*, in George Demko, Grigory Ioffe & Zhanna Zayonch (Eds) (1999) Population under Duress, Boulder, CO: Westview Press.

Person, J., Jr (Ed.) (1993) *Statistical Forecasts of the United States*. Detroit: Gale Research.

Phillips, David (1989) Neither a Borrower nor a Lender Be? The Problems of Cross-national Attraction in Education, *Comparative Education*, 25, pp. 267-274.

Polanyi, Karl (1944) *The Great Transformation: the political and economic origins of our time*. Boston: Beacon Press.

Popkewitz, T.S. (1993) *Changing Patterns of Power: social regulation and teacher education reform*. Albany: State University of New York Press.

Population Division of the Department of Economic and Social Affairs of the United Nations Secretariat, World Population Prospects: the 2000 revision and world urbanization prospects: the 2001 revision. Retrieved 28 January 2003, from: http://esa.un.org/unpp.

Postlethwaite, Neville & John Wiley (1989) *The IEA Study of Science II: science achievement in twenty-three countries*. New York: Pergamon.

Powell, Arthur G. (1996) *Lessons from Privilege: the American prep school tradition*. Cambridge, MA: Harvard University Press.

Powell, Walter W. & Paul J. DiMaggio (Eds) (1991) *The New Institutionalism in Organizational Analysis*. Chicago: University of Chicago Press.

Purta, J.T. & C. Hahn (1988) Values Education in the Western European Tradition, in William K. Cummings, S. Gopinathan & Y. Tomoda (Eds) *The Revival of Values Education in Asia and the West*. New York: Pergamon.

Purta, J.T. & J. Schwille (1986) Civic Values Learned in School: policy and practice in industrialized countries, *Comparative Education Review*, 30, pp. 30-49.

Putnam, R. (1996) *Bowling Alone*. Cambridge, MA: Harvard University Press.

Ragin, Charles C. (1987) *The Comparative Method: moving beyond qualitative and quantitative strategies*. Berkeley: University of California Press.

Ramirez, F.O. & J. Boli (1987) The Political Construction of Mass Schooling: European origins and worldwide institutionalization, *Sociology of Education*, 60, pp. 2-17.

Rasell, M. Edith & Lawrence Mishel (1990) *Shortchanging Education: how US spending on grades K-12 lags behind other industrial nations. Economic Policy Institute Briefing Paper*. Washington, DC: EPI.

Ravitch, Diane (1983) *The Troubled Crusade: American education, 1945-1980*. New York: Basic Books.

Reich, Robert (1991) *The Work of Nations*. New York: A.A. Knopf.

Reisner, Edward H. (1923) *Nationalism and Education since 1789: a social and political history of modern education*. New York: Macmillan.

Ringer, F. (1974) *The Decline of the German Mandarins*. Cambridge, MA: Harvard University Press.

Ringer, F. (1979) *Education and Society in Modern Europe*, pp. 1-31. Bloomington: Indiana University Press.

Robitaille, D.F. & R.A. Gardner (1989) *The IEA Study of Mathematics II: context and outcomes of school mathematics*. New York: Pergamon.

Rohlen, Thomas P. (1983) *Japan's High Schools. Berkeley*: University of California Press.

Rohlen, Thomas P. (1996) Differences that Make a Difference: explaining Japan's success, in William K. Cummings & Philip G. Altbach (Eds) *The Asian Educational Challenge: implications for America*. Albany: SUNY Press.

Rostow, F. (1960) *The Stages of Economic Growth: a non-communist manifesto*. Cambridge: Cambridge University Press.

Rotberg, Robert I. & Theodore K. Rabb (1986) *Population and Economy: population and history from the traditional to modern world*. New York: Cambridge University Press

Rubinson, R. & Fuller, B. (1992) Specifying the Effects of Education on National Economic Growth, in B. Fuller & R. Rubinson (Eds) *The Political Construction of Education: the state, school expansion and economic change*, pp. 102-115, 136. New York: Praeger.

Russell, Nancy Ukai (1994) The Kumon Approach to Teaching and Learning. *Journal of Japanese Studies 20*, pp. 87-113.

Rust, Val D. (1999) Aminata Soumare, Octavio Pescador, and Megumi Shibuya. Research Strategies in Comparative Education, *Comparative Education Review*, 43, pp. 108-109.

Rust, Val D. & Per Dalin (1990) *Teachers and Teaching in the Developing World*. New York: Garland.

Sachs, Wolfgang (Ed.) (1992) *The Development Dictionary: a guide to knowledge and power*. London: Zed Books.

Sadler, Michael (1900) How Far Can We Learn Anything of Practical Value from the Study of Foreign Systems of Education? Address of 20 October, in H. Higginson (Ed.) Selections from Michael Sadler. Liverpool: Dejall & Meyorre.

Sansom, George (1950) *The Western World and Japan*. New York: Knopf.

Sansom, George (1962) *Japan: a short cultural history*. New York: Appleton-Century-Crofts.

Sansom, George (1963) *A History of Japan: 1615-1867*. Stanford: Stanford University Press.

Schiefelbein, Ernesto (1997) Trends in the Provision and Design of Self-learning Models of Education, in William Cummings & Noel McGinn (Eds) *The International Handbook of Education and Development: preparing schools, students, and nations for the twenty-first century*. Oxford: Pergamon.

Schmidt, William H., Richard T. Houang, David E. Wiley, Curtis C. McKnight & Leland S. Cogan (2001) *Why Schools Matter: a cross-national comparison of curriculum and learning*. San Francisco: Jossey-Bass.

Schumpeter, Joseph (1947) *Capitalism, Socialism, and Democracy*, pp. 12-13. New York: Harper & Brothers.

Selden, William (1960) *Accreditation: a struggle over standards in higher education*. New York: Harper & Brothers.

Senge, P.M. (1990) *The Fifth Discipline: the art and practice of the learning organization*. New York: Doubleday.

Shimahara, Nobuo (1995) *Learning to Teach in Two Cultures: Japan and the United States*. New York: Garland.

Shore, Maurice (1947) *Soviet Education: its psychology and philosophy*. New York: Philosophical Library.

Slack, W.V. & D. Porter (1980) The Scholastic Aptitude Test: a critical appraisal, *Harvard Educational Review*, 50, pp. 154-175.

Smethurst, Richard J. (1974) *A Social Basis for Prewar Japanese Militarism: the army and the rural community*. Berkeley: University of California Press.

Smiles, Samuel (1866) *Self-Help*. New York: A.L. Burt.

Somerset, H.C.A. (1987) *Examinations as an Instrument to Improve Pedagogy, Examination Reform in Kenya* (World Bank Education and Training Series No. EDT 64). Washington: World Bank.

Soo, Alvin Y. (1990) *Social Change and Development*. Newbury Park: Sage.

Spaulding, R.M., Jr (1967) *Imperial Japan's Higher Civil Service Examination*. Princeton: Princeton University Press.

Spencer, Herbert (1891) *Essays Scientific, Political, and Speculative*. New York: D. Appleton & Co.

Stevenson, D. & D. Baker (1991) *State Control of the Curriculum and Classroom Instruction, Sociology of Education*, 64, pp. 1-10.

Stevenson, H., H. Azuma & K. Hakuta (1986) *Child Development and Education in Japan*. New York: W.H. Freeman.

Stevenson, H. & Stigler, J. (1992) *The Learning Gap*. New York: Touchstone.

Stigler, James W. & James Hiebert (1999) *The Teaching Gap*. New York: Free Press.

Stinchcombe, Arthur L. (1965) Social Structure and Organizations, in James G. March (Ed.) *Handbook of Organizations*. Chicago: Rand McNally.

Stromquist, Nelly P. (1997) Emerging Families and Democratization in Gender Relations, in William Cummings & Noel McGinn (Eds) *The International Handbook of Education and Development: preparing schools, students, and nations for the twenty-first century*. Oxford: Pergamon.

Swanson, Guy (1971) Frameworks for Comparative Research: structural anthropology and the theory of action, in Ivan Vallier (Ed.) *Comparative*

Methods in Sociology: essays on trends and applications. Berkeley: University of California Press.

Tan, Jason, S. Gopinathan & How Wah Kam (2001) *Challenges Facing the Singapore Education System Today*. Singapore: Prentice-Hall.

Tatto, Teresa (1997) Teachers Working in the Periphery: addressing persistent policy issues, in Dean Nielsen & William K. Cummings (Eds) *Quality Education for All: community-oriented approaches*. New York: Garland.

Teese, R. (1986) Private Schools in France: evolution of a system, *Comparative Education Review*, 30, pp. 247-259.

Teichler, U. (1985) The Federal Republic of Germany, in B.R. Clark (Ed.) *The School and the University*. Berkeley: University of California Press.

Teichler, U. & B.C. Sanyal (1982) *Higher Education and the Labour Market in the Federal Republic of Germany*. Paris: International Institute for Educational Planning.

Thayer, V.T. (1965) *Formative Ideas in American Education: from the colonial period to the present*. New York: Dodd, Mead & Co.

Theisen, Gary & Don Adams (1990) Comparative Education Research, in Murray Thomas (Ed.) *International Comparative Education*. Oxford: Pergamon.

Thomas, R. Murray (1979) *Comparing Theories of Child Development*. Belmont: Wadsworth.

Thompson, E.P. (1963) *The Making of the English Working Class*. New York: Vintage.

Tilly, C. (Ed.) (1975) *The Formation of Nation States in Western Europe*. Princeton: Princeton University Press.

Tilly, Charles (1993) *European Revolutions 1492-1992*. Oxford: Blackwell.

Tilly, Charles (1989) *Coercion, Capital, and European States AD 990-1990*. London: Blackwell.

Tomoda, Y. (1988) Politics and Moral Education in Japan, in William K. Cummings, S. Gopinathan & Y. Tomoda (Eds) *The Revival of Values Education in Asia and the West*. New York: Pergamon Press.

Trow, Martin A. (1961) *The Second Transformation of American Secondary Education*, International Journal of Comparative Sociology, 11, pp. 144-166.

Tristram, Henry (Ed.) (1952) *The Idea of Liberal Education: a selection from the works of Cardinal Newman*. London: Harrap.

Trow, Martin (1974) *Problems in the Transition from Elite to Mass Higher Education, in Policies for Higher Education. General Report of the Conference on Future Structure of Post-Secondary Education*. Paris: Organization for Economic Cooperation and Development.

Trow, Martin (1977) The Second Transformation of American Secondary Education, in J. Karabel & A.H. Halsey (Eds) *Power and Ideology in Education*. New York: Oxford University Press.

Tsurumi, E.P. (1977) *Japanese Colonial Education in Taiwan, 1895-1945.* Cambridge, MA: Harvard University Press.

Tyack, D.B. (1974) *The One Best System: a history of American urban education.* Cambridge, MA: Harvard University Press.

Tyler, Ralph (1949) *Basic Principles of Curriculum and Instruction.* Chicago: University of Chicago Press.

Ulich, Robert (1947) *Three Thousand Years of Educational Wisdom.* Cambridge, MA: Harvard University Press.

UNESCO (1973) *World Survey of Education Handbooks, vol. 1-4,* 1966-1971. Geneva: United Nations.

US Department of Education. *Digest of Educational Statistics.* Annual.

Ushiogi, M. (1986) The Transition from School to Work: the case of Japan, in William K. Cummings, Edward Beauchamp, Shogo Ichikawa, Victor N. Kobayashi & Morikazu Ushiogi (Eds) *Educational Policies in Crisis: US and Japanese perspectives.* New York: Praeger.

Van Doren, Charles (1991) *A History of Knowledge: past, present, and future.* New York: Ballantine.

Veysey, Lawrence (1965) *The Emergence of the American University.* Chicago: University of Chicago Press.

Von Laue, T.H. (1987) *The World Revolution of Westernization.* New York: Oxford University Press.

Walford, Geoffrey (1986) *Life in Public Schools.* London: Methuen.

Wallerstein, Immanuel (1976) *The Modern World-System: capitalist agriculture and the origins of the European world-economy in the sixteenth century.* New York: Academic Press.

Wallerstein, Immanuel (1980) *The Modern World-System II: mercantilism and the consolidation of the European world-economy, 1600-1750.* New York: Academic Press.

Wardle, D. (1971) *Education and Society in Nineteenth Century Nottingham.* Cambridge: Cambridge University Press.

Webber, Stephen & Ilkka Liikanen (Eds) (2001) *Education and Civic Culture in Post-communist Countries.* London: Palgrave.

Weber, Max (1930) *The Protestant Ethic and the Spirit of Capitalism.* London: Allen & Unwin.

Weber, Max (1949) *The Methodology of the Social Sciences.* New York: Free Press.

Wechsler, H.S. (1977) *The Qualified Student: a history of selective college admission in America.* New York: Wiley.

Weinberg, Ian (1967) *The English Public Schools: the sociology of elite education.* New York: Atherton.

Weiner, Myron (1991) *The Child and the State in India: child labor and education policy in comparative perspective.* Princeton: Princeton University Press.

Wheeler, David (1984) *Human Resource Policies, Economic Growth, and Demographic Change in Developing Countries*. Oxford: Clarendon Press.

White, M. (1987) *The Japanese Educational Challenge: a commitment to children*. New York: Free Press.

Whyte, W.H. (1956) *The Organization Man*. New York: Simon & Schuster.

Williams, J. (1997) The Diffusion of the Modern School, in William Cummings & Noel McGinn (Eds) *The International Handbook of Education and Development: preparing schools, students, and nations for the twenty-first century*. Oxford: Pergamon.

Williamson Jr, Eugene L. (1964) *The Liberalism of Thomas Arnold*. Alabama: University of Alabama Press.

Williamson, Jeffrey (1993) Human Capital Deepening, Inequality and Demographic Events along the Asia Pacific Rim, in Naohiro Ogawa, Gavin W. Jones & Jeffrey G. Williamson (Eds) *Human Resource Development along the Asia-Pacific Rim*. Oxford: Oxford University Press.

Willinsky, John (1998) *Learning to Divide the World: education at empire's end*. Minneapolis: University of Minnesota Press.

Wilson, James Q. (1989) *Bureaucracy: what government agencies do and why they do it*. New York: Basic Books.

Winkler, D. (1987) Decentralization in Education: an economic perspective. Paper prepared for the Research Division, Education and Training Department, Washington, DC: World Bank.

Wittfogel, Karl A. (1957) *Oriental Despotism*. New York: Vintage.

Woolcock, Michael (1998) Social Capital and Economic Development: towards a theoretical synthesis and policy framework, *Theory and Society*, 27, pp. 51-208.

World Bank (1993a) *The East Asian Miracle: economic growth and public policy*. Oxford: Oxford University Press.

World Bank (1993b) *Social Indicators of Development*. New York: Oxford.

World Bank (2002) *World Development Indicators*. Oxford: Oxford University Press.

Young, Michael (1958) *The Rise of the Meritocracy: 1870-2033*. London: Thames & Hudson.

Yukichi, Fukuzawa (1969) *An Encouragement of Learning*. Translation with an Introduction by David A. Dilworth & Umeyo Hirano. Tokyo: Sophia University Press.